From
Netsie & Joe
Oct. 23, 1981

why they call him

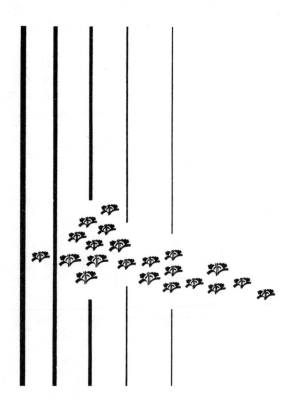

THE
BUFFALO
DOCTOR

by Jean Cummings

HARLO PRESS, DETROIT, MICHIGAN

Why They Call Him The Buffalo Doctor
by Jean Cummings
Copyright © 1971 by Jean Cummings

ISBN 0-8187-0035-1
Library of Congress Catalog Card Number: 73-147172

Printed in the United States of America · T
Prentice-Hall International, Inc., London
Prentice-Hall of Australia, Pty. Ltd., Sydney
Prentice-Hall of Canada, Ltd., Toronto
Prentice-Hall of India Private Ltd., New Delhi
Prentice-Hall of Japan, Inc., Tokyo

Second Printing . . . . September, 1972

Harlo Press
50 Victor, Detroit, Michigan 48203

Third Printing . . . . February, 1980
Fourth Printing . . . . June, 1980

To
Kahtanka's Friend

Contents

■
Morning Rounds

1   The thunder of an approaching buffalo herd at feeding time is a familiar sound to residents of a rural village in central Michigan. Daily, they witness the following scene.

A battered, blue Jeep truck bounces across the field toward the galloping herd. The shaggy animals churn to a stop at a fence corner and mill about, charging and hooking each other. As the hay-filled truck approaches, the buffalo shake their black manes and amble toward it.

Quickly the driver stops and scrambles from the cab to the top of the high-stacked hay bales in the box. Already the herd has the truck surrounded. Clad in a torn, brown wool coat, navy stocking cap and faded coveralls, the driver begins his daily chore of feeding the buffalo. Braced against the chill winter wind, he breaks apart and throws heavy bales of hay to the ground, then drives on a way and throws down more, thus spreading the hay so the animals have horn-room to eat.

By the time the feeding operation is finished, the driver is snowy and dirty, with blades of hay caught in his cap and seeds matted into his coat. The blue truck roars out the gate and parks beside a white building just outside the pasture.

In a short while the truck rumbles up a gravel roadway toward the yellow brick hospital standing atop a gentle knoll overlooking the buffalo pasture. The

1

rusty truck swings into a parking place at the rear of the hospital building. As on all other mornings, the driver is transformed from the hay-covered figure just recently feeding his herd, to a neat, slender man in well-cut business suit and topcoat.

Flakes of snow catch in his black hair as he strides in soft, polished cowboy boots across the doctors' parking lot toward the rear entrance. This is the man known as "The Buffalo Doctor."

When "The Buffalo Doctor" became his nickname, I feared people would think he was a veterinarian, or a zoo-keeper; yet no one seems to get confused. They know he is a people-doctor who also raises buffalo with zest and affection.

I know The Buffalo Doctor well. He is my friend, my confidant, my doctor, the father of my children, and my husband. To others, he may be The Buffalo Doctor, but to me, he is Bill. I knew him long before his name became synonymous with buffalo. We were college sweethearts, and when I met him, I didn't know quite what he was, or what he was going to be, but I knew he wasn't ordinary. A threadbare and impoverished pre-medical student, Bill didn't fit the pattern of carefree young college boys to whom I'd become accustomed. He considered life an individual challenge rather than a spectator sport. He created big dreams and small dreams, and they were all infectious. Soon I was caught in with his aspirations, and our talk of the future became "we."

I never suspected his grandest dream would be a small, struggling, country hospital nestled in the second-growth timber of Michigan. Or that as a diversion for the recuperating patients, Bill would install a buffalo herd on the grassy hillside beneath the hospital windows. As a cheerful college coed I knew nothing about backwoods villages, or livestock, and my wildest imagination could never have created anything so strange as life with a buffalo herd.

2

■
Whither
Thou Goest

2   "Are all those buffalo yours?" the lady asked. Two well-scrubbed children gaped at me from the rear window of her station wagon.

"Yes," I admitted. I set aside the post-hole digger and brushed a wasp from my mud-spattered white blouse.

The lady took off her jeweled sunglasses and peered closer at me. "But why?"

I looked at the dark, shaggy animals chewing their cuds in the shade of the lone elm. Everyone wanted to know why we had buffalo. Maybe it's a reasonable question, but I can never think of a reasonable answer.

Sometimes I say that Buffalo Bill was my grandfather, and I'm trying to atone for his sins of destruction. Since this lady looked so serious I was afraid she might believe me, I just shrugged and said, "Oh, I guess we just like buffalo."

That didn't seem to be a reasonable answer. She gave me a distrustful look and quickly drove away. There was always an implied meaning behind that question, "Why do you have buffalo?" What they really meant was, "What are you?—some kind of a nut, or something?"

How do you justify having even one buffalo, to say nothing of harboring a whole herd?

Becoming the owners and caretakers of a buffalo herd isn't something that just happens to you, like

3

breaking your leg. Giving consent is involved. In other words—we asked for it.

Ever since the arrival of Kahtanka, our monstrous black devil of a herd bull, and his retinue of young buffalo heifers, our lives have been decidedly changed.

Whenever our planned course takes a right-angle turn in an unexpected direction, most of us search back through our memories to find the original incident that set in motion this chain of events. The Romantic says, "If I hadn't turned that corner at that precise moment, I'd never have met my true love." The Fatalist says, "It was just meant to be."

It's hard for me to believe we were destined to be buffalo breeders. Bill and I had always been such a practical, sensible couple. Out of necessity we had to be. When we were married shortly after Bill's graduation from college, he still had eight years of medical school, internship, and residency ahead of him, so being "sensible and thrifty" was the motto of our newly formed household. Our whole concern those eight years was somehow to make enough money to meet the next tuition payment, pay the rent, and buy macaroni and cheese.

Our student marriage didn't seem at all rash during that post-World War II period when most of the students were married and struggling along just as we were. Getting married was the sensible thing to do. After all, the man didn't take a wife, he took a partner who brought in a paycheck. The wives were investing in their husbands' futures, and grateful they had an ambitious mate. Frugality was the rule, and hobbies had no place in our lives. Our one extravagance was starting our family. Not wanting to postpone children until we were past thirty, we decided that when the babies arrived, we'd manage somehow.

In February, during Bill's senior year of medical school, our son Bruce was born. As Bill helped the

4

intern wheel me out of the delivery room, his glazed eyes stared at me in awe.

"You did it, Pinkie! You gave me a son! Of all those babies in the nursery, he's the only boy!" Bill spent the rest of the day passing out "It's-a-Boy!" cigars and boasting to anyone who approached the newborn nursery, "The boy in there—that's my son!"

Still wearing that typical new-father smirk, Bill swaggered into my hospital room that evening. After describing his son's superiority to other infants, he outlined future plans. "Now that we have our son we must chart our course. Since you're so good at producing what I want, I'm putting in my order for a daughter, a flaming redhead, just like you."

(And on a chilly St. Patrick's Day two years later, after working all day at my secretarial job, I again filled Bill's order. Our daughter Beth, a redheaded livewire, was born. Bill was impressed. "Pinkie, you're really terrific! For the rest of the children, I guess you can pick whatever you want.")

Soon after Bruce was born, I found a reliable baby-sitter and returned to my secretarial job.

In June, Bill received his sheepskin proclaiming him a doctor. Upon our husbands' graduations, we students' wives were given little parchment diplomas with the P.H.T. (Putting Hubby Through) degree. Instead of the official golden seal, a safety pin was fastened through the diploma for each baby we had produced. We accepted the degrees cheerfully, and looked ahead to the glittering, stimulating, and luxury-flooded life we felt sure every doctor's wife enjoyed.

But first, there were four years of internship and residency to complete. During that interminable stretch I became very stoic over the current situation, but starry-eyed and expectant about the future. We students' wives eagerly watched the full-fledged doctors' wives and how they lived. I studied everything—the

5

mink stoles, the twice-weekly cleaning lady, the automatic dishwasher, the alligator handbags, professionally done coiffures. We students' wives built up great expectations.

When Bill's surgical residency neared completion and our time to go out into the world approached, I confess I left the choice of a place to practice entirely up to him. I was retiring from my typing job, and he was now going to take his turn as breadwinner. The birth of our third child was due at any moment. What with advanced pregnancy, caring for Bruce and Beth, and packing our belongings for the big move, I didn't pay much attention to *where* we were moving. I was certain that going out into practice meant the end of toil and the beginning of a life of ease.

I should have suspected that we were leaving the well-beaten path of the ordinary when Bill chose his location to set up practice. Instead of heading for the city as most specialists do, he chose the tiny rural village of Stanwood, Michigan, halfway between Nowhere and Nowhere.

Vaguely, I was aware that Bill had chosen Stanwood because the small hospital there badly needed a surgeon. When they said, "We need you," he was hooked.

I was delighted at the thought of our moving to a rural community where the children could play freely, away from traffic and danger. Both Bill and I had been raised in small towns where we had roomy backyards for play. It seemed so unnatural, our having to take Bruce and Beth to a neighborhood playground so they could run, jump, and ride their three-wheelers.

Bill suffered his own private misery, trying to raise a son in a city apartment. There were no chores for Bruce to do. How Bill fretted over this!

Frequently, he reminded Bruce, "When I was your age I had to herd thirteen goats out to the pasture every morning, and then collect garbage for the hogs."

6

Not yet five years old, but a serious, responsible little boy, Bruce always answered, "I wish we did have goats and hogs. I'd take care of 'em." His earnest eyes, the color of a June morning sky, implored Bill to bring on the animals.

"Me, too. I'll help," chimed in Beth, whose chief occupation was keeping up with her older brother. "Let's live on a farm."

We couldn't afford a real farm, but with a hasty plane flight to Michigan, Bill found and placed a down payment upon a house with five acres of land. After our near-downtown city apartment, five acres sounded like a magnificent expanse of property.

When Bill described our future home, the children were ecstatic. "Now we can have animals and chores," said Bruce, relieved that he soon would have a chance to prove his manhood.

During the hubbub of the packing and moving preparations, Kerry Ellen was born. Even before we were dismissed from the hospital, Kerry's remarkable eyes intrigued me.

"Look at her eyes," I told Bill. "She has the eyes of a wise old patriarch. Her look seems so penetrating and serious."

"Mmm," Bill murmured. "I've noticed that, too. Her eyes are different, rather dusky." Grinning, he added, "Maybe that means she'll have my brown eyes."

It was a sultry June evening when Bill, the children, and I started our long drive to Michigan. The radiator of our aged car insisted upon boiling over if driven at thirty miles an hour in the sunshine, so we solved that problem by driving at night. Darkness lulled Bruce and Beth into sleep which lasted the whole trip. Just three weeks old and a tiny bundle in my arms, Kerry grew hungry every two hours, but since I was nursing her, there was no problem, as there would have been with formula and bottles.

7

Dawn was just breaking as we approached Stanwood. Though we'd had no sleep, Bill and I weren't the least bit drowsy. This was the Big Moment, the beginning of our new life. I leaned forward in the seat, being careful not to waken little Kerry on my lap. Bill turned slowly off the highway. Our sagging, trunk-heavy car bounced over the railroad tracks, and we rolled to a stop. There was Stanwood before us, the corn-yellow rising sun behind it. Surely the dazzling sunlight was obscuring the main part of town! I blinked, shielding my eyes. Then I saw that we were *in* the main part of town. Stanwood was exactly one block long. One side of Main Street was taken up with a grain elevator and feed-store operation. The opposite side of the street consisted of a locker plant, a grocery store, a bank, a post office, and a hardware store. Aside from four gas stations located back on the main highway, those six enterprises made up the business district of Stanwood.

Oh, where was my beauty parlor I'd so long antici-pated? Where would I buy my alligator handbag? Where was a dentist, a golf course—or worse thought—where would I even *wear* a mink stole?

At the end of the block, we were, of course, out of town. Open country faced us. In the midst of the farmland ahead stood the two-story brick building which had to be the hospital.

After the shock of Stanwood's business district, the hospital was a pleasant surprise. Its neat yellow bricks peered sedately through huge green cedar trees, taller even than the building. A vast, neatly mowed lawn framed the structure. The pastureland surrounding the hospital gave a sedate and quiet tint to the picturesque scene. With great relief, I thought: It looks just the way a hospital should!

Imagine my chagrin when I discovered it hadn't been built as a hospital at all! Just ten years earlier this proper-looking rural hospital had been the old county poor farm—the horror of an older generation. Before the advent of social security and retirement pensions, the poor farm was the fearsome limbo where the poverty-stricken were sent to die. There, in great austerity, they subsisted on public charity, suffering pangs of homesickness and shame. Those who were able, helped run the farm and tended the gardens, growing food to help offset the expense of maintaining the poorhouse. The need for a poor farm vanished with the more affluent times of World War II and the proliferation of pensions and retirement plans. The building was converted into a hospital, and the surrounding one hundred and sixty acres of farmland were allowed to lie fallow and unused.

As we drove around behind the building, I saw that this was no ordinary hospital. A mammoth red barn stood close by the rear of the hospital building, and a long white implement building sat nearby. The barn seemed in good repair, and not long out of use. A long, shiny tube a yard in diameter stretched diagonally across the rear of the hospital, reaching from the second floor to the ground. This was evidently the fire escape for the patients, or the inmates of a decade before.

At ground level the basement windows were protected by vertical iron rods like those seen in jail cells.

"Why do they have iron bars on those windows?" I asked Bill.

"The violent inmates were kept down there in the basement," he explained. "The old county poor farms were often called upon to house the insane, especially those who were senile or paupers."

As we studied the building in the quiet of the June sunrise, I noticed a white signpost crudely lettered "Dr. Cummings."

"Look, Bill, a parking place for you!" I cried. "Your own private parking place. You've really arrived!" We laughed jauntily, pretending to make light of such a little thing, but we were honestly thrilled. This simple gesture welcomed us and said, "We're glad you're here. We want you here."

As we drove away from the hospital toward our new home and the ordeal of getting moved in, Bill looked lovingly back over his shoulder at the rolling green fields surrounding the hospital.

"The perfect setting for a hospital," he murmured. "Clean air, quiet and beautiful surroundings—exactly what a hospital should have." His deep-set hazel eyes misted over dreamily. Perhaps that was when the first tiny seed entered his mind, the zygote of imagination which decided that a buffalo herd should be grazing over those grassy hillocks beneath the hospital windows. There was a six-year incubation period for his dream to turn into a buffalo herd grazing on the long-unused pastures surrounding the hospital. It took a little doing. You don't just order a herd of buffalo from your Sears Roebuck catalog.

Only two hours after my first glimpse of Stanwood and the hospital, while Bill was attempting to assemble the children's bunk beds and I was madly searching for our coffee pot among the dozens of cardboard packing boxes, he received his first emergency summons to the hospital. Since our telephone was not yet connected, one of the nurses had driven to our house to locate the doctor. Bill quickly fled to the hospital, and it was several days, long after we were unpacked and settled, before he had any leisure time again. Doctors always find marvelous excuses for escaping household chores.

Along with surgery, Bill soon discovered he had a busy general practice. Colicky babies, fishhooks caught in elbows, mangled accident victims from the tourist-clogged highway, and unusual, exotic diseases all seemed to arrive at this country hospital.

"Why?" people ask us. Why did we choose a small hospital in a declining crossroads village?

10

During his training Bill had developed a philosophy of the purpose of a hospital. He felt that the hospital's role was similar to that of the old philosophy of sanctuary. "A hospital is a place where people go to get well," is how he puts it. Helping the patient become well is the only service a hospital of any size has to offer. Bill believes this can be done best when the hospital is located in a quiet, rural setting where the patients are insulated from the bustle and noises and bad smells of everyday city life. A pleasant, quiet atmosphere amid beautiful scenery is more conducive to healing and recovery.

In the small hospitals Bill had visited he discovered an informal atmosphere infused with friendliness and personal attention. He felt this was very helpful to patients, psychologically. When a patient enters a hospital, he is necessarily exposed to strangers. Doctors and nurses prod and poke and examine. Bath time, using the bathroom, and too-short hospital gowns contrive to strip one of his dignity. Embarrassment is a constant emotion to the patient, but the informal atmosphere of a country hospital with its camaraderie helps dispel it. Bill also felt that smaller hospitals excelled in treating each patient as an individual, a human being, not just "a case," or "Bed C, Room 341." Personal and individual care was given thoughtfully, and rules were not abided by so strictly as to clog the mechanism. If Mrs. Thornton's husband couldn't come to visit her until ten P.M., well, then, the rules were changed for Mrs. Thornton.

When Bill arrived at Stanwood he found the hospital pervaded with what he called the Underdog Philosophy. This, he said, was that the personnel knew the hospital was an underdog, and they put great effort into getting out of this position—basically the we-try-harder attitude. Nurses and personnel willingly worked very hard to prove that something small could be mighty. Bill learned that practicing in a rural hospital made a doctor

11

out of him quickly. Cases and crises were so diversified that he needed to use all the information he'd received in training. Nurses who came from large hospitals to Stanwood were presented with quite a challenge. No longer did they care for only one type of patient, such as maternity patients, or surgical patients. At Stanwood, they were required to anticipate the needs of the whole spectrum of patients.

Doctors often argue over whether medicine is an art or a science. They usually agree that it is a combination of the two. It sometimes seems, though, that at the large research-oriented hospitals medicine becomes heavily weighted with science and gets pretty short on the art. In a small hospital where heart transplants and artificial kidney machines are out of the question, the practice of medicine uses more art. This doesn't mean that scientific devices are shunned. Soon after Bill arrived at Stanwood he persuaded the hospital guilds to begin a long series of bake sales and chicken suppers to raise funds to buy a cardiac monitor and pacemaker for the hospital. The cardiac monitor is a machine which, when attached to the patient, keeps track of the heart rhythm and warns of a heart stoppage. The pacemaker sets the normal rhythm of the heart, and the defibrillator stops abnormal rhythm. After these expensive machines were purchased, they were used daily and were attached to every patient undergoing surgery. In large hospitals these machines are hooked up only to selected high-risk cases, as they don't have enough machines for all their operating rooms being used simultaneously.

The fact that the hospital had no surgeon and desperately wanted one was very important in drawing Bill to the cut-over scrub land of Mecosta County. But the most influential reason for his picking Stanwood was its location in the country with acres and acres of surrounding empty land. Bill strongly feels that health care

12

is something to be handled in different kinds of medical units, the units in one grouped complex. First, the hospital cares for the acutely ill, those who require a great deal of attention. Second, near the hospital building, there should be a nursing-home facility; this would care for those who are only slightly ill and need only a minimum of medical watchfulness and care. The third part of his dream-complex would be a senior-citizen housing area, made up of duplexes and apartments for the elderly.

Though a great amount of capital is needed to build a comprehensive three-service facility like this, Bill still hopes that one day such a medical care complex shall become reality at Stanwood.

Bill envisions a free movement of people between these different types of medical units. When one of the elderly people becomes too sick to stay in his own little apartment, he is moved to the hospital for care. His spouse may visit him easily, take meals in the common dining room, or if unable to live alone, can be moved temporarily into the nursing home division. This movement of patients back and forth between units, depending upon their medical needs, is an ideal situation, and Bill believes this can be done best around a rural hospital where there is plenty of room for such a complex.

Many, many elderly people have great need for this type of medical-care complex. A typical example was a couple Bill treated early in his practice. In the middle of the night a woman called to report that the elderly wife of a neighboring couple was terribly ill. "You'd better get out there right away, Doc. It sounds like she's dying," was the warning.

This was another one of those backwoods calls, and Bill had learned through experience to get detailed directions for finding the house in the darkness. He scribbled a map from the neighbor's directions and, grabbing his medical bag and throwing a snow shovel in the trunk, he left.

After driving several miles west on gravel roads he found the directed landmark, a roofless barn, then turned onto what the local people call a two-track. A two-track is just what it says, two tire trails instead of a graded road. The trail wended into a heavy forest, and after a half mile it forked. As directed, Bill took the right fork and wound on through the woods. Another half mile and the track ended at the door of an unpainted shack, hopefully the right destination. The path to the door was walled in with stacked wooden crates, which Bill discovered were full of cabbages.

Upon entering the home, Bill found a couple well into their seventies. The two-room house was chilly and damp, the wood-burning stove hardly effective against the ten-below-zero weather. The wife lay in the unheated bedroom, heavily covered with layers of tattered quilts. It took very little examination to discover she was suffering from a severe case of pneumonia and needed hospital treatment immediately if she were to live. As Bill gently told the husband that his wife must go to the hospital, he glanced about the kitchen. Cabbage, cooked in every conceivable manner, was everywhere. Nothing else but cabbage. This old couple had been living, for who knows how long, on a diet of cabbage.

Bill drove to the neighbors a mile away to phone for an ambulance.

After ten days of hospitalization, the woman was nearly well enough to return home, but just at that time Bill received another phone call from the watchful neighbor. Now the husband was very ill, the neighbor said. Living alone and caring for himself had nearly done the old man in. After the husband was admitted to the hospital and under care, the wife was well enough to be dismissed, but Bill feared sending her home alone to their isolated shack and cabbage diet.

This is when the nursing home and housing facility for the elderly is needed. If these facilities were available, the wife could have gone to the nursing home or to their little efficiency apartment, and still been under a watchful medical eye with proper diet. She could have visited her husband frequently to cheer him up, and he could be dismissed from the hospital earlier if he lived nearby.

Those elderly people who are not seriously ill can live alone, and most of them prefer having their own home or apartment. Their one big fear is not dying alone, but dying with unnecessary suffering. Everyone hears too frequently about the elderly man who fell down outside and broke a leg, but died from exposure before being discovered. Or worse, of the woman who broke her hip falling in her own living room and died painfully after long, struggling hours not twenty feet from her telephone. Older people know these deaths are especially sad because they are unnecessary if routine checks are made upon those living alone. In housing geared especially for the elderly, these periodic checks are made. Also, push-button alarm systems are installed in bathrooms and bedrooms so aid can be summoned.

With the many acres of inexpensive land around the hospital, Bill knew all sorts of things could be done to give a medical complex pleasant surroundings—even a buffalo herd.

These are the reasons Bill chose this country hospital in remote surroundings. He knew he was swimming against the current. The rapid transfer to bigness in the medical field meant that present-day small hospitals are rapidly being closed down and sacrificed to large hospitals. He was willing to take the chance with a small hospital, working to surround it with a nursing home

15

and housing complex, and thus allow a small hospital to survive and perform with excellence.

We liked living in a rural area. During Bill's schooling we had suffered through eight years of city living where the view from our windows ranged from the neighbor's garbage cans to a used-car lot, to a sooty brick wall of the adjoining building. We breathed the stench of polluted air and lived with the grime which filtered onto our window sills. Now, at Stanwood, the air was clear and clean, the only odors being those from the vast forests of pine trees and the honey-sweet fragrance of newly mown hay.

Bruce and Beth explored the woods behind our house, climbed the smaller trees, and fashioned a wobbly clubhouse from woodpile logs. Too young to join in outdoor activities, Kerry gurgled and grinned from her playpen, enjoying the kaleidoscopic movement of leafy tree branches through the windows. The perceptive wisdom in her watchful eyes continued to amaze us. It made me feel almost uneasy. A baby shouldn't look like a wise old man, I thought.

Quickly, Bruce and Beth grew acquainted with our farming neighbors and adjusted to our new environment. We wanted our children to grow up with trees to climb and build treehouses in, brooks to wade and fish in, and fields and woods to explore. With these toys of nature, the fragile baubles from Santa Claus seemed paltry and dull.

Bill and I also shared a theory that children should be raised with all kinds of people. We feared that if we settled in a city, we would soon be walled into a middle-class suburban ghetto, where our children would go to school and play only with children similar to themselves. In a rural area you have all kinds of neighbors, successful and unsuccessful farmers, airline pilots, hillbillies in dirt-floored shacks, writers, and bankers. The children of all these people mingle at the one school. Our children would learn from the outset that there are many kinds of people and many ways of living a life.

Life at Stanwood was very different—another world. We left our city apartment, the humming brick pavements, the whining electric buses, the sirens, and moved to utter stillness. The expression, "rolling up the sidewalks at sundown" isn't an exaggeration at Stanwood. The businesses (all six of them) are closed by six P.M. After that, Main Street is in darkness except for the lone street light swinging from its wires overhead.

The people of the community were pathetically anxious that I like Stanwood. "Do you really like it here?" they asked at every opportunity. "In the past," they explained, "all the doctors who came here seemed to like Stanwood. It was their wives who made them leave for the city."

Always, I reassured them, "I'm a small-town girl. City living holds no allure for me."

Still, they remained wary and concerned for my happiness. Perhaps they were troubled because I seldom left the house to socialize those first few months at Stanwood. With a small baby and two other children not yet of school age, motherhood and homemaking duties occupied most of my time.

Only five months after our moving to Stanwood, little Kerry died very suddenly. "Acute fulminating meningitis" was the pediatrician's diagnosis. Smiling and well at breakfast, she became ill late in the morning, and passed away before midnight.

Bill and I were stunned with grief. For a long time we just stared at each other, unbelieving. However, there were things to do.

The laboratory tests showed that a particularly virulent and contagious germ had struck Kerry. We left the hospital, rushing home to begin administering preventative medication to Bruce and Beth. Suffering with grief and trying to explain Kerry's death to Bruce and Beth without unduly alarming them, we hurriedly scrubbed and sterilized all the baby equipment, clothes, and toys which might harbor deadly germs. The preventative medication made us slightly ill, and we moved through the nightmare of funeral arrangements in a miserable daze.

The winter's first severe blizzard was in progress, preventing travel. Our families in Iowa agonized over our being among strangers at that sorrowful time. But the "strangers" immediately turned into loving friends who rallied to our home in sympathy and concern. They listened to our bewildered ramblings, our "Why did this happen to Kerry?" protests, and showered kindness upon Bruce and Beth, both badly frightened by the sudden topsy-turvy state of their world. Especially comforting were the complete strangers who risked driving the snowy highway to tell us that they, too, had lost a child. Some of them had lost an only child; others lost a child from a fall or poison. We wept in shared grief with these strangers, and the realization that others had lost and suffered more than we, swept away our self-pity. Sorrow remained, but as a regret for Kerry herself and her too brief life.

In the weeks that followed, the memory of Kerry's wise, perceptive eyes haunted us. It almost seemed as if all along Kerry had been aware of something which was beyond our knowledge. Her life spanned only half a year, but that brief life changed Bill and me a great deal. Losing Kerry taught us that we were stronger than we'd suspected, that we could bear what we'd thought unbearable. Her death also erased a growing trait of smugness in us. We'd been managing our destinies pretty well, planning for children and reaching our goals. When the lives of other people had gone awry, we'd secretly suspected them of mismanagement or careless planning. Kerry's brief stay ended such arro-

18

gance, reminding us that we are not always masters of our fate.

As the months went by the ache of grief retreated. We no longer felt like strangers in the community, but a real part of it. I began hoping that we might have another baby, and thinking of that made the future cheery.

Like everyone else in a rural village, we spent our evenings at home. Perhaps it was those silent, dull evenings that got Bill to dreaming. He often had a thoughtful look about him. I should have guessed he was contriving something to combat the dullness, but I wasn't prepared for the announcement he made one morning.

"I'm going to raise buffalo," he said, tossing it out casually, the way one would say, "I'm going to get a haircut."

I think I said, "Oh?" as I'm not any good at clever retorts. Anyway, I wasn't worried. I knew buffalo were extinct.

After breakfast Bill insisted the children and I join him in our backyard to walk the land, all five acres of it.

"Can't you just see a herd of buffalo peacefully grazing out here?" he asked.

I could just see a herd of buffalo stampeding through my clothesline and flower beds and trampling the children, but I said, "Yes, dear." I was quite sure they were extinct, living peacefully in their happy hunting ground with the dodo bird and the passenger pigeon.

That evening I discovered Bill was serious. He was actually preparing to write a letter ordering ten buffalo. He hadn't the slightest idea where to write, but decided it had to be somewhere in the West. He picked Wyoming as a nice, typical western state and wrote a letter to the Conservation Department of Wyoming, asking where we could purchase a small herd of buffalo.

I was so embarrassed. I could just imagine the tittering and giggling at the Wyoming Conservation Department when they received his request. I hoped none of his patients ever found out he had written such a letter.

Surprisingly, we received a prompt reply informing us that according to their records, such-and-such ranch in Wyoming did have some buffalo.

Bill wrote to the ranch and hopefully awaited their answer. A reply never came. An extinct ranch, too, I figured. Or else the Conservation people thought they'd have a little fun with that nut who wanted some buffalo.

Bill wasn't about to give up, though. He went right on sending letters, and I went right on blissfully thinking buffalo were extinct.

Besides, I really wasn't concentrating on buffalo. Preparations for our expected baby occupied my thoughts. At last, we were rewarded with a beautiful daughter, Brenda, whose sweet and sparkling disposition brightened our household. Her birth alone assured her of prestige within the family. As our only Michigan-born member, she was unique, but it was her Stanwood hospital birth which greatly elevated her position. Bruce and Beth were seven and five when Brenda was born, and how they envied her! She was a native, while they were foreign-born Iowans.

With a baby in our home again, I put my energies to diapers, playpens, and nursery rhymes. In that busy maternal fog I paid little attention to Bill's mail search for buffalo.

One day Bill got a response from the Department of the Interior. They sent a leaflet actually showing pictures of buffalo and claimed to have four game refuges, all harboring buffalo. Now I began to worry. Evidently buffalo weren't entirely extinct. There still were buffalo, but they were scarce.

We wrote to all four federal game preserves, asking if we could buy some buffalo. The Montana preserve suggested we try the Oklahoma preserve. In the same mail, a letter from the Oklahoma refuge suggested we try Montana. No one seemed eager to part with a buffalo. I began to suspect that, after all, the buffalo was just a mythical creature like the unicorn. Perhaps the government game preserves didn't really have any preserved buffalo. The government might be just trying to cover up their bungle of once having minted a buffalo nickel.

Bill continued writing letters, and I kept right on thinking it was all a big joke, a harmless pastime. Writing letters seemed a nice inexpensive hobby.

But the day came when Bill announced, "I've been looking hard for our buffalo ranch."

I went along with it. "Just what specifically do you look for when you look for buffalo-raising land?" I asked, not even trying to keep the sarcasm out of my voice.

His answer confirmed my fears. He *had* been giving it a lot of thought. "I want at least one hundred acres," he said. "It's got to have a creek or river or lake on it for watering the buffalo. It can't be too remote or off the beaten path, or deer hunters will be poaching my buffalo." Bill's forehead wrinkled deep as he pondered the problem. "I'd really like to find some land right on the main highway."

For nearly two years Bill kept up his search for suitable buffalo land, checking out leads and exploring the countryside for miles up and down the highway.

Then one day his car sped into the driveway, spinning up a cloud of dust. I stared out the kitchen window, flabbergasted. Bill—home in the middle of the day—an unheard-of occurrence! Bill dashed into the house, taking the back steps in one long leap. His eyes gleamed with excitement.

"I've found it, Pinkie! I've found it!" he cried, picking me up and whirling me around.

Though a bit dizzy and dazed, I gasped, "Found what?"

21

"Why, our buffalo ranch, of course!" Bill said, putting me down suddenly. The I'm-disappointed-in-you look on his face told me I should know that nothing but finding the buffalo land could be so exciting.

He raised his chin defiantly. "I've found our buffalo ranch, and I'm going to buy it!"

Who else would buy it? I wondered silently. Were there other prospective buffalo breeders lurking about?

I poured us each a cup of gritty, warmed-over coffee and sat down at the kitchen table to hear the details.

The land Bill wanted was ideal for his purposes. It seems the county needed a new jail, and in casting about for various sources of money, they thought of the long-unused county poor farm upon which the hospital was located. They could retain several acres for the hospital building, and sell the unneeded farm land. Of course, farm land for sale isn't exactly a hot item in Mecosta County. For years, Mecosta County's farmers had been leaving its thin, sandy soil for the more dependable weekly paycheck from General Motors and Ford Motor Company.

For his office Bill had been using three rooms on the first floor of the hospital, rooms the hospital badly needed, and Bill was worried about what to do for an office. By buying the hundred acres of poor farm, he would have his buffalo patch, a construction site for his office building which would be stone's-throw handy to the hospital, and land for the future nursing home and senior-citizen complex. It was perfect.

Bill eagerly offered to take the old poor farm off the county's hands, and they, just as eagerly, agreed to sell it to him.

That day marked the end of Phase One of our buffalo hobby. I fondly remember Phase One as the inexpensive phase, the postage stamp phase. A few dollars' worth of stamps pasted on letters searching for buffalo hadn't upset my household budget.

Without Reservation

3 Bill insisted that the children and I accompany him in exploring our newly-acquired buffalo breeding grounds. We parked the car at one side of the narrow gravel road which formed the south boundary of the farm. I stared glumly at a huge tangle of brush which formed a thick screen from one end of the pasture to the other.

Like two young deer, Bruce and Beth frolicked into the dense thicket, vanishing into their own world of adventure and exploration. Occasional soprano war whoops assured us of their whereabouts.

In the midst of that tangled jungle ran the needed water supply, Bill informed me. "Once we get all that brush and tag elder cleared out of there, it'll be the most beautiful brook you've ever seen," he said. "Come look. I'll lead the way."

Swinging a machete, Bill struggled ahead, breaking trail. I followed, trying to carry Brenda, but thorns kept snagging her ponytail until she begged to "go it alone." Her stocky little body moved ahead, maneuvering through small openings and creating her own low-to-the-ground trail.

After fighting our way through fifty feet of thorny, ripping overgrowth, we arrived at the clear, bubbling creek. It was a beautiful creek, cold and clean, hurrying noisily over rocks, curving and weaving its way through

the thicket. Bill said the creek coursed the whole length of our land and never dried up or froze solid. This was important. Not being a farm girl, I didn't realize then (I do now) the importance of a constant drinking supply for animals.

Beyond the creek to the north lay acres of grassy pastures. But somehow it just didn't look like a farm to me.

When I think of a farm or a ranch, I picture a neat white farmhouse, a red barn, some sheds, and a windmill. This farm was just land. Nothing more. If you looked carefully, you could see there had once been fences, but that was long ago, in better days. Now all the fence posts lay prostrate on the ground, and there's nothing more useless than a fence that's lying down on the job.

"The poor fences are dead," Brenda commented, as she toddled around. Bill ignored her. After all, what does a three-year-old know about real estate investment?

"Isn't it beautiful?" Bill breathed as we stared at the one hundred acres of desolate, scrubby land. "Doesn't it just smell like buffalo country? Perfect buffalo land," he murmured over and over.

Being no authority on the preferences of buffalo, I kept quiet. If all that fresh air hadn't addled my brain, I might have remembered that Bill was no authority on the preferences of buffalo, either. But he had a big advantage over me. He was born and raised on an Indian reservation in South Dakota. (And you know about Indians and buffalo.) Since I'm a native Iowan (this makes me an Easterner to Dakotans) I have to bow to his superior advantage of birth, at least when it comes to things like buffalo, blizzards, and dust storms.

Bill gets a lot of mileage out of his Indian reservation childhood. As the tenth of eleven children growing up in the droughty depression years of the early 1930's, he

24

never runs out of tales to widen our children's eyes. If one of the children balks at eating something, Bill reminds them of his childhood winters where home-canned goat meat was all that held off starvation. He tells them how a little boy feels going to bed so hungry he wants to cry, and dreaming of the small portion of mush that would be his breakfast. "Back on the reservation" this and "back on the reservation" that is a common phrase in our household.

Until we got the buffalo, the children weren't quite sure of their ancestry. They knew they were Scottish from my side of the family, but they had been dubious about their true inheritance from their father. He didn't wear moccasins or feathers, and couldn't speak much Indian. His entering the buffalo business changed their uncertainty.

People would ask, "Why do you raise buffalo?"

Bill would begin, "Well, I was born and raised on an Indian reservation in South Dakota . . . "

"Oh," they'd interrupt, nodding that they understood. Somehow, everyone accepted that as reason enought for raising buffalo.

The three children, of course, absorbed all this. When they had to fill in a "nationality" blank on a school record form, they wrote, "half-Scottish, half-Indian." The school accepted this (maybe on the basis of the buffalo) but it gave me the nervous giggles. You really couldn't find three children more blue-eyed and less Indian-looking than ours. According to the genetic tables, Bill's brown eyes and my blue ones should have produced a preponderance of brown-eyed children, but the blue genes won the battle each time.

And you might know, it was our middle child, Beth, who took greatest pride in her Indian-reservation ancestry. She inherited my copper-colored auburn hair, blue eyes, and abundant nose freckles. A more Scottish-looking lass you'd never see, but when asked

25

for her nationality, she'd proudly brag, "I'm half Indian!"

Every time the television Indians begin speaking their grunts and ughs, the children bedevil Bill for a translation. Sometimes his imagination works well, but other times he has to remind them that he left the reservation when he was fifteen.

It was in 1942 when Bill's parents went to Illinois to visit an uncle. To their surprise they found our country had come out of the great Depression several years before and was in the midst of a war-boom. People in Illinois weren't just subsisting, they had highly paid jobs. Both parents were hired for defense plant jobs, and Bill's mother returned to South Dakota to gather their belongings. Only Bill and his younger sister were still of school age, but three older sisters were still unmarried and living at home.

A farm truck was rented to move the furniture, and Bill was selected to go with the driver. Adjusting to civilization proved traumatic even the first hour's travel away from the reservation. At a gas station, Bill was exposed to his first sight of a flush toilet. It was one of those ancient devices with the tank suspended high against the ceiling. Bill pulled the chain, but the noisy roar of rushing water terrified him, and he raced back to the truck, his heart pounding. He was sure he'd broken the strange contraption.

Bill's early life of kerosene lamps and outdoor plumbing made his adjustment to the rural practice of medicine easier for him. Even so, he was taken aback by some things.

One of his first days at the hospital he was questioning the supervising nurse about the availability and location of some of the equipment. "And how about the emergency electrical system?" he asked her, wondering where the auxiliary generator was.

She motioned him to a small broom closet, where she

26

reached in and brought out a very long flashlight. Thrusting it toward him, she sighed apologetically. "This is our emergency electrical system."

She must have noticed Bill's face turn a pasty gray, for she quickly added, "The power company here is very good. We hardly ever have power failures, even in a bad thunderstorm."

Bill shuddered and went on with his investigating.

The three-room doctor's office just off the hospital lobby proved to be very adequate. He did not need X-ray or laboratory facilities because the patients could be sent to the hospital departments for that. This also helped the hospital's income, which was always precariously low. There was one disconcerting thing about the office, however. That was the view from the windows. Directly in line with them was the towering red barn, the remnant of the poor farm days. Bill thinks a barn is a thing of beauty, so he didn't mind that at all, but directly to the north of the barn and still very prominent in the view from his office windows was the village cemetery.

Local people thought this quite a joke. "Yup, Doc," they'd say, "you can look right out your windows and see your mistakes." Bill would laugh with them, but without mirth. Doctors don't like to think of mistakes—they're much too final.

That cemetery was a proper one, used for those who had the means to pay for a proper burial and a monument to mark their final resting place. It was sometime later when Bill found out about the other cemetery. In fact, he really stumbled upon it.

Bill had begun the habit of taking a relaxing walk after lunch, before office hours. He usually walked around the barn, which fascinated him, or to the pine tree plantings and meadows near the hospital. One day while walking through very high grass about a hundred feet from the barn, he stumbled upon something and nearly fell. As he crouched to see what had tripped him, he was startled to see a small tombstone. Just across the quiet road was the cemetery. What was this tombstone doing all by itself on this side of the road? Bill's first thought was that vandals had moved it, but he found it to be upright, and firmly cemented to a foundation. It was most puzzling.

That afternoon, while seeing patients, he questioned each of the local people about this strange lonely headstone, but none of them was aware of its being there. Late in the afternoon Bill finally got his answer from an eighty-three-year-old patient.

At one time the elderly man had been the caretaker at the poor farm. The old gentleman explained that the stone marked the grave of an inmate who had died.

"That's pauper's field out there, you know," he said, nodding toward the barn.

Most startling was the information that there were nearly a hundred and fifty other bodies buried out there, those who had died while inmates. Only one had relatives who later placed a marker over the grave, and that explained the one lonely tombstone.

Bill and the former caretaker walked out to the grisly area. Now that he knew what to look for, Bill could see it was, indeed, an old, unmarked burial ground. By peering through the long unmown grass and feeling the uneven contour of the ground with his feet, he could make out grave-size depressions, neatly arranged in rows, and laid out two-by-two.

What an ignominious end, Bill shuddered. All those people, obscure in life, and even their final resting-place forgotten. A whole forgotten cemetery!

The old man pointed to the far row. "Black Sal's over there. I recollect helping bury her. Sal come here through the underground railroad, runnin' away from slavery. She was a good woman, but Sal never could find a job."

He waved a wrinkled hand toward the barn. "Willy

and Frank are nearer the barn. They're buried together, you know."

Bill didn't know, but he got the story out of the man,
and it was truly a strange story. Willy was a poorhouse
inmate all his adult life, which came to an end before he
reached fifty. Stanwood children knew of him as "Silly
Willy from the county farm." Willy never bathed, he
spoke in grunts, and he drooled profusely. Everyone
avoided Willy, except Frank. Willy loved to walk about
the poor farm, through the fields, and down to the
creek, but once he got beyond the barn, he forgot how
to get back. Fortunately, Frank accompanied Willy on
all his walks, and Frank knew the way home. Frank was
smarter than Willy. There was no question about that.
Frank was a large, dapple gray horse.

Near sundown Frank always started home, and since
Willy loved his only companion, he followed the big
horse back to the poorhouse. The county farm supervi-
sor relied upon this convenient comradeship, and the
arrangement went on for years. When Willy died, Frank
was a feeble, twenty-two-year-old horse. For many years
his only usefulness had been in keeping Willy from
getting lost. It was decided that it would be fitting to
shoot Frank and bury the two companions together.
Comrades in life, they could spend eternity together.
Thus the grassy, innocent-looking meadow conceals the
remains of scores of unfortunate paupers and at least
one devoted equine, elevated to the honor of being
buried with man.

That meadow bothered Bill. He thought about it a lot.
Something should be done, he felt, to set it apart, to
commemorate it as a cemetery. The planting of trees
and bushes, with a hedge border, would make a pleasant bird sanctuary and lend a bit of dignity to this
anonymous burial ground.

Bill found the local citizens reticent about this cemetery on the wrong side of the road from "the real

cemetery." Their frowns said, "Forget it. Don't bring up the unpleasant past."

Perhaps you can't blame the people. Though poorhouses and poor farms are a part of the history of nearly every county and borough in our nation, it wasn't an admirable solution for the impoverished. No one points with pride to the old poorhouse. Stanwood prefers to think of the yellow brick building as "the hospital," which it had been for only ten years, forgetting its long history before.

Except for the county poorhouse, Stanwood's past was more grand than its present. The village began a century ago, carved out of the vast forest which covered northern Michigan. Just three miles to the north, the spring floodwaters of the mighty Muskegon River annually floated thousands of huge white pine logs to the sawmills located at its mouth on Lake Michigan. There, they were sawn into the boards which rebuilt Chicago after Mrs. O'Leary's incendiary cow caused the great fire. Though surrounded by the virgin pine forest, Stanwood was located in a shallow valley of clay soil, which produced an abundance of hardwood trees. Stanwood was situated in this stand of hardwoods, thus, its name for "stand of wood." Huge kilns were erected, and the beautiful old hardwood forest was chopped down and fed to the kilns. The hardwood was baked into charcoal, much in demand for the busy forges of nineteenth-century blacksmiths.

The village straddled the railroad line linking Indiana to the Straits of Mackinac, and for a few years Stanwood grew and prospered. Three hotels lodged the many travelers and visitors. There was even an opera house boasting a grand ballroom.

When the hardwood forest was gone, as were the pine forests to the north, miles upon miles of desolate stump-covered land surrounded Stanwood. It took a very stubborn or desperate farmer to pull all those huge

stumps from the earth before the land could be culti-
vated. Many residents went farther south, or out West
where the soil was richer and more productive. Others
moved to Detroit to get jobs in Mr. Ford's new auto
factory. Frequent fires, common in those days of
wooden buildings, destroyed the three hotels and many
business places, none of which were replaced. Stanwood
became a ghost of its former promise.

Today, second-growth trees cover much of the land,
and once again Stanwood is surrounded by the same
mixed forest of hardwoods and pine as a century ago.
Brushy undergrowth pushes closer to the village,
threatening to reclaim even the town.

In the business section vacant lots gape between the
stores like toothless spaces in a mouth. These are the
fire scars which gnawed away at the town. Older citizens
point to these empty, weed-grown lots and sadly recall,
"That's where the old opera house was, and over there,
the pickle factory, the blacksmith shop, the hotel."

Fewer and fewer of the inhabitants still farm. Most
have turned to the greater income and security of
factory jobs. They drive as far as Grand Rapids, a
hundred-mile round trip. Many of the car pools have
gone on for twenty years, with a twenty-year poker
game continuing among the riders. The riders not only
have traveled to work together for twenty years, but
they grew up together and went through school together. Those who remain in Stanwood are a closely-
tied group.

Stanwood is by no means a picturesque little town like
the quaint New England villages pictured on Christmas
cards. But there are two structures in the village which
save it from being an ugly town. These are the two
churches. The small white clapboard church on the hill
points a graceful steeple to the heavens, and is a
charming little rural church. The other church, a next-
door neighbor to the hospital, is a fieldstone structure,

31

faced completely with round, glacier-scoured stones. Bill and I had never seen this type of stone masonry until we moved to Michigan, and we found the surviving examples lovely. These grapefruit-sized rocks were common in the area, and in the past a few stonemasons had lovingly specialized in this craft. The church on the corner is not only unique in its stonework, but zealous in its evangelism. On his first Sunday morning in Stanwood, while making rounds on the hospital patients, Bill was surprised to hear church music clearly ringing through the corridors. He discovered the stone church has an outdoor loudspeaker system, and every Sunday morning hymns fill the whole valley with music. The hospital patients get great comfort from this broadcast music, and no one in Stanwood can forget that it is Sunday morning. Perhaps the calling music persuades a few would-be Sunday fishermen to attend church.

Like most rural houses of worship, Stanwood's churches practice the good old-time religion. Their religion is not a passive discussion period, and modern theologians with their God-is-dead theories are considered blasphemous pagans. The hymns in these country churches have a beat and rhythm which begs the feet to tap and the hands to clap. Theirs is a participating religion in which everyone sings with gusto and feeling. Their rules of morality harken back many years. Liquor, tobacco, cosmetics, dancing, playing cards, and women wearing slacks are strictly forbidden.

Included in Bill's Dakota upbringing was a heavy dose of this type of old-time religion. My church education had been regular and sincere, but of the restrained and decorous type. Again, Bill was better prepared for Stanwood than I.

My first intimate exposure to evangelism occurred a year after we settled in Stanwood.

I'd finally met a congenial friend near my age, and she had undertaken the task of teaching me the game of golf. She was an expert and enthusiastic golfer, and I clutched eagerly to golf as a symbol of worldly sophistication amid my pastoral living conditions. I think I reasoned that taking up golf might keep me from becoming a complete country bumpkin. We tried to play once a week, but it took a bit of doing as we both had small children and thus, baby sitters to arrange for. If weather cooperated and baby sitters could be located, I drove ten miles to her house to pick her up. Then, together, we had a twenty-five mile trip through a sparsely populated national forest to reach our golf course. With all these preliminaries, our golfing preparations had to start early in the morning.

One warm summer morning it was just slightly past seven when I wheeled my golf clubs out of the garage. I was frantically hurrying the children through their grapefruit and Rice Krispies when a strange car pulled into our driveway. Since I was trying to wipe grape jam off my white golf shorts, Bill went to the door.

"We're here," said strange voices.

I went to the hall to see who "we" were and found Bill decorously leading a very, very old gentleman and two women (his daughters, I learned) into the living room.

"We'd like the whole family here," they said, and I dutifully brought the children from the kitchen.

After we were all seated, the old patriarch stood and made his presentation. A ninety-six-year-old retired minister, he had made a gift of appreciation for Bill. He took great pains with his speech, just as he had with the lovely wooden chest he'd constructed. Though his voice was thin and shaky, his seventy-five years in the pulpit still stood by him. There was fervor in every sentence, and I began to see what is meant when one hears of the old "fire and brimstone" preachers.

During the speech I suddenly became aware of my golfing shorts and my long, bare legs. Though the three visitors seemed to be ignoring my attire, I felt absolutely unchaste even in my own living room. Frantically, I looked about for a sweater or a dish towel or something to toss over my nakedness, but, for once, there was nothing lying about.

After the speech, Bill rose to accept the gift, and I glanced uneasily at my watch, thinking of my golf partner waiting vainly for me. But there was yet more ritual for the occasion.

The elder of the two daughters strode toward the piano. A tall, robust woman with florid complexion haloed by white hair, she arranged herself carefully at my baby grand. She debated a moment about the most appropriate song, then launched into it with gusto. She had the bosom and the build of a Wagnerian soprano, and also the volume. Her zealous voice easily could have filled a concert hall or a church; but in our average-sized living room, the sound overflowed.

Bruce, who was only five years old then, scrambled behind the davenport. Three-year-old Beth threw her chubby little hands over her ears and ran to me. I quickly pushed her down out of sight beneath an end table. Our big Weimaraner scurried under the coffee table, and Cleo, our fat mongrel, ran wild-eyed under the piano, of all places. There Cleo hunched, quivering, her big brown eyes fastened on me, while the decibels rained down upon her.

The aged minister enthusiastically joined his daughters in song. The trio threw back their heads and sang joyously with the true abandonment of devoted Christian evangelists.

I prayed steadily through the renditions of those rousing hymns. I prayed that the dogs wouldn't howl, that the children wouldn't cry, and that I wouldn't do or say the wrong thing.

I did finally get to the golf course that day, and surprisingly, I shot the best round I'd ever done. It just couldn't have been that sunrise revival service, I told myself.

That evening when Bill got home I was filled with questions. I was uneasy about whose soul they'd been trying to save—his, or mine? Why the prayer meeting?

Bill explained that the old preacher was merely showing his gratitude for Bill's having saved his life during a recent illness. The elderly man felt he wouldn't be able to repay Bill for his services. He was doing what is commonly done in rural communities where a neighborly attitude means that you exchange talents. Each man gives of his own talent to his neighbor. The old man's talent happened to be saving souls and religion, and he did the best he could for Bill by honoring him with a personalized church service.

"The old gentleman doesn't know it," said Bill, "but at one time I was on the road to becoming a minister of the gospel myself."

Now this was a surprise—something Bill had never told me about.

Bill went on. "When I was fourteen I spent a summer with a traveling evangelist, preparing myself for a life in the ministry. We held tent revival meetings in most of the villages across the reservation. I led the singing and the prayer groups. I think I got into this because I felt guilty about something I'd done a couple years before that." Bill chuckled, remembering.

I fidgeted uneasily, wondering what his childhood sin could be.

"In Rosholt we had a basement Pentecostal Church which periodically held revival meetings," Bill continued. "On warm summer evenings my buddy, Moon, and I used to sit in the darkness by the basement windows, peeking at the goings-on at these revivals. We'd heard that some of the blessed ones would speak in tongues when they got saved. Moon and I watched many nights to see this. The meetings all were pretty humdrum and dry. No one seemed to be touched by the Lord.

"One night Moon and I decided to liven up the services. We had foot-long pea shooters with which we'd become deadly accurate. Large tapioca was our ammunition. We each poked a hole through the screen and waited. Finally, one of the parishioners went forward to the altar to be saved. The minister laid his hands on her bowed head. Both had their eyes tightly closed and were deep in prayer when I let go with a tapioca missile aimed at her backside. Instead, I hit her on the shoulder, but what a response! She thought she'd been touched by the Lord. The stout woman fell to the floor with wild gyrations, grunting unintelligible gibberish. Voices cried out, 'She's talking in tongues!'

"Moon and I were amazed at the reaction. We hadn't come there with true evangelistic spirit, but apparently we'd been instrumental in helping someone on her way to salvation.

"As the woman rolled on the floor, freeing herself from sinful spirits, a changed atmosphere came over the congregation. With tears in their eyes and glory in their voices, the crowd bellowed, 'Praise the Lord! Hallelujah! The Lord is with us tonight!' "

At this point in Bill's confession I was convulsed in tears of laughter. Bill described how the people began leaving their seats and filing up to the altar.

"When the altar was full," Bill continued, "those remaining knelt in the aisles and prayed. Moon and I were kept busy touching each kneeling person with gifts from the Lord. We'd gotten everyone at the altar worked up and were starting in on those along the aisle. We'd been getting pretty giddy and careless. Suddenly we noticed there was a great deal of tapioca spread over the church floor. Prudently, we stopped the heavenly missiles and just watched.

"The pandemonium was still raging when we reluctantly headed home. The minister was still giving thanks to the Lord for the most successful revival meeting he'd ever experienced. Talk of that successful revival went around town for months after that, and Moon and I always felt a little bit guilty."

Bill's early life back in Dakota prepared him for understanding a wide variety of experiences. Understanding the rural mind, evangelistic religion—these new strange things weren't bewildering to him as they were to me. My piano lessons, summer camps, and college education had left me sadly inadequate to cope with our life in Stanwood. Bill had to educate me for our life in the bush.

After we'd purchased the buffalo ranch, Bill's job as my teacher became enormous. My knowledge of farming was even less than my knowledge of country life. But Bill is courageous. For his first agricultural lesson, he undertook teaching an inept wife and three young children how to construct a buffalo fence.

■
"Hevy"
Fences

4 Now the buffalo hobby became more expensive. We bought the hundred acres of "buffalo land," and with the purchase price we could have built a road out of five-cent postage stamps from here to the Little Big Horn. We christened our land the Rx Ranch, in deference to our neighbor, the hospital.

With the optimism only found in the innocent—or fools—we painted a ranch emblem on the front doors of my black car. We started with a background of a large, fleecy white cloud, and upon this we painted a brown buffalo. The cloud symbolized the ephemeral, dreamy character of our project. Because of our nonexistent artistic talent, the large brown buffalo resembled a fat camel with horns.

The local reaction to our announced enterprise was strictly Suppressed Smiles. We might have painted a unicorn on our car and announced we were going to breed unicorns. The citizens of Stanwood shook their heads and grinned. Their smiles said, "Some people sure have a weird sense of humor."

By publicly announcing we were starting a buffalo farm, we were going out on a limb in a big way. We'd exhausted all our leads and hadn't located even one scrawny buffalo for sale. Yet Bill is a great one for positive thinking, and his attitude was infectious. I found myself almost believing that someday we would have a herd of buffalo. That's faith. Of course a few elderly Indians still believe the buffalo will come back some day, and a lot of good their faith has done them.

The deed was signed, the Rx Ranch was ours. It awaited its fate—being turned into a buffalo stamping ground. Now we had to figure out what a self-respecting buffalo would want.

Grass. That was Number One, and we had plenty of that, it seemed. But it wasn't buffalo grass. What if buffalo ate only buffalo grass? This horrifying thought sent us collecting and researching Department of Agriculture bulletins. Our vocabularies became enlarged by learning that buffalo grass is really *Buchloe dactyloides,* and that it is a stoloniferous perennial grass, etc. We finally decided to stop worrying about it. If our buffalo were going to be Michigan buffalo, they'd have to learn to relish Michigan grass. We'd show them right from the start—they couldn't buffalo us!

Number Two on the list of buffalo needs was water, and the little creek meandering across the pasture would take care of their drinking needs nicely.

Number Three was trees for shade, and for rubbing and scratching against, and blessedly, enough trees were already growing there.

Those first three necessities were easy enough, but the fourth, and last, turned out to be a real problem. Number Four was a tight, strong enclosure to keep the buffalo confined to their stamping ground. Namely, a Superfence.

I knew absolutely nothing about building a fence, but a faint voice within me whispered that this was one of those Big Projects. Bill, with his infernal positive thinking, absolutely adores Big Projects, but I'm a foot-dragger from way back. My one Big Project was undertaken in childhood. I spent an entire summer behind our garage with a teaspoon, digging a hole to

China. I had finally dug to the two-foot level when my father stepped into the hole one dark night. He filled in my Big Project with a few scoops of a spade, and I learned a lifelong lesson: "Don't tackle big jobs with a teaspoon"—or Do-it-yourself means doing something the hard way.

Oldtimers say a good fence should be horse-high, bull-strong, and pig-tight. Our fence had to be a Super-fence—buffalo-high, buffalo-strong, and buffalo-tight. Bill decided to start by fencing in "only" fifty acres. Sort of a practice drill, he said. After some complicated arithmetic, we discovered this would be over a mile of fencing, and the cost of the new fencing materials would be over a thousand dollars, not counting labor.

Our whole project faltered temporarily while Bill reconnoitered. He finally decided that much of the old wire fencing lying about the pastures could be salvaged. The wooden posts were decayed and rotten, but the woven wire, though buried under years of accumulation of grass and leaves, seemed miraculously preserved.

Resurrecting a dead fence is a job no mortal should undertake. During election time you hear the term "grassroots" thrown about casually, but we learned there's nothing casual about grassroots. The prairie farmers learned how strong grassroots can be when they first tried to plow the virgin sod, and broke their plows. Our horizontal, dead fence had been lying there so long the grass had grown attached to it—very attached.

Reviving the fence was real drudgery. It required no brains, just brute strength. Ten-year-old Bruce was strong enough to be an able hand. Volatile Beth, through her continual striving to keep up with big brother and his cronies—and succeeding—was far sturdier than most eight-year-olds. Brenda was our problem. Our ranch work was a family project, and Brenda insisted that she be included in our family labors. Bill and I proposed that a three-year-old's greatest contribution could be running errands, but Brenda felt demeaned by that sort of childish task.

"Run get this! Run get that!" she complained, "I want to help, too."

So she joined the rest of us as we lined up along a dozen feet of buried fence and grabbed hold of a bit of wire peeking through the grass. As Bill called the yo-heave-ho pep calls, we pulled. Usually, Brenda either stood on the wire or leaned against it. Thus, her "help" forced us to lift her weight along with the fence. We tugged and heaved to free the wire. First to give were our fingernails, then our jacket seams, and finally the grassroots creaked and tore. Up from its grave came twelve feet of wire fence. Then we moved on to the next twelve feet. When a long section of dead fence was loosened in this way, we rolled it up.

Bruce and Beth discovered that rolling the wire was fun, like pushing a snowball through wet snow and watching the ball grow larger and larger. As with making a giant snowball, the roll of wire eventually became too heavy for them to push farther.

As the children grunted and heaved those rolls of wire across the meadow, often they were rewarded with delightful treats of nature—a nest filled with big-eyed, nose-twitching baby rabbits, or a mother possum, her hairless babies clamped to her underside. Bruce and Beth were careful not to tamper with the wild animals they discovered. Through the code of a children's grapevine, rural youngsters at an early age learned that human interference upset the balance of nature.

However, once when they discovered a nest of pink, hairless field mice, the children couldn't resist. Apparently, they convinced themselves that the mother mouse had abandoned her babies. Upon arriving home, Bruce removed eight newborn mice from his pockets. An ardent detester of mice, I felt sure they'd never survive. Tenderly, for three weeks, the children administered to the baby mice, feeding them warm milk from a medicine dropper. Not a mouse succumbed. I thought it bizarre that in my basement and garage were traps set to catch invading rodents, while my children were nursing eight mice toward prolific maturity. The mice finally were declared mature enough for independence. On our next fence resurrecting detail, after carefully searching out their nest, Bruce released the pampered mice near their birthplace. From that time on, the children always worried about rolling heavy wire over one of "their" mice.

After weeks of pulling wire from matted grass, then rolling it up, our Rx Ranch was decorated with dozens of cumbersome rolls of wire fencing.

We gazed, misty-eyed, at these first products of our labor. With hands pressed into our aching backs, we consoled each other with how much money we were saving. After salvaging over half-a-mile of fencing, we gratefully put down our money and purchased the other half-mile of new fencing wire.

The posts for our Superfence had to be Superposts. Bill scouted the countryside, and finally, after much searching, wangled a good price from a nearby land clearance project and bought four hundred cedar posts.

These so-called posts didn't look at all like fence posts to me. They looked like logs. Each post was nine feet long, a foot thick, and covered with bark. Bill informed us that for every log to be transformed into a post, the bark had to be peeled off. This job was considered women's and children's work, while Bill went on to some of the heavier jobs of clearing brush and moving boulders.

We learned lots of things, the children and I, as we peeled those four hundred posts. On some, the bark peeled off neatly in nine-foot strips, as if from a banana.

Others absolutely refused to give up their bark without a fight, and these we attacked with butcher knives and fingernails. We became wary of the logs with reddish tinged bark—those were the real toughies. We pushed them aside until the bitter end. During this bark-peeling period we were enjoying beautiful Indian-summer weather, and friends sometimes stopped by to chat and get a breath of fresh country air. I became crafty at hoodwinking a visitor into helping me turn a log, and before he or she realized it, they were busy peeling posts, and wondering how they could take their leave without appearing lazy and unhelpful. Not long after we'd finished the last post, we were informed by a passerby that there was an instrument called a post-peeler which would have prevented all our bruised and scraped knuckles. There's always someone who spreads The Word too late!

The next stage in the erection of Superfence was the digging of the holes to receive the posts. There was great urgency now because winter was approaching. The holes had to be dug before the ground froze. While the children and I were still peeling posts, Bill began this awesome project. A post-hole digger is a strange tool, sort of a hinged spade, and if you've never wielded one, there's no point in trying to describe the feel of it. Only if your muscles have knotted and throbbed from post-hole digging, could you possibly understand. Now there's such a thing as digging post-holes by machine. There's a big attachment that goes on a tractor, the way a buttonhole attachment goes on a sewing machine. The tractor post-hole digger looks like a big screw and bores a post-sized hole in the ground. After the first few handmade post-holes, we decided we'd hire a farmer to machine-dig the holes for us, but a huge number had to be dug by hand, anyway. There were two swampy areas to cross, and a tractor couldn't get through these bogs. All those holes had to be dug by muscle power.

44

By no stretch of the imagination can I say that we made a game of post-hole digging, but a certain amount of suspense did add interest. Our Rx Ranch seemed to have a strange soil pattern, kind of a calico print. As we'd dig one post-hole, we'd be digging yellow clay soil, hard as concrete. Then the next hole, just twelve feet distant, might be pale sand. Every so often we'd dig into bright red soil—not common red clay, but rust-colored, sandy dirt. It didn't make the labors exactly fun, but our curiosity about what lay ahead kept us digging. It really got exciting after we found rainbow-hued oil slicks floating on the ground. With oil wells pumping twelve miles to the north of us, and eight miles south of us, we had our moment of wild glee. Then we remembered it takes tens of thousands of dollars to drill an oil well, and if it's dry—tough luck, Charlie! Our wildcatting impulses died a-borning. We picked up the post-hole digger and went back to work. But to this day when I get to wishing I had an automatic dishwasher or a new model stove, I remember that oily ground and wonder if our buffalo's hoofs are trampling over subterranean black liquid riches.

We needed lots of muscle power for our post-hole digging. One local teen-ager whose weight approached three hundred pounds dreamed of becoming a professional wrestler—one of those beefy performers who are one-quarter wrestler and three-quarters actor. The young man thought that digging post-holes would be an excellent way of developing shoulder muscles, and Bill quickly offered to help him train. For his professional gimmick, the boy would be called "Buffalo Bill," and he'd gain fame by his loud, guttural buffalo grunt when securing a hammerlock. He practiced the rasping grunt with each thrust of the post-hole digger. The deep sound echoed across the fields to the hospital, where the patients thought a wild boar was loose in the swamp. After a few days of this, the would-be wrestler decided

45

post-hole digging was too strenuous a training regimen and went back to his bar bells.

We labored on, digging Superholes for our Superposts, and the weather grew frostier, threatening to freeze the ground solid. At last the farmer came with his miraculous tractor-powered post-hole digger. This machine did in one minute what had been taking us a half-hour of hard digging. It was enough to make you sit down and cry.

One more job had to be finished before the big freeze-up. The four hundred posts had to be distributed along the fence line and set into the holes; the dirt must be tamped back around them to make them firm and solid. We borrowed an old pickup truck, and Bill gave me a quick course in truck driving.

After loading the logs on the truck, Bill climbed atop the teetering pile. My driving instructions sounded simple: I was to drive *slowly* along the imaginary line where our Superfence was to be erected, a line at this stage marked only by gaping holes. I was supposed to stay close to the holes, but somehow the holes concealed themselves in the tall grass, and occasionally one of the truck wheels gouged into a gaping abyss. It's a good thing the truck's engine was so noisy. I think our marital relationship would have suffered if I could have heard everything Bill kept shouting from the back of the truck. I drove along grumbling under my breath that I never claimed to be a truckdriver.

The holes were spaced twelve feet apart and I was supposed to drive slowly enough for Bill to throw a huge post out every twelve feet. Now driving along slowly isn't supposed to be hard (as Bill kept informing me every few minutes), but there was a problem. I had been instructed *not* to put on the brakes; for if I did, Bill would go flying off his precarious log pile perch. Driving along slowly without braking was easy on flat stretches, but unfortunately our Superfence had to coil up and down a few hills. As the truck started down the first incline, it picked up speed, but Bill had said *not* to put on the brakes. The truck rolled faster and faster, and my view in the rear-view mirror showed Bill throwing the posts faster and faster. His frantic tossing movements reminded me of something out of the old jerky silent movies. When we reached the bottom of the first hill I collapsed against the steering wheel in wild laughter. Bill felt wild, too, but not from laughter.

I knew he was furious because he called me "Jean" five times. On one of our first dates Bill dubbed me "Pinkie" because of my red hair. I've been "Pinkie" ever since, except when I've irritated him. Then I become "Jean."

Since our marriage survived that afternoon, I believe it can survive anything. The only other divorce-stimulating episode I recall was the first time I cut Bill's hair. That was back during his internship days, when we'd try anything to save money. That first haircut took three hours, and we were both in tears during most of that time. We weathered that storm; in fact, I was soon doing a pretty professional barber job in twenty minutes. But Bill never gave me another chance with my truck driving.

After the posts were all distributed into the holes and standing upright, we had to tamp the dirt around them until they were as solid as telephone poles (and about as big, too). With broomsticks and steel rods we thumped and pounded until the last post was firmly set. The buffalo pasture was outlined now by the not-so-straight line of naked posts surrounding it. We breathed a big sigh at the completion of that task, for the freezing winds could come upon us. The attaching of the fence wire could continue even though the ground was frozen, if the snow just didn't get too deep.

We unrolled our salvaged woven wire along the back fence line, using our shiny new purchased wire for the edge of the pasture facing the road. This was partly for appearances, but mostly because the wire facing civilization had to be strongest.

We stretched the fencing wire by pulling it taut with our car, then pounding the U-shaped metal staples into the posts, securing the wire. Superfence was really shaping up.

We shaped up, too, during this time. Bill looked glorious with his bulging biceps, while I tried to hide mine in long-sleeved blouses. Even when camouflaged, my muscles gave me away, for I swiftly took thirty strokes off my golf score. Though the golf ball manufacturers never came, I was ready for them with my testimonial: "I owe it all to Superfence."

All that autumn as we built Superfence, people stopped by and asked what the fence was for.

"Buffalo," we'd answer, and they'd grin at our big joke and drive on.

By the time the fence really began to look like a buffalo fence, panic started to creep over us. Where in the name of William Cody were we going to get a herd of buffalo?

We practically had their home made for the buffalo, but it wasn't like building a birdhouse and waiting for the birds to show up. Buffalo weren't going to just show up, in spite of the old beliefs of the plains Indians. Evidently the wild Indians of the West didn't know much about the birds and bees, for when the buffalo herds became scarce in the wintertime, the Indians never worried. They knew the buffalo had just gone into huge caves in the South in an "underground country." Come spring, the buffalo would swarm out of the caves and return to the hunting grounds to provide sustenance to the Indians.

Unfortunately, Bill and I did know about the birds and bees, and we just couldn't subscribe to this faith. We

48

were getting more and more uneasy. How were we to save face?

Here we had told everyone that our Superfence would soon be enclosing a herd of buffalo. We thought of conjuring up a herd of ghost buffalo, *a la Harvey.* We could pretend the buffalo were there, but only *we* could see them.

The Christmas season approached. Superfence was done, needing only two rows of barbed wire on top. We continued sending out letters inquiring about buffalo, following every possible lead, but with no results.

We finally gave up on letters and applications for buffalo from government-owned herds. They required bidders to be present at their auction corrals with cash and a stout truck, ready to haul away any buffalo won in the bidding. The hospital's struggles and the wintertime increase of sick people kept Bill running sixteen hours a day. We had no time to go traipsing off to Montana or Oklahoma to buffalo auctions.

We wrote to a private buffalo breeder who had a goodly number of animals, hoping he might sell us some. In a few weeks his answer came, scribbled hastily on the back of a corn and oats feed-bill on which the large amounts reminded me of the national budget. This breeder had quite a few buffalo, but none he wanted to sell. He carefully outlined the procedures we should go through to apply annually for buffalo from the government herds. We sighed wearily as we read this too-familiar story, but chuckled when we read his P.S. It said, "Frankly, it's easier to adopt a baby."

An important afterthought struck him, though, for he added a P.P.S. Its very simplicity was ominous. Misspelled and in all capital letters, it said, "HEVY FENCES." We thought of Superfence and wondered just how heavy was "HEVY."

So often you just don't see things that are right under

your nose. In a fit of childhood reminiscing I recalled an Iowan who raised buffalo just twenty miles from my home town. There returned a hazy memory of having seen grazing buffalo there along the highway to Mason City.

"Write to your father," Bill suggested immediately, "and find out if buffalo are still there."

I didn't really want to let my parents know Bill was trying to buy some buffalo. Even though we'd been married for thirteen years, like many protective parents, they weren't quite sure of this strange son-in-law from the reservation. He hadn't endeared himself to them any by taking me and their only grandchildren to the wild forests of Michigan.

However, I wrote to them requesting the name and address, and my father immediately replied that the man was no longer living, but his son continued the buffalo-raising tradition, and gave us his name and address. With little spirit we wrote another letter asking about buffalo for sale.

The absolutely unbelievable reply arrived the day after Christmas. We opened it listlessly, expecting another negative reply to our inquiry. After all our will-o'-the-wisps, the stationery looked authentic and impressive. In green ink the letterhead read, "Sherman Buffalo Farm, Nora Springs, Iowa." And beneath, the motto explained: "Breeder of Fine American Bison." A picture of a shaggy buffalo bull added to the realism. This was obviously no phantom buffalo farm, but the real thing.

The letter began: "Received your letter inquiring about buffalo this morning. I believe I could fix you up with the kind and number of animals you want."

We could hardly believe it. Was it possible that at last we had found buffalo for sale? Ironically, after years of writing letters all over the North American continent, we'd found buffalo practically in the backyard of my home town.

Bill answered immediately, asking Mr. Sherman to put ten buffalo on lay-away for us. Nine heifers and one bull was the specific order. Many letters were exchanged, a price agreed upon, and the buffalo scheduled for shipment to us in late March. Mr. Sherman suggested that we get an extra bull. Buffalo bulls are nearly impossible to ship once they become mature, and if our one young bull didn't mature into a productive bull, we would be stuck with nine spinster heifers and lose a year or two while we shipped in another young bull and waited to see if he were productive. Mr. Sherman had been around buffalo most of his life, so we took his advice and increased our order to two adolescent bulls and nine heifers.

Activity really picked up. Superfence had to be finished, strong and ready.

Bill had what he thought was an excellent idea for testing the holding qualities of Superfence. As a boy growing up in Dakota he'd always had a herd of goats to tend. For years he'd been hinting strongly that our son could never grow to real manhood without caring for a goat herd. Now Bill saw his chance. It seems that goats are very good fence-testers. If there's any kind of hole or weak place, the curiosity of a goat soon seeks out that spot.

We drove through back country roads looking for goats, and finally one chilly Sunday afternoon we spotted a bearded nanny goat tied outside a small unpainted shack. The owner gladly exchanged the goat for a ten-dollar bill. Nannie climbed cheerfully into the back seat of our car. I drove, while Bill and the children sat with Nannie, petting her and talking soothingly. I think the attention was unnecessary, for Nannie took the ride calmly, as if she always took Sunday afternoon drives. I

51

drove, red-faced and blushing, the ten miles to the ranch, trying to ignore the stares from passing cars.

Even without a goat passenger, our car was something to invite stares. Once it had been a beautiful, shining black sedan with white sidewall tires, but that was eleven years before. It was kind of a one-owner car, or at least a one-family car. My father had bought it new, then sold it to my brother, who sold it to us. They both had been fastidious owners. Not a scratch or rust spot marred its ebony finish. It stayed in fine shape so long as I just drove it to the store.

Then we bought the Rx Ranch and began building Superfence. The black car was our truck, our tractor, our bulldozer, and our fence-stretcher. It hurdled boulders and tree stumps, thickets and creeks. The back seat soon broke loose from the flooring, so we just removed it. That opened the whole trunk into the back seat area and was much better for cargo-hauling, though a bit drafty. After tearing out a few mufflers on rocks, Bill had the garage install a tractor-style exhaust pipe. The exhaust thrust straight up through the right front fender, and the muffler perched high on the pipe. When we stretched fence with the wire fastened to the door handles, they ripped off. The gas cap jiggled off somewhere, and we couldn't get a replacement for such an early-model car. Bill solved that problem with forthright farm ingenuity. He stuck a corncob in the hole. Gas station attendants always appeared startled when they reached for the gas cap.

After only a few months of farm labor the poor old sedan was reduced to an apparition. It still proudly sported the buffalo emblem on what was left of its front doors, and it was widely known and recognized as the "buffalo car." It wheezed and sputtered, but chugged on proudly, the perfect car for hauling goats.

We soon acquired an odorous billy goat and two other

nanny goats to join our first Nannie in the buffalo pasture to pursue their job of fence-testing.

Superfence passed the goat-test. Not a single goat found a way to freedom.

The rest of the winter we shivered and froze as we put the finishing touches on Superfence. By the end of March the last gate was hung and all was in readiness. Bring on the buffalo!

■
Our
Own Peace
Corps

5 Threatening clouds gathered over our struggling small hospital. Our six years of country practice at Stanwood had been six years through constantly stormy seas.

From the very beginning Bill was buffeted by overwork and strange new worries. During his first four months of rural practice Bill lost thirty-five pounds, and these were pounds his lean frame needed.

There were so many things medical school hadn't told us. We had assumed that a hospital was a reasonably permanent institution, like a church or a school. Because it was there yesterday, it would surely be there tomorrow. With Mecosta Memorial Hospital, our hospital at Stanwood, we found this was not so. Its precarious existence was almost a day-to-day survival. Only a few weeks after our arrival, we were startled to learn that the hospital financial situation had grown so dismal that the Board of Directors was considering closing the hospital. Bill and I were aghast. It seemed impossible that a hospital could be forced to close its doors. Besides, we'd gone into debt to purchase a home and equip an office. Now it seemed the rug was being pulled from under us. Bill's embryo dream was about to miscarry.

Though the hospital building was owned by the

county, no tax support was given the hospital. It is very difficult for a hospital to break even if it has no outside financial aid from either taxes or church support. Mecosta Memorial was especially hard pressed because of its old reputation as a charity home. Patients without funds or health insurance chose our hospital because it seemed the place to go when you were destitute and ill. Consequently, the uncollectable bills carried on the hospital's account books were well up into five figures. Mecosta Memorial was constantly in the position of having to provide nursing care, food, and drugs to patients who were unable to pay anything. The hospital's monthly expenses nearly always exceeded its monthly income. A crisis arose every two weeks when it became time to pay the nurses and other hospital personnel. As the administrator and the hospital-board president labored over the books, the people of Stanwood agonized with them. At these times, the main topic of conversation among the citizens was, "Can the hospital meet its payroll this time?"

Bill and I had been blissfully unaware of this situation when we chose Stanwood. The national shortage of hospitals and hospital beds had received so much publicity that we assumed every hospital to be indispensable. We knew the hospital was needed, as were Bill's services. It seemed so unjust that it was all in danger of being lost.

Bill spent many hours discussing the situation with hospital officials. They agreed upon one obvious solution for the hospital's financial troubles: more paying, non-charity patients were needed to raise the hospital's income to cover its fixed expenses. This could be done by getting doctors to settle and establish practices in some of the neighboring small towns, and their patients would tip the balance sheet in the right direction. The job of recruiting these doctors was delegated to Bill.

56

This suited Bill fine. He passionately wanted other doctors to come to the area; he needed colleagues, not just to stabilize the hospital's finances, but to work with him.

The bleak financial prospect wasn't the only blow introducing Bill to the rigors of country practice. We should have realized that the flashlight serving as the emergency-lighting system was only a portent of things to come.

A crisis arose during one surgical procedure which might have made a less courageous surgeon turn in his scalpel. The operation was a prostatectomy, the removing of a prostate gland from a seventy-six-year-old woodcutter.

A rusty, rattling pickup truck had delivered the old man to the hospital emergency entrance one frigid morning. Writhing in terrible pain, the man groaned, "Doc, I'm dying, I'm dying. Take my water so I can die in peace. Please, Doc, help me."

With a large-bore needle, Bill punctured the man's bladder, and nearly two quarts of urine were drained out slowly, to prevent rapid decompression and resulting shock. From the time this procedure began, the suffering woodcutter felt relief, and by the time the bladder was drained, he could smile wanly, saying, "Doc, I think I'm not going to die."

Roy was typical of the many backwoods relics found in the dense timberland around Stanwood. An old bachelor, he lived with his also unmarried brother. These old men still worked daily, just as they always had, cutting pulpwood in the forests. Dirty and disreputable as they appeared in their torn, grimy clothes, they were not destitute, or wards of the county, but confident, self-supporting citizens. It was just that bathing and washing were habits they'd never acquired. Winter bathing in a drafty, one-room shack would

57

probably have been pneumonia-inducing, and since the body went unwashed, it never occurred to them to wash the clothes they wore. Clothes stayed on until worn out and discarded, and a new shirt and overalls were purchased to sheathe the body.

Once Roy was comfortably settled in his hospital bed and Bill had finished with the examinations and tests, Bill told Roy that his prostate gland must be removed. Like most older men, Roy had heard of this operation and was very skittish about the whole procedure. Though he didn't know the name of it, Roy even knew there was a type of prostate removal which did not involve cutting through the skin.

"Can I have that kind, Doc?" he asked Bill hopefully.

Bill explained that the trans-urethral approach wouldn't be sufficient in Roy's case, that a better job could be done if he cut through the skin and removed all of the gland. Roy agreed that the surgery must be done, and pre-operative preparations were begun. X-rays, heart tracings, and blood work showed that Roy should tolerate the surgical procedure well, if it weren't prolonged. The nursing staff was briefed on the special post-operative care Roy would need. Continuous salt water irrigation of the bladder would be necessary for several days following surgery. A steady stream of water must flow into the bladder and return, washing out any blood before it could clot inside the bladder. Clots would cause an obstruction of the bladder outlet, and the patient would have to be operated on again.

On the morning of the surgery, Bill instructed the surgical nurses to move especially fast. He believed Roy would tolerate no more than fifty minutes of surgical time, and Bill hoped to finish in forty-five minutes. The initial incision was made, the bladder opened, and the prostate gland exposed. All went well. Bill had just cracked the gland and was starting dissection along the backside of the gland when two hard raps jolted the door to surgery. No one paid any attention. Interrupting surgery was unheard-of.

There were two more loud bangs, the door opened a foot, and Jake, the janitor, thrust his head into the operating room. One of the nurses gasped at this improper intrusion. Bill cleared his throat as he gathered harsh words to fling at the impudent janitor.

The janitor spoke first, saying, "The well's just gone dry."

A cold, bristly feeling crept up Bill's spine until he felt the back of his neck prickle. No water, he moaned inwardly. His first thought was to stop the operation, but the procedure was at the point of no return, and large amounts of irrigating water were going to be necessary no matter what. Bill continued enucleating the prostate gland.

"Okay, Jake, I hear you," Bill spoke as he went on working. "If the well's gone dry, you're going to be carrying a lot of water for the next five days. Go to some of the dairy farms around here and get five ten-gallon milk cans. Find someone in town who can give you fifty gallons of water every day. Start hauling water right now. I want fifty gallons here by the time we get this man back to his room."

Jake's voice quivered. He was nearly crying. "It's not my fault, Doc. I can't help it."

Bill continued without looking up. "I know it isn't your fault, Jake. That doesn't matter. We've got to have water, though. Bring it as fast as you can."

Jake ran out, enlisting the aid of all the neighbors in the area.

The crucial water arrived on time and was delivered in plentiful supply over the next five days.

Roy progressed beautifully following his surgery. The chief casualty was one country surgeon. Bill had acquired a few hundred more gray hairs. The absence of running water was another one of those things they

59

don't tell you about in medical school. Actually, that was the only time the hospital lost its water supply. There were two wells, but with extraordinarily bad timing, the emergency well froze in the six-below-zero February weather just at the time when the point on the regular well became clogged with gravel.

For forty-eight hours following his surgery, the old woodcutter lay in an incoherent fog. On the third day, while Bill and a nurse were changing his dressings, Roy's eyes became clear and bright. His gnarled hand crept slyly across the sheets and covered the hand of the pretty young nurse. Roy was getting well.

Bill saw Roy weekly after his dismissal from the hospital. On each of these office visits, the old bachelor quizzed Bill thoroughly about the operation he'd undergone. He wanted to make sure his cords had been tied securely so he couldn't get a woman pregnant. Each time Bill assured him that this was so, the procedure being a necessary part of the operation to prevent infection.

When the third visit brought a repetition of the previous line of questioning, Bill figured the old fellow was making too much of his lack of fertility.

"What's the problem, Roy?" Bill asked. "What's worrying you?"

Roy's answer gave Bill a new outlook on the romantic activities of old bachelors. Unlikely though it seemed, the unwashed old woodsman, just recovering from a severe prostate operation, was having a torrid affair with the young housekeeper he'd acquired to help during his recuperation. An illiterate, retarded woman who had been abused by her own family, she was warmly receptive to old Roy's kindness and affection. Bill didn't moralize over the situation. He knew the woman was better off than before, and the twinkle in the old woodsman's eye clearly told of his new-found interest in life.

"I sure thank you, Doc." Roy squeezed Bill's hand and hurried out of the office with his hunched-over gait.

From the very beginning, Bill knew he wanted to concentrate on caring for older patients. He liked older people and found their health an interesting challenge. Performing surgery on these elderly, poor-risk patients required a well-trained anesthetist who could "breathe" for that patient during surgery. Bill realized that his scope of surgery was limited by the ability and knowledge of his colleagues, especially the anesthetist. Some rural surgeons manage with a nurse-anesthetist or a family doctor giving anesthetic, but Bill knew immediately he would never do this. Bill also needed an internist adept at taking care of patients with bad hearts, diabetes, and strokes. A radiologist to pick up signs of tumors and cancer also was necessary. A team of good doctors had to be gathered to care for these poor-risk patients, and this wouldn't be easy. Few specialists are willing to live and practice in a rural area. An added complication was that any specialist who came to Mecosta County would have to carry on a general practice along with his specialty. The volume of patients in his particular field wouldn't be sufficient for an income.

Bill spread the word throughout his profession that we desperately needed doctors in our area. He wrote countless letters and made dozens of long-distance telephone calls.

I was certain it was a hopeless search, but Bill was optimistic. Surprisingly, a few doctors did show up to look us over. They were all hunting, fishing, and skiing enthusiasts. We wined and dined them, drove them through the forests, pointing out herds of deer and scenic trout streams. We especially emphasized the uncrowded backwaters of the hydro-electric dams along our Muskegon River, and the vast acres of untouched land awaiting the population explosion touted in the news media.

61

As soon as the visiting doctor began to show interest, talking of the farm he could have for raising registered cattle or homing pigeons, his wife always intervened.

Firmly, she'd notify her husband that this country might be a nice place to visit, but who'd want to live here?

If the husband reminded her that Bill and I seemed to be enjoying rural living, she had to think fast to be tactful. "The symphony is so important to me, dear," was a typical wifely rebuttal. "I have to be able to attend the symphony."

Even Bill, with his super-optimism, couldn't promise that Stanwood would someday boast a symphony orchestra: not Stanwood, where Lawrence Welk was considered too avant-garde and sophisticated.

On one occasion our hopes were raised high by a visiting doctor and his wife. She was an ardent trap-shooter and skier, and never once did she mention symphonies, Junior League, or Little Theater. They both thought the countryside beautiful. But that evening after dinner our hopes were shattered. The doctor, a much-needed anesthetist, was recounting some of his exploits in administering anesthesia, intending to impress Bill with his great abilities. In relating one instance of giving an anesthetic to an older woman, he told of a misjudgment or mistake he'd made.

Snapping his fingers, he chortled, "She died, just like that!" He broke into gales of wild laughter, and his wife joined him in the mirth.

Appalled, Bill and I gulped, staring at each other across the room. Things were difficult enough at Stanwood. We didn't need a colleague who thought it funny when he'd killed a patient.

The couple continued to talk, and it became apparent that they were sold on Mecosta County, as they began making plans for moving to join us. A sickening feeling spread through me until I heard Bill begin to speak.

"Oh, it's fun in the bush," he said, "if you think of it as being missionary work. You can't make any money, of course. Pinkie plans to get a job soon to help out, but it's so satisfying to know you're being of service to people who otherwise couldn't afford care."

I caught on right away to what Bill was doing. He cleverly managed to bring up and magnify every disadvantage of rural practice and living. Before their coffee was finished, the visitors were glancing around uneasily for their coats and wondering how to get away quickly from this peculiar clearing in the forest. It was disheartening to cut the line and let the fish get away, but we didn't want that species of fish in our pond.

We continued to court and entertain any visiting doctors who happened our way. After a time I could have driven, blindfolded, the grand tour of our countryside. I knew by heart Bill's sales pitch on the wonderful opportunities and potential in Mecosta County. Sometimes, if Bill was tied up with patients, I was called upon to conduct the auto tour and promotional talk. I really hated this because I was so poor at it. Bill was completely sincere when he spoke glowingly of the wonderful potential in our area, while my attitude was half-hearted and skeptical.

After several months of fruitless doctor-hunting, Bill thought of a former classmate who was not only an able anesthetist, but an avid outdoorsman.

"Dave is our man!" Bill exclaimed. "We've got to get him up here."

After many phone conversations and a visit to look us over, Dave agreed to join us. Like Bill, he saw the possibilities of Mecosta Memorial. With five young children, four of whom were boys, he liked the thought of his sons being able to explore the creeks and forests.

He hadn't brought his wife along, and warily, I asked, "But how do you think your wife will like it?"

"She'll be happy if I am," he shrugged.

Later, when I met Johanna, his intelligent German-born wife, I realized she was in the same position I'd been in when Bill picked Stanwood. So busy and involved with small children that we could think of little else, all we could say was, "Whither thou goest, I'll follow."

Delighted to have an able anesthetist working with him, Bill intensified his search for other doctors.

Over the next two years a few family doctors settled in neighboring villages. Then Bill heard of a former classmate who was completing a residency in internal medicine in Cleveland. Frank and his wife had been living in cities for some time, and I was sure making country converts of them would be an impossible task.

Weekends, we met them in Detroit and made the round of dinner clubs and current shows, while Bill preached the advantages of practicing in a small hospital. When Frank complained of the delays and inefficiencies of his present metropolitan hospital situation, Bill quickly pointed out how the very smallness of a country hospital brought efficiency due to the personal attention given each doctor and each patient by the technical personnel.

I enjoyed these urban weekends, so completely different from our rustic life, but Bill never quite adjusted. We'd have a big steak dinner early in the evening, then take in a few nightclub shows and perhaps a movie. At the close of the evening we might try the barbecued ribs at some recommended spot. However, Bill just couldn't imagine eating twice in one evening.

"But we've already had our dinner," he'd protest, bewildered at the strange eating habits of urbanites. Though no urbanite, I'm always ready to eat someone else's cooking, so the double dinner didn't upset me a bit.

It was mostly luck and timing that brought Frank to Stanwood. We'd just purchased a huge old log house,

64

picturesquely situated on the banks of the beautiful Muskegon River. We'd fallen in love with the huge cedars and pine forming a canopy over the house and the clear trout stream rippling through the backyard. Fearing someone else might beat us to it, we bought it without waiting to sell our little brick Cape Cod house. So it happened that just as Frank's residency came to an end, our former home, nestled in its five-acre woods, was sitting empty. Frank hadn't decided where to practice, so Bill used this advantage.

"The house is empty," Bill said. "Come on up and live in it for a while. Try life in the bush. It will give you a change."

Bill reasoned that if Frank once got started taking care of the great number of heart and stroke patients in Mecosta County, he'd be hooked. Happily, the patients were numerous, interesting, and grateful, and we had acquired an internist.

The hospital was also fortunate to have a jovial, soft-spoken general practitioner settle in a town twelve miles south of Stanwood. Extremely energetic, George soon had a practice that kept him racing night and day. He functioned well on four or five hours sleep a night, but was too busy and too soft-hearted to collect his fees. When the end of each year came around, his accountant would show him that he'd done nearly eighty thousand dollars worth of work, but had collected only seven thousand.

This situation happened with other doctors over the years. It was easy to become so immersed in the zealous missionary atmosphere of country practice, and the challenge of bringing a dying hospital back to its feet, that making a living and providing for the future seemed crass. Such fervor could be maintained for a year or two, but ultimately, the realities of money in raising a family were realized, and the once-dedicated practitioner left for the more lucrative city.

65

After two years of man-killing busy practice, George, too, left the area to begin a residency in radiology. But George didn't leave for good as other doctors had. The cause of our struggling hospital had become part of him, and all through his years of residency training he returned to Mecosta Memorial on weekends, helping in every possible manner. He read X-rays, cared for emergency-room patients and even painted the walls of the obstetrical ward. The call of the bush was so strong that when George completed his residency, he returned to Mecosta Memorial as the radiologist.

Now the team was complete. There was a surgeon, an anesthetist, an internist, a radiologist, and two general practitioners. An immensely capable group, these men excelled in the special challenge of caring for acutely ill older people.

The formation of a group of specialists in a poverty-stricken remote area amazed many people. One day while writing orders in the chart room, Bill overheard a conversation between two nurses in the corridor.

One of the new R.N.s brought in from Detroit was voicing her surprise to another nurse. "I can't get over this group of osteopathic specialists gathered out here in this little country hospital," she said. "In Detroit they always grumbled that the osteopaths took the moneyed practices, tending to care for a wealthy clientele, and avoiding welfare patients. Was I surprised to see all the different types of patients in this hospital!"

With several doctors putting patients in the hospital, Mecosta Memorial's revenue increased, and the old dismal financial picture was brightening. Mecosta Memorial was waging successfully the battle to meet its bi-monthly payroll and other fixed expenses.

Government rules and regulations always seem to be extra tough on the little man or the small business, and this is also true with the small hospital. Every year saw

66

an added number of regulations, and compliance with these was a constant headache for Mecosta Memorial's administrator and governing body. Whenever new regulations demanded changes, the ladies of the hospital guilds rolled up their sleeves, donned their aprons, and proceeded with fund-raising chicken suppers to finance these changes. In the past, a few hundred dollars usually had been sufficient.

With the doctor-shortage problem solved, everything had seemed promising. But worse problems were on the way. First, the state fire marshal decreed that the fire escape tube on the rear of the hospital building was no longer acceptable. Enclosed, fireproof stairwells must be constructed at a cost of fifteen thousand dollars. The guild ladies gasped; there weren't enough chickens in the whole county to bring in that much money.

Stanwood people were bewildered that outsiders from Lansing, the state capital, could exert such control over their local institution. Once, not many years before, local housewives had furnished a goodly share of the food served in the hospital. During vegetable and fruit harvests, the guilds had met in the hospital kitchen, where they canned hundreds of quarts of peaches, corn, beans, cherries, and applesauce. Nowadays, only food from approved canning factories is allowed.

Frequently housewives had brought to the hospital kitchen a donation of warm, newly-baked loaves of bread, saying, "I baked today and thought the patients might enjoy some warm bread with their supper."

Now any such delicious contribution would have to be given to the garbage pails. Only food from commercial processors may be used. Perhaps it's safer that way. Yet if I were a patient, just the aroma of freshly baked bread might spur me to recovery.

The hospital guild ladies still sew for the hospital, making infant and pediatric clothes, hospital gowns, and draw sheets. This probably won't continue long. Someone, somewhere, will decree that homemade items are not regulation.

Miraculously, construction of the required stairwells began. This was accomplished through a concerted fund-raising drive, a large amount of donated labor and material, and a bank loan.

As Bill watched the basement-to-second-floor stairwells grow skyward, he sadly shook his head.

"I don't get their reasoning," he said. "If the hospital were smoke-filled and burning, I'd much rather slide the bedfast patients down the chute than struggle to carry them down a stairway." Bill shuddered as he imagined trying to carry a comatose two-hundred-fifty pound woman down steps and, perhaps, dropping her. Sometimes the manifestations of progress seemed strange indeed.

Even before the stairwells were completed, other agencies instituted new regulations with which Mecosta Memorial must comply. Bill began spending every evening in desperate conferences with the hard-pressed hospital administrator and board of directors.

After one of these nightly meetings Bill came home very late, looking discouraged and despairing. That evening the hospital administrator had laid out the whole picture before them.

I pushed a plate of cookies and a glass of milk toward Bill while he summarized the troubles for me.

"The fire marshal wants a new sprinkling system in the building. The plumbing inspector wants new toilets throughout. The sewage commissioner wants a new dry well and drain field. The food-handlers' inspector wants a completely new kitchen," Bill said, pausing for a gulp of milk. "The building inspector wants seven-foot hallways throughout the hospital instead of our present four-foot hallways. Moving walls is difficult enough, but we're having trouble finding out which of our corridor walls are weight-bearing walls. Pull down the wrong wall and your roof falls in." Bill groaned and rubbed his forehead. He looked so pale and tired that it frightened me.

"Oh, that's terrible," I sympathized. The hospital was being visited by the scourges of Job.

"That's not all," Bill said, with a wry smile. "There's more. The welfare department says they won't pay for any more welfare patients admitted to our hospital until we correct all the physical deficiencies of the building. The drug companies won't sell the hospital any more drugs or supplies on credit. Everything must be strictly cash on delivery. The administrator is so discouraged he's ready to throw in the towel."

Just as a football coach must bear the brunt of angry public opinion when he has a losing team (even if the team is made up of ninety-pound weaklings), so must a hospital administrator bear the wrath of local citizens when hospital functions go awry. Those of us closely connected with the hospital knew that Mecosta Memorial was a tough problem, but the local people needed a scapegoat. In the past few years several administrators had abdicated their position in the face of local wrath. The reign of one of these adminstrators came to an end rather colorfully.

Early one morning as Bill was approaching the hospital, he noticed something hanging from the tall flagpole on the hospital grounds. It appeared to be a human figure, but as he drove closer, he saw that it was a straw-filled dummy dressed to resemble the hospital administrator. Hospital supporters, angry again, had hung the administrator in effigy.

Thinking it best to get the thing out of sight before news media heard of it, Bill and another doctor got the dummy down from the flagpole and carried it to the hospital furnace room. There they laid the effigy out, covering it with a sheet. Just then the other doctor's office nurse opened the door, looking for her doctor. She stared at the supine figure, its shoes poking out from beneath the sheet, and gave a loud scream. The two doctors drew her closer, showing her the figure was not a human casualty, but a straw man.

Hospital administrators do not have an easy time of it, especially those at Mecosta Memorial.

At the next evening conference, the administrator had more bad news for the doctors and the hospital board members. For some time Blue Cross had been putting heat on the hospital, maintaining that the small rural hospital wasn't needed. The administrator had just been notified by Blue Cross that Mecosta Memorial had been removed from the approved list of participating hospitals. Losing Blue Cross patients as well as welfare patients would be a final blow. The administrator advised that getting accredited once again by Blue Cross would take some time and might even be an impossibility. However, the withdrawal of payment for welfare patient care was based upon a misunderstanding. After a call to the state office, the administrator was assured that this withdrawal was a premature action. Mecosta Memorial could count at least on revenue for caring for the destitute: one small consolation among a swarm of disappointments.

Like a flock of vultures, every inspector and agency in the state seemed to be descending upon Mecosta Memorial to take a nip at something. Money in large quantities was needed to comply with all these new regulations, and all attempts for funds thus far had been futile. Bill and the administrator had made numerous trips to the state Hill-Burton office, the Farm Home Administration office, the Wolverine Foundation, and had approached the Kellogg Foundation, the Kresge Foundation, the Sears Roebuck Foundation, and even the Ford Foundation. No funds were forthcoming from any sources.

Every year it had been necessary for Bill to work more and more on these time-consuming tasks necessary for the survival of the hospital, but he resented the time these tasks took. It was a constant source of irritation to him that so much of his energy, time, and thought must go to hospital problems when he wanted to spend his time doing surgery and helping people get well, with some spare time left over for his family.

With no federal loans or grants available, and no prospects of a helping hand from any wealthy philanthropist, the continuing financial problems of the hospital became a grim burden. The hospital was like a moribund patient. But just as Bill would fight fiercely to save the life of a dying patient, so he continued to battle for the continued life of the hospital.

Bill's reaction to this kind of pressure was something lighthearted and entertaining, yet not frivolous. He believed his buffalo herd might alter the failure-pattern of the little hospital out in the bush. Buffalo would bring a sense of action, change, and progress, and especially a sense of uniqueness. Downhearted hospital supporters could once again strive to support the hospital. Buffalo would surely be a tourist attraction, drawing people to this unknown village. Patients' families and relatives would be more inclined to visit hospital patients, if they could also see a buffalo herd as a side attraction. The patients themselves would benefit by watching the buffalo, for this would provide an outside interest for them during the long, boring days of hospital recovery. Instead of turning inward toward their own illness, they would be benefited by an interest in something outside themselves. With fund-raising, a buffalo barbecue should be a bigger success than the countless chicken suppers of the past.

The hospital was down on its knees and everyone seemed to be giving it a whack; yet Bill was enthusiasti-

71

cally preparing to bring in a buffalo herd. To me, this seemed the height of audacity and stubbornness, and I told Bill so.

"Now, look, Pinkie," Bill tried to explain patiently, "I know the buffalo will be beneficial to the patients. Boredom and depression is a big problem among hospital patients. Buffalo will add a bit of levity and interest to being hospitalized at Mecosta Memorial. And, who knows," he added, "buffalo may help us in fund-raising, by drawing interest and sympathy to our hospital. Lending agencies might be more receptive."

In these ways Bill hoped buffalo would help our situation. My interests in buffalo were more wifely. Bill had always craved and thrived upon hard outdoor work, and caring for a buffalo herd would surely provide exercise and diversion. Buffalo would be an interesting approach to hobby-farming and a relaxing change for Bill from the problems of his patients. One advantage of buffalo was that they required less care than domestic cattle, needing only a high, strong fence, good grassland, and water. Farm buildings weren't necessary. A herd of buffalo could be obtained at the same cost as a small herd of registered domestic beef, but buffalo had the added intriguing potential of cross-breeding. Bill had always been fascinated with the possibility of crossing buffalo with different kinds of beef stock to create a new, hardy, superior line of beef to improve northern beef herds.

When people asked us why we were getting buffalo, our answers were usually flippant and uninstructive. But with the critical situation of the hospital, Bill actually had valid and powerful reasons for bringing buffalo to Stanwood. Getting buffalo was not just a whim; it was more an act of desperation.

What's
in a
Name?

6 We didn't have an invoice, or bill of lading, or whatever you call an order for ten (10) American bison—buffalo to everyone but a zoologist. There was just a gentleman's oral agreement between two buffalo buffs. As we tore the February page from our calendar, we realized that the arrival of our buffalo was imminent. We placed a call to the Shermans to see if the loading had begun. We found that the Shermans were wintering in Hawaii, but they would return in a week.

When the third week of March arrived and there was still no sign of approaching buffalo, we called the Shermans again. Mr. Sherman explained that the weather had been irregular and stormy and the buffalo impossible to work with. Out in the buffalo pasture his men had constructed a stout corral to use in getting our buffalo separated from the rest of his herd, altogether about fifty animals. They thought the corral would serve to separate the animals to be shipped to us, but one night his monstrous old herd bull took offense at the barricade and ripped the corral into a heap of toothpicks.

Mr. Sherman assured us, however, that we would receive our buffalo in due time.

Another week passed and we began to get really

worried. We knew it was not financially necessary for Mr. Sherman to sell us any buffalo, especially at the agreed price of three hundred dollars a head. Perhaps he had decided not to part with any buffalo after all, and these delays were his way of letting us down easy.

Bill called him again, this time offering to go out to Iowa and help with the round-up. Bill explained that he had been raised out West and was accustomed to handling range animals.

"Sure, come on out if you want to," Mr. Sherman agreed. "We can always use good help."

To himself, Bill thought, "I've never seen any wild range animals yet that a man couldn't maneuver where he wanted them in two or three weeks' time. This must be a delaying tactic of some kind."

The next weekend was Easter weekend and the children had two days' school vacation, so we all headed for Iowa. After the seven-hundred-mile drive, Bill dropped me and the children at my parents' home in Charles City, hardly saying hello to his in-laws, and sped off for Nora Springs and the buffalo herd.

Bill enjoyed meeting another buffalo buff, and Mr. Sherman was friendly and helpful in his suggestions. He had inherited his interest in buffalo from his father who had purchased four bison in 1940. Later, ten more animals were added from the Montana National Bison Range. The herd increased and Mr. Sherman maintained the herd at about forty head by selling off as many as fifteen buffalo yearly. On the fifteen-hundred-acre farm, the buffalo herd occupied a sixty-acre wooded pasture. Buffalo were just a hobby on this fertile corn-growing vastness. One single field of corn stretched over a hundred and seventy-five acres.

After a couple of hours of visiting and talking buffalo, Bill and Mr. Sherman had begun a first-name friendship. It was "Francis" and "Doc." Bill agreed to return there the next morning for the big round-up.

It was bitter cold in the morning when Bill crawled out of bed. "Come on, Pinkie," he urged, "let's go get our buffalo."

"It's too cold," I complained, and rolled over in bed, pulling the blankets tighter. Bill tip-toed out, grumbling about dainty white squaws.

The day was frigid, but clear—a beautiful day, Bill thought, for herding buffalo. At seven A.M. he arrived at Shermans' where Francis, already up and around, handed Bill a cup of steaming coffee. The first gulp of the hot brew surprised Bill—it was coffee royal.

Francis laughed at Bill's surprise. "Doc," he said, "when it's five below zero like this morning, whiskey is the only thing to put in coffee when you're going to work buffalo. Cream or sugar won't do a thing for you."

After draining their cups, they bundled up and went out into the crackling cold where three huge heavy-duty diesel tractors awaited them.

Francis shook his head, frowning. "I really doubt if we can do anything today, Doc," he said. "The herd's been pretty edgy for a couple days so there must be a storm coming."

Bill glanced at the cloudless sky, unconvinced.

The other men agreed with Sherman. They thought it best to just forget it all for today.

Francis reminded his men that Bill had just driven seven hundred miles to round up his buffalo. "Let's make a try at it," he said.

Francis climbed on one of the wide-front-axle tractors and motioned Bill to ride with him. With a roar, the three tractors chugged out three-quarters of a mile into the pasture where the herd had been bedded down for the night. Lining up on the far side, the tractors slowly neared the herd.

The huge herd bull stood up and glared at the trespassing tractors.

"It's too cold to fiddle around long!" Francis shouted

75

at Bill over the roar of the engine. "We might just as well find out right now whether we can do anything today or not."

He drove the tractor slowly up to the menacing bull and stopped a foot short of the dark monster. For five minutes the men and the bull stared at each other in the biting wind.

Francis finally shrugged. "We might as well go home. We aren't going to do anything with them today."

"Look, I didn't come seven hundred miles just to spend five minutes staring down a bull," Bill protested. "Can't you nudge him a little, and maybe he'll start toward the corrals?"

Sherman replied firmly that nothing in the world could make him nudge that bull. Seeing Bill's disappointment, he relented a little. "We'll try pushing a cow and see what he does."

Backing the tractor away from the immovable bull, he headed for a cow. The cow quickly jumped to her feet and ran ahead of the tractor. Bill was hanging onto the seat of the tractor and thoroughly enjoying the chase, which lasted for about fifty feet. Suddenly, the rear tire was struck a powerful blow from behind, and the tractor lurched ahead eight feet. Bill thought one of the other tractors had hit them from behind until out of the corner of his eye he saw a churning mass of brown fur, and snow flying in all directions. The herd bull was riled.

Francis stopped the vehicle immediately, but the furious animal went up to the front end, and placing his horns under the wide front axle, lifted the massive tractor nearly eighteen inches off the ground. Growling and roaring, he swung his head and shook the tractor. He put the tractor down and danced in the snowdrifts, wheeling on himself, as agile as a goat, but mad as a charging elephant. The big old bull circled the tractor at a distance of twenty-five feet. Suddenly he lowered his head and charged, hitting the six-thousand-pound tractor on the left side. The tractor rocked back and forth while Bill clung tightly to the seat. The collision of his head with the heavy vehicle seemed to stun the bull for a moment, and Sherman took the opportunity to throw the gears into high and make a dash for the gate. The other two tractor-drivers joined the flight, and all three made it safely through the gate and out of the pasture.

Safely back in the Shermans' toasty warm kitchen, Bill was again poured a cup of the special buffalo-handlers' coffee. With shaking hands, Bill sipped it gratefully. He was now a wiser Future Buffalo Owner.

Refills were deemed necessary. After the second cup, Francis asked with a twinkle in his eye, "Are you warmed up enough to go back out and try again, Doc?"

Bill groaned, sheepishly admitting that he would be patient. Now he understood the problems of handling buffalo. "Whenever you're able to cut them out of the herd and ship them is fine with me," he said.

Francis explained that it would now be a week before they could do anything further with the herd. They'd have to let the herd bull settle down and forget his irritation.

Early the next morning we started back for Michigan. The buffalo weren't rounded up, but we were more prudent people. Having a buffalo herd was going to be somewhat of a challenge, and we suspected there might be further new experiences ahead.

Though the cold sky was cloudless when we left, after less than an hour on the road, a thick, whirling Midwestern blizzard whistled down upon us from the northwest. We'd been fooled by the brilliant blue sky, but the shaggy hump-backs weren't! Sherman had said that edgy buffalo meant a storm coming, but we had smiled condescendingly at the idea of buffalo being good weather forecasters. Only buffalo would dare predict a blizzard for Easter Sunday.

We struggled homeward on slippery, snow-clogged highways. Until we got east of Chicago, we would have made better time on snowshoes. In the dim hours of dawn we gratefully pulled into our driveway.

Now that we had seen our unruly animals, it was easier to stifle our impatience for their arrival. We appreciated the difficulties of separating and loading on a truck several tons of sharp, swinging horns. We'd just have to let the buffalo pick the departure time for their journey from Iowa to Michigan. The waiting days we spent pacing our fence line, making final fence-sturdiness inspections, and tacking signs to posts and trees surrounding the pasture. We'd painted dozens of signs reading, "Danger, Buffalo! Keep Out!" and "No Hunting." We wanted no surprised hunter shinnying over our Superfence after a pheasant, to come face-to-face with a buffalo.

After seeing Mr. Sherman's corral demolished by his sixteen-year-old herd bull, we were inspired to doubly check the strength of our Superfence. Before, Superfence had appeared strong and invincible, but now it looked weak and silly. How could a few thin strands of wire possibly keep a herd of buffalo in a pasture?

We began investigating insurance policies for runaway buffalo, but even the insurance companies wouldn't take us seriously. A buffalo liability policy?—nonsense! You'd have thought we were desert nomads trying to get flood insurance.

The people of Stanwood finally took us seriously after we put up the "Danger, Buffalo!" signs.

"There it is in black-and-white," they said. "It must be true."

Bets and side bets were taken on the date and time of arrival of the herd. A small splinter group formed the

"Buffalo, Go Home!" faction. It seems they feared the streets of Stanwood would no longer be safe for women and children if a buffalo herd were pastured nearby. "They're dangerous animals," they protested. "Leave them out West where the cowboys and Indians know how to handle them." Though these protesters didn't picket us, they did draw up a petition attempting to halt the project before the buffalo arrived, but were unable to get enough signers.

A "buffalo pool" was formed, similar to a ship's anchor pool, where one donated a dollar to pick the day and hour he guessed the buffalo truck would arrive, the winner to get the whole pool.

At bedtime on April 8, the call came from Iowa.

"The truck left this noon heading east. It should be at Stanwood sometime tomorrow morning," Francis Sherman announced wearily. "But . . ."

Our hearts sank. A "but" like that is always like a slap with a wet dishrag.

"We couldn't get just ten on the truck," he continued. "More kept getting on and we kept prodding some off, and finally when we had twelve animals on the truck I said 'heck, ship 'em all!' So you're getting twelve buffalo."

We groaned. That meant several hundred more dollars, but an even dozen sounded nice, anyway.

Then Francis went on to explain that since the buffalo were on the truck, they were ours, and our responsibility. "The way my man drives, I figure he should be going over the Chicago Skyway about now. Sleep well, Doc!" he chuckled.

Bill didn't sleep well. In fact, he didn't close his eyes all night. He said every time he'd close his eyes he'd see the truck having an accident on the Chicago Skyway, and all those buffalo, *our* buffalo, running amuck over the Skyway and through the Windy City.

Bill spent the night pacing the floor and drinking

warm milk. A nervous father-to-be never suffered more than this buffalo-owner-to-be.

At seven the next morning, when I was getting the children ready to catch the school bus, the phone rang. An excited voice shouted, "A big stock truck just went by. I think it's the buffalo!"

Two minutes later another caller repeated the announcement. It seems that for days everyone in Stanwood had been peeking through their curtains, watching for the arrival. All thought of school was forgotten, and we bundled up to go welcome our buffalo.

The whole surgery schedule was postponed three hours while the surgeon welcomed his buffalo herd.

The huge semi-trailer stock truck was a sight in itself. A massive red truck, it had specially reinforced steel beams inside. From a safe distance we peered through the slats into the darkness, but could see only moving shapes and hear strange kicking and thumping noises. It could have been a truck full of monkeys.

As I stood there shivering from both cold and excitement, an odd feeling kept tugging at me. Perhaps it was just a natural fear of the unknown, but I kept thinking of Pandora's box. What were we about to release upon our quiet countryside? Up to now it had been a game, a challenge to see if we could get a herd of buffalo. It was speculative. One could always quit. But once those creatures were released from the truck, there would be no turning back.

When the big truck backed up to our Superfence gate I shuddered. The fence looked more and more like a puny cobweb flung across the land. A large crowd had gathered in spite of the cold, early hour and the stinging snow blowing out of the west.

Twenty feet short of the gate the truck became stuck, mired down in the sticky gumbo soil. My heart sank. Now what? The truckdriver looked depressed, resigned to a long wait. Bill and some of the men in the crowd conferred briefly, then one of the onlookers sped off in his car.

Soon a long flat-bed truck bearing a bulldozer drove up, greeted by welcoming cheers. The day was saved.

First, the bulldozer operator scooped out an area of ground at the gate opening, so the rear wheels of the truck would be lowered and the buffalo wouldn't have to jump so far down in getting off the truck. Then the dozer turned its attention to the mired truck. With seemingly little effort, the small but powerful machine pushed the huge truck out of the mud and into position at the open gate.

When the truck was lined up perfectly with the opened gate of our pasture, the rear door was swung open and we held our breath, awaiting the grunting monsters' mad charge for freedom. Nothing happened. No great stampede for the wide open spaces. Nothing.

Several men and the truck driver seized long poles and began poking through the slats of the truck, trying to goad the buffalo off. Finally, one solitary buffalo either tripped or was crowded out. She leaped off the truck, heading at a fast gallop along the fence line, off into the sunrise and out of sight. One more shaggy beast soon followed, but the rest seemed to have grown attached to their mobile home. The men yelled and prodded the animals through the slats. The buffalo fought back angrily, banging into the sides of the truck and kicking at the steel reinforcing bars with a terrific clang. One of the men glanced down at the broomstick he had been using as a prod. It was broken off neatly by a well-placed hoof or horn.

Two newspaper photographers impatiently stamped their chilled feet as they awaited the grand de-trucking.

Suddenly, the rest of the buffalo poured off the truck in one churning brown mass, some frontward, some backward. As soon as their hoofs hit the ground, they were off, loping *en masse* down the fence line and out of sight.

One sharp-eyed lady standing next to me counted rapidly as the pounding mass rushed by. "Thirteen buffalo!" she exclaimed. "Isn't that something!"

I corrected her. "No, just twelve."

Twice the buffalo galloped around their fifty-acre pen, following close to the fence, while we crossed our fingers, hoping they didn't bump into it. Each time they came thundering by we all furiously counted shaggy heads, and most of us kept coming up with thirteen.

By afternoon it became obvious that we had not twelve buffalo, but thirteen. Evidently one beast had stowed away in the crowd. By that time the trucker had left with payment for twelve buffalo. Now we had to come up with quick payment to Mr. Sherman for yet another animal. Only six hours in the buffalo business and already in danger of being accused of buffalo rustling!

On the second day, the herd began to settle down, having gotten acquainted with every square inch of their new pasture. We began to settle down, too, for it seemed they were going to respect our Superfence after all. Their strange grunting noises seemed contented enough. I'd expected buffalo to moo as cattle do, but they don't. They blow, snort, and make grunting sounds like a baritone pig.

Our next task was obvious. All thirteen buffalo had to be named so we could tell them apart. At first, they all looked alike to us. But after squatting in the snow for a day or two, watching them, it was apparent that the brown mass of shaggy buffalo consisted of thirteen individual animals, with distinct appearance and personalities.

The first name came easily. That was Bleeding Horn. When she disembarked from the truck, we all noticed the broken-off and bleeding stump where a horn had recently been. She was easy to tell from the others in the herd.

Next was Ringo, a sad-looking, hornless beast whose black shaggy bangs hung over her eyes and made her resemble the Beatles. I hate to admit such ignorance, but for the first few days we thought Ringo was a bull. She had the heavy, dark head that bulls have, and this confused us. (Yes, I know—you don t tell a bull by the shape of its head!) We worried about her hornless state, but later Francis Sherman told us a previous owner had dehorned her. And what a cruel thing to do to a buffalo! She was a complete outcast, always having to hang out on the fringes of the herd, waiting until last for her food and drink. She knew she was no match for those swinging horns. The rest of the herd had her buffaloed. All one had to do was swing its head at her and she retreated fast. We had installed Angie, a black Angus heifer, in the pasture before the buffalo arrived, and Ringo soon found she was more compatible with the hornless Angus, and they became buddies.

We had been sent ten cows and three bulls for our assortment. One of the bulls stood out from the others, immediately attracting our attention as a magnificent specimen. He was obviously the future herd bull, when he grew up a bit. Resplendent in a thick black mane, from which his square, heavy dark head emerged, he glared at us with regal disdain. He was promptly christened "Kahtanka"—a Sioux word meaning Chief Bull.

While the other twelve animals seemed to accept the indignities of their transfer, this bull's arrogance seemed to say, "Don't think you can civilize me. I am an American bison, monarch of the plains."

The second largest bull became Bull-in-the-Bush, since he was strictly second-string varsity, to be sent in only upon failure of Number One, Kahtanka. Mr. Sherman had advised us that not all bulls are capable of becoming fathers. And if a bull can't become a father, he hasn't really much *raison d'être,* has he? Mr. Sherman insisted we get a couple of second-stringers to keep until we were sure we had one "good" bull.

The third bull was a scrawny little yearling, really only a potential bull. We called him Sitting Bull because it appeared he would be doing very little but sitting.

Now with five of the animals identified and named, we were making progress. Only eight to go.

One of the cows was larger than the other cows, with longer, more curving horns, and as we watched them, we realized she was leading the herd about the pasture. When she moved to the stream to drink, the whole herd followed her. This checked with reports of old-time Westerners who said the buffalo herds had a wise old cow who was the actual leader of the herd, the bulls being protectors and sentinels. That seemed to be so in our herd, and our cow-leader became Old Cow. Old Cow was two years old, a young teen-ager in buffalo years, but since most of the other animals were only yearlings, she dutifully assumed her role and her name.

Another cow appeared rather sleepy and gentle, so she was named Good Cow.

About this time it began to dawn upon us what we were doing. All the very descriptive names of Indians came to mind, like Shoots-the-Bear, or Rain-in-the-Face, or Sits-down-Spotted (now what on earth did *that* mean?). The name of an Indian meant something, describing a personal characteristic or an important event in his life. We seemed to be reverting to the Indian method of christening, by naming each animal with a descriptive name. Perhaps the Indians really had something going there. John Jones tells you absolutely nothing, but Drinks-a-Lot Jones, or Lots-of-Money Jones would kind of clue you in.

Our worst goof with names was with Worms. As a yearling, she appeared to be on the scrawny side and

84

extra shaggy. We thought she probably had parasite worms, and thus the name. She turned out to be extremely healthy and wormless, but by the time we discovered our misnomer, the name "Worms" had stuck. It's embarrassing when spectators ask the names of the animals, and we have to admit to "Worms." Most unappetizing.

Gray Fox seemed to have a slightly silvery gray coat. Doe Eyes had expressive, large eyes, with long lashes, looking like a Walt Disney cartoon characterization of a deer or a cow. Cow-With-Square-Black-Face and Cow-With-One-Good-Eye are just what their names say.

I'm afraid if we had any more children, their names might be Red-Wrinkled-Raisin, or Howling-Lips, or Cries-in-the-Night. One gets carried away with these things.

The first tender green shoots of grass began to peep through the ground soon after the arrival of the herd, and the buffalo settled down to graze and ruminate in the spring sunshine. Though Michigan never really had been a natural habitat for buffalo, our herd seemed perfectly contented with Michigan grass, water, and air.

Buffalo came to North America sometime during the early Ice Age, crossing to Alaska on the land bridge, above sea level at that time. They thrived and spread out until they eventually covered nearly the whole North American continent, although they were always most numerous in the plains between the Mississippi River and the Rocky Mountains. All the buffalo seemed to ask for was a good supply of grass and water, and plenty of hoof-room.

Weekends, the quiet gravel road bordering the buffalo pasture was gorged with cars of sightseers, anxious to glimpse a real American bison. They brought their children for the educational experience of seeing an historic animal, but were often sadly disappointed. For in the pasture with the buffalo we had Angie, the black

Angus heifer, two horses, two ponies, a donkey, and seven goats.

The excited parents would hold their children high on their shoulders. "See, Johnny! See the buffalo? Those are real, live buffalo!"

Johnny would hardly look. He was too excited. "Yeah, Daddy, yeah. But look at the donkey! Look at the goats! Look at the horses!"

Times when we worked at the ranch, building more fence and making log bridges across the creek, sight-seers questioned us constantly about buffalo, their big concern being what we were going to do with them come wintertime.

"You don't have a barn!" they'd worry.

We explained that buffalo need no shelter in the winter, that their woolly coats protect them. Even as far north as Alaska, they paw and root through snow to forage for themselves. The people looked at us skeptically, wondering if they should report us to the humane society. Can't you just see a herd of buffalo being driven into stalls in a barn every night? We'd remind them that there were no barns for them out on the plains where they once roamed, yet they thrived and multiplied fantastically under those conditions.

Occasionally a spectator who fancied himself knowledgeable in buffalo lore would ask, "What kind of buffalo are these—plains or wood buffalo?"

"Wood buffalo," we'd answer, as that's what Mr. Sherman had told us they were.

Oldtimers, contemporaries of the great herds, strongly believed there were three different kinds of buffalo. Modern scientists believe these were only minor variations, natural to an animal with a wide range of living habits. They maintain it is natural for a species to change in adapting to its environment, but still be all of the same species: *Bison bison.*

The popular belief of the western frontiersman and

many present-day buffalo raisers, is that there were three types of buffalo:

1) The wood buffalo, said to be largest and darkest.
2) The plains buffalo, medium-sized, and lightest.
3) The mountain buffalo, the smallest, and of dark color.

Back in Phase One, our letter-writing phase when we were attempting to purchase buffalo, one breeder advised us to get the "northern" kind, by which he meant the wood variety, as they were bigger-boned and nearly one-third larger. He said he'd purchased twenty buffalo from a southern plains herd a few years before and they were such a scrawny, scraggly bunch that he soon disposed of them. Of course, we could assume these animals came from a diet of desert-type vegetation, rather than the thick, nutritious grasses of our northern pastures. It seems likely that a scanty diet could have a stunting effect upon any group of animals. Even with humans, we've found that a nutritious diet over two or three generations increases height and weight of the new generation. The Japanese clothing and shoe manufacturers are now making larger sizes since the Japanese diet has undergone a generation of Westernization.

We fed grain to our herd those first few weeks until the grass became longer and more nourishing. Bill got in the habit of making a loud, grunting call. I think he intended it to sound like one buffalo calling another, but it sounded more like a hippopotamus with a toothache. He made this deep, guttural sound, then called "Kah-tanka!" while pouring feed on the ground in spaced-out piles.

At first the herd seemed to come out of curiosity, but within a few days they learned this weird throaty sound meant "grain to eat!" The animals might be nowhere in sight, but when the dinner call went out, a brown mass of real "thundering herd" appeared over the hill, and it was a sight to behold. Bill always poured out separate mounds of grain, spread at twelve-foot intervals, so the animals could space out to eat. This was when we first discovered the "pecking order" within the herd. A definite hierarchy existed as to who was boss over whom.

Old Cow was Top Bison. Every other animal quickly moved out of Old Cow's way as she moved from one pile of grain to another. No one hesitated or argued. She had first choice of everything.

Next in line was Good Cow. Each animal, except Old Cow, gave way to her.

The budding adolescent Kahtanka was third in line. He lorded it over most of the herd, but forfeited authority to the two higher-status cows. Bull-in-the-Bush ranked fourth, just behind Kahtanka. This orderly hierarchy progressed through the herd, reaching down to hornless Ringo, who was truly low-man-on-the-totem-pole.

It was amazing how this hodgepodge of buffalo established themselves as a group, with leadership, power structure, and a definite pecking order (although this lasted only until July, when Kahtanka matured). It was especially surprising since all these young animals had been the teen-agers and calves of a larger herd, undoubtedly having absolutely no position or prestige in their home herd. After having been bundled together, jammed into a dark, strange vehicle, moved seven hundred miles eastward and dumped together in an unfamiliar place, you'd expect a certain amount of chaos, like the bewilderment of the characters in *Lord of the Flies* or *Swiss Family Robinson*. Yet the buffalo seem to have done better at setting up an orderly society for themselves than did these fictional humans.

Area newspapers and television stations soon learned of the presence of the buffalo and began requesting interviews. It was embarrassing at this particular time in May because the buffalo couldn't have looked worse.

They were half-way through their shedding period, the sloughing off of their woolly winter fur coats. Huge chunks of matted fur dangled from their bodies. Nothing looks more bedraggled than a shedding buffalo. We tried to convince the newsmen to come back a month later when the animals didn't look so moth-eaten, but they insisted they wanted pictures "now." They cold-heartedly snapped their photos while the buffalo frantically rubbed on trees or rolled on the ground, trying to hasten the loosening of their tattered fur.

Poor Ringo's shedding cycle was all mixed up. On the hottest days of July, when the other buffalo had lost all their heavy fur, she still sweltered in her winter coat, only just beginning to shed. In September, when the other animals were growing their new fur, huge patches still hung from her body. Our only explanation is that because of her hornless state and her consequent isolation from the herd, she didn't get the rubbing and nuzzling which the other animals exchanged. Perhaps this rubbing and butting hastens the shedding process.

We started a Buffalo Journal—sort of a ship's log. Some days our only entry was "Good Cow sneezed twice," but we dutifully recorded our various experiences with our animals.

After the publicity in the newspapers and on television, more and more people came to see the herd. They asked so many questions that even though we had been boning up on buffalo lore for some time, we were kept busy trying to learn more.

We learned that the buffalo is really a bison, and not a true buffalo such as the Cape buffalo of Africa or the water buffalo of India. Our buffalo have fourteen pairs of ribs, while the true buffalo have only thirteen. To the zoologist the American buffalo is a "bison," but to generations of Americans it has been known as a "buffalo."

According to zoologists, many other American animals have been misnamed, chiefly because they were first encountered by uneducated frontiersmen. I say, more power to the illiterate adventurer who risked his life beating back the frontier. He ought to have the right to name the animals he discovers. If the scientists want to name the animals, they'd better get there first. Even when zoologists do get there first, they come up with names like "hippopotamus" and "rhinoceros."

The prairie dog is one of these misnamed animals, for he isn't really a dog, but a squirrel. To the practical-minded explorer, however, squirrels had to live in trees, not in holes in the ground, so obviously they weren't squirrels. One oldtimer said their name probably saved them from extinction. Once, in extreme hunger, he had eaten a prairie dog and found it delicious despite its doggy implications. If they had been called "prairie squirrels," he figured they'd have been eaten up by hungry plainsmen long ago.

Being misnamed didn't help the buffalo, though. Books on buffalo are more rare than buffalo themselves, and information had to be searched from mostly out-of-print sources. We were always delighted when we encountered a new tidbit to add to our collection of buffaloiana. What this country needs, we decided, is a good book on "How to Raise Buffalo for Fun and Profit."

Kahtanka's Honeymoon

7 The more we learned about buffalo, the more awesome became our thirteen charges. We felt great respect for them, the survivors of the survivors. The responsibility of their care and protection began to worry us.

You know how it is. You finally give in and let little Suzy keep that poor, homeless kitty, hoping it won't be much trouble once it learns what a sandbox is for. But soon you're involved in veterinary bills and coaxing a neighbor to keep it while you're away on vacation. You *have* it, or does it have you?

We were *had* by thirteen buffalo, tons of grazing, chewing remnants, and there was no sending them back for refunds.

We were so proud of Superfence. In spite of its do-it-yourself appearance with its bends and waves, it was holding the buffalo. Then one day a spectator jolted us with his question, "What's going to happen in the fall when your buffalo decide to migrate south for the winter?"

We were aghast at the image of Superfence lying crumpled, our buffalo loping through Grand Rapids, then Kalamazoo, and on to Indiana. We rushed back to our buffalo information studies and read frantically. At last our worries were soothed. It seems that most of the oldtimers and even some present-day students of the

91

West believe the buffalo herds migrated as geese and robins do, in an instinctive movement in a definite direction. Yet most experts discount this theory, saying that the movement of the great herds was erratic, the herd often moving for no reason at all. Though the buffalo moved several hundred miles in various directions, there was no instinctive or purposeful migration, as with geese. Of course, seeking grass, they tended to move in a southerly direction in winter, and back north come summer. Through their herd movements they sought water, but mainly new grazing lands, since any large herd must be nomadic, as their large numbers soon exhaust grass in one region.

We trusted that as long as we furnished our animals with sufficient food, they wouldn't go "shufflin' off to Buffalo." Southern Michigan would be spared an invasion of the hump-backs.

We spent hours squatting outside Superfence gazing at our shaggy-haired pets. As I watched these imprisoned roamers, I thought of the plains Indians and their sad confinement upon the reservations, with their ponies and weapons taken from them. It would be like taking away modern man's automobile and job, then saying, "Now be a *man*."

The reservation Indians withered in sullen boredom and near-starvation. Some of the old warriors remained dignified and haughty even while coughing themselves to death from the white man's tuberculosis. I suspect those proud old warriors glared out at the white man's world with the same imposing arrogance that Kahtanka fastened upon us.

From beneath his black, tousled forelock, Kahtanka sullenly observed us. I shivered when I saw the power housed in his heavy, square body, and grew uneasy about the unknown thoughts lurking behind his brooding eyes. Bill immediately adopted Kahtanka as his special pet, his pride and joy, but I'd as soon hire a cannibal for a baby-sitter as become pals with the mighty Kahtanka.

Eventually, Kahtanka and Bill established a certain relationship. Kahtanka learned that Bill was the "Man-with-the-Golden-Grain" and permitted him certain familiarities he would tolerate from no one else. So long as Bill had grain in his hand, Kahtanka allowed him to thrust his hand through the fence and place the feed on the ground. If Bill put an empty hand through the fence, however, Kahtanka allowed him one mistake. Kahtanka would sniff the empty palm once, then if it wasn't removed immediately, Kahtanka swung his horn at the offensive empty hand. It was a case of horning the hand that feeds you, but Kahtanka would tolerate no foolishness. Always, Kahtanka gave the one warning sniff, but that one warning was all he allowed. The game was played by Kahtanka's rules.

As people peered through Superfence at the herd, they often shook their heads sadly and murmured, "To think there were once millions of them."

It is estimated that at the time Columbus discovered America, there were from fifty to one hundred million buffalo roaming our land. No other continent—not even Africa—has produced a wild game animal in such numbers. Yet now the buffalo is a curiosity, only narrowly saved from extinction. Many Americans have never seen a buffalo except on a buffalo nickel. Although it's still in circulation, the buffalo nickel was last minted in 1938, and in time it will undoubtedly follow the fate of the buffalo, becoming a rarity, a collector's item.

For forty years the Department of the Interior has used a buffalo insignia as its official seal. Now, influenced by all the trends toward modernization, they feel this symbolism is too old-fashioned for them, and they are planning to retire the buffalo seal.

The official United States emblem, the American bald

eagle, projects a bad image of our country. Perhaps our forefathers chose this threatening symbol to give an aura of might and power to our weak, emerging nation. Now, in these days of the Ugly American, when much of the world is suspicious and fearful of our power, this symbolic bird of prey fortifies their apprehension. Evoking a picture of a powerful nation searching for victims, the eagle is bad public relations.

It would be far better, I think, to have a positive and productive symbol such as the buffalo. The buffalo presents the more favorable image of a powerful animal wishing to live in peace, fighting only when attacked or threatened. The buffalo will fight not only to protect his species as a group, but also for the safety of the most insignificant calf. The United States should seek to project its true image, a protector of the species—the whole human species—as well as every individual human being. I propose the buffalo as a more appropriate national emblem.

The buffalo actually contributed to our nation's development. The dog and the horse were probably more influential, yet they had to be tamed before they became useful, while the buffalo was used in its natural state, without domestication.

It's common knowledge that many of our present highway routes and railroad beds follow the paths of old Indian trails. Many people don't know, however, that something preceded the Indian trail. The Indians usually followed wildlife trails, which in many cases were those of the buffalo. The huge herds of buffalo followed river valleys and picked out the paths of least resistance in their wanderings, breaking the very first trail. These trails were followed by the Indians, then by white travelers on foot or horseback. Ultimately the trails were widened for wagons and a roadbed was formed. The buffalo, then, can be regarded as surveyors and engineers, the trail-builders of yesterday.

The Indians living near the huge herds, mainly the plains Indians, had for centuries lived off the buffalo. Their whole way of life was dependent upon the shaggy animals. Even their religion was centered in some degree upon buffalo. They used the furry robes for blankets, the scraped skins for their tepee shelters. Buffalo meat fed them, and preserved as pemmican, prevented starvation during the lean months. Buffalo bones became their tools, and the horns were used as cups and spoons. Except for the Caribou Eskimo, no other people have ever become so dependent upon one animal as the plains Indians were upon the buffalo.

Even after the buffalo had disappeared from the plains, their remains were useful to the economy of the area. Many a prairie settler earned much-needed cash by gathering buffalo bones. Thousands of tons of pulverized buffalo bones were shipped east to be used as fertilizer.

The abundance of buffalo greatly speeded the westward settlement of our country. Without this readily accessible supply of fresh meat, starvation might have postponed expansion, for the explorers, trappers, settlers, and the workers who built the first transcontinental railroads all relied upon buffalo for meat.

Our horses and goats stayed out of the way of the buffalo. When they saw the herd moving in their direction, they made tracks fast. No integration for them. But the donkey was different. Right from the day we got him, he attached himself to the buffalo herd and moved about with them, usually staying close to the hornless Ringo. But when he was really hungry, he'd move right into the middle of the herd, getting himself a good place at the table. Recklessly, he braved the swinging horns to mingle and graze with the humpbacks.

When school recessed for the summer, we moved the horses to a small adjoining pasture so the children could ride them, safe from the buffalo. As we opened the gate and let the horses and the donkey into the new pasture, the horses galloped off joyously, seeming to sense they were free now of those ominous pasture-mates with the sharp horns. The donkey plodded in reluctantly, then stopped to gaze back at his shaggy friends. All that day while the horses romped and grazed in peace, relishing their new security, the donkey stood by the fence gazing mournfully at the buffalo pasture. Occasionally, he threw back his head and shattered the hospital-zone silence with an idiotic "Hee-haw!"

The next day the homesick donkey still stood as a sentinel, watching the distant buffalo. So long as we watched him, we never saw him either eat or drink. All donkeys have sad, brown eyes, but our donkey looked absolutely heartbroken.

"I guess he thinks he's a buffalo," Bill said, giving in. "If he'd rather be with them than with the horses, I guess there's no harm."

Bill opened the gate into the buffalo pasture, and the donkey needed no further invitation. He trotted happily through the gate and rejoined his preferred company.

Perhaps the Donkey-Who-Thought-He-Was-a-Buffalo had gotten a bit too cocky, for a few days later he was painfully reminded that he was *not* a buffalo.

Bill had spread two dozen piles of hay along a fence row. The donkey rushed up to one of the piles and began eating. Good Cow sauntered up and stood behind the donkey. Not wanting to lose his place, he backed toward her, kicking her squarely between the horns with his right hind hoof. Good Cow shook her head and gazed at the donkey.

Having stopped a buffalo, the donkey seemed to feel his power. He decided to follow through, establishing his authority. He backed toward Good Cow and kicked, this time with both hind legs, and again hit her between the eyes. This powerful double kick didn't seem to hurt Good Cow any more than the single kick had, but it did bring a reaction.

Slowly and deliberately, Good Cow lowered her head, and with a fast, twisting sweep of her head, she buried a horn in the donkey's posterior. Good Cow raised her head, and this brought the donkey's hind legs off the ground so he was unable to kick or get free. She gave him two remonstrative shakes, then lowered her head. The donkey limped off in a hurry.

When the donkey stopped bleeding fifteen minutes later, Bill felt relieved. He kept a watchful eye on the donkey's injury over the next three weeks, but the wound healed well, leaving only a slight residual limp. Nature provides well for her animals.

In three weeks the donkey seemed fine, physically. He had received more than a physical injury, though. He had received the word that he wasn't one of them. Pouting and keeping to himself for a time, he nursed his emotional scars. Eventually he rejoined the herd, warily now, keeping on the fringe near Ringo. Perhaps he decided being a poor relation was better than being an outcast. Several times since, we've offered the donkey the safety of the horse pasture, but he haughtily refuses.

The goats continued to share the pasture with the buffalo. One weekend we tried moving them out of the buffalo pasture and into the horse pasture, but that lasted only a few hours. The Superfence of woven wire was goat-tight, but not so the barbed wire horse-pasture fence.

Only an hour after we had put the goats in the barbed wire pasture, I got a phone call, "Your goats are out."

The children and I hurried to the ranch. Sightseers were having a ball with the escaped goats. Some were playing with the smaller nannies and kids, while the more fastidious spectators had fled to the safety of their cars. I shuddered when I saw Billy, the huge odorous male goat, his front hoofs leaning on the windows of a blue sedan. I was relieved to see the occupants laughing. They had rolled the window down two inches and were feeding Billy Lifesavers and cigarettes through the crack.

After nearly two hours of chasing, we caught the last goat and sentenced them all to permanent confinement within Superfence.

The goats' presence within the buffalo pasture confused some visitors. Bill and I always enjoyed mingling anonymously with the crowds of spectators and overhearing their comments. Since many of the local people stopped by periodically, our anonymity didn't last long, but was fun while it did. It was one of those rare opportunities to be a fly on the wall and overhear conversations we normally wouldn't hear.

The goats were constantly being mistaken for something else. Once, when the goats were grazing in the distance, I heard a man exclaim, "Why, he's got a white buffalo in there!"

His companion snorted. "That's not a white buffalo, Harry! It's an antelope. See? There's a whole herd of antelope there." Then he proceeded to lecture Harry on the history and feeding habits of antelope. To this day, I suppose those two men are telling people about the herd of antelope they saw at Stanwood.

There were spectators of all kinds. Some amused us. Some interested us, and some irritated us.

Nothing riled Bill so much as the spectator who said, "Aren't they ugly critters!"

Anyone who uttered that remark received a murderous look from Bill. "Buffalo are beautiful," Bill would reply quietly through gritted teeth. The determination in the reply convinced the hapless onlooker that he had said the wrong thing, and in fact, was probably mistaken in the first place.

There were spectators who were really constructive. One day a middle-aged couple had been watching the herd for some time. We were busy planting trees and hadn't paid any attention to them, but they finally approached us with a question.

"What's that building over there across the field?" the man asked, pointing toward the hospital.

Bill explained that it was Mecosta Memorial Hospital.

The couple expressed surprise that a hospital could exist in this rural area. The wife explained that until recently she had been employed at a small hospital in Detroit, but that it had gone bankrupt and closed down.

We told them that Mecosta Memorial was in pretty rough shape, too. They seemed interested, so Bill explained some of the regulations that had to be met. When he got to the required new kitchen equipment, the woman exclaimed happily. It seemed that the excellent kitchen equipment of her defunct hospital was for sale at very low cost.

Through this bit of information, the hospital acquired new kitchen equipment and complied with one of the troublesome new regulations.

Another time Bill was visiting with a buffalo-watcher who mentioned that he was a building contractor. Bill began recounting to him some of the construction remodeling problems the hospital couldn't seem to solve. When explaining the seemingly insurmountable problem of the too-narrow corridors, the builder smiled easily.

"That's no problem nowadays," he said. "With the new steel studs you can put up a fireproof wall easily, anywhere. Just take a sledgehammer and knock out one of the corridor walls and build a new wall with the easy steel studding. You people can do the work yourselves, it's that easy."

Another miserable problem facing the hospital could

be solved. In this indirect manner, the buffalo herd already seemed to be making concrete contributions toward the survival of its neighbor, the hospital.

Onlookers always seem to be impressed when Bill calls the buffalo to feed them grain. One time when he was far up the fence line and gave his deep, guttural grunt and then called, "Kahtanka!" I noticed a man and wife exchange puzzled looks.

The woman asked, "What'd he say?"

"I don't know," the man replied, "but he told 'em something."

Many people accept unquestioningly the fact that Bill talks to his buffalo. It started as just joking conversation. In the Sunshine Ward at the hospital, Bill once told the roomful of elderly men, "Cheer up. Kahtanka says the sun will shine tomorrow."

Of course Kahtanka was right. From then on, the men wanted a new weather forecast from Kahtanka each day. I think it keeps Bill busy thinking up these imaginary conversations.

When some of the elderly patients ask, "What has Kahtanka had to say lately?" you get the feeling they're only half-kidding, so eager are they to hear the latest words of wisdom from Kahtanka.

Those early summer months we waited anxiously for our buffalo to begin rolling in the mud and making a genuine buffalo wallow. All the encyclopedias said that buffalo wallow in mud to protect themselves from insects. Either the books are mistaken, or we have an unusually fastidious group of animals. When we were Superfencing our pasture, we had enclosed an area of low, swampy land, congratulating ourselves on how thoughtful we were to provide a wonderfully natural spot for a buffalo wallow. We'd gaze sentimentally at the swamp, saying, "After we get our buffalo this will be the biggest buffalo wallow east of the Mississippi." History books describe the huge cup-shaped indentations in the prairies which are supposedly buffalo wallows of the past. We thought now we could watch one in the making. We could write a scientific paper: "A Study of the Development of a Buffalo Wallow." Who knew where it all would lead?

Our buffalo cheated us out of any scientific renown. Not once has one of our beasts wallowed in mud. Instead, they picked a spot of their own on the top of a hill, a very sandy, dry spot. There they roll in the sand, raising mighty dust clouds with their "wallowing," if that's what you call it. Perhaps we should be grateful. They'd be a terrible caked-up mess with their long shaggy hair all mud-coated. It isn't as if you could give them a bath or curry them as you would a pet dog or horse.

With their shedding now complete, the buffalo were left with a long forelock and beard, long hairs over the neck, shoulders, and forelegs, stopping in an abrupt line just behind the shoulders and hump where the short, smooth, shiny hair covers their slender hind-quarters. They looked a little like clipped poodles.

One day in late July, Bill noticed the cows making a big fuss over Kahtanka. They were all grouped around him, nuzzling and licking him. Bill studied the celebration quite awhile before he discovered what all the excitement was about. Kahtanka had reached puberty. His testicles had descended, and he was now a full-fledged bull. The silly heifers fussed over him like swooning adolescents over a matinee idol.

Either Kahtanka's hormones told him that he was now a big, fierce bull, or all the adoration of the heifers went to his head, for he soon turned the previous pecking order topsy-turvy.

Now Kahtanka was boss. He had free choice of everything. No one argued with him as he moved from one hill of grain to another, munching a mouthful off the top, then shoving another buffalo out of his way as

101

he moved on to taste the next mound. Second in line was Worms—why she became elevated to this slot we've never figured out. Maybe she's just naturally one of those popular individuals who charm everyone. Next in the power structure came Old Cow, the matriarch leader of the herd. She gave way to Kahtanka and Worms, but to no one else. Fourth in line was Bull-in-the-Bush, fifth was Good Cow, and so on down the line. Last of all was, of course, Ringo, who had to stand on the outskirts of the feeding herd and wait until they moved on, hoping they might have overlooked a few tidbits. Ringo's friend, the black Angus heifer, kept her company.

Aside from being recognized as Big Man on Campus, Kahtanka soon began boasting of another achievement. He fancied himself as a fine judge of character. Occasionally he took an instant dislike to a person on the outer side of Superfence. Then he growled, swung his head, and snorted monstrously. Most of the human victims of this insult didn't even realize they were being insulted. They just thought he was a fierce, wild buffalo acting himself. But we knew differently. Kahtanka usually treats human observers with sullen tolerance. When he singled out someone for his wrath, he must be showing his contempt for that individual. We found ourselves casting a wary eye at anyone Kahtanka disapproved of. It was really very peculiar. Perhaps Kahtanka knew something we didn't know.

Bill and I are very guilty of anthropomorphic beliefs. If you don't know what "anthropomorphic" means, don't feel bad. I didn't either, until I was accused of being that way. I didn't even know whether I was being complimented or insulted until I looked it up in the dictionary. It means ascribing human attributes to animals. Naturalists and zoologists tell us animals don't really think like men, acting under human motivations. I'm sure they're right, but everyone gets a little anthro-

102

pomorphic with pets. It's more fun that way. How many dog or cat owners think their pet is just an ordinary animal? Most animal owners who put up with the inconveniences of having a pet aren't doing so for a dumb animal. They enjoy their pet because it seems to resemble a person imprisoned in an animal body. How often an owner says of his pet, "He's almost human!" That's anthropomorphism.

By August, we knew mating season (rutting season, if you want to show off your animal husbandry knowledge) should be near. We didn't know what to expect, but from historical reports, it might be quite terrible. In old journals we read, "The roaring of the bulls could be heard for miles." Perhaps if our herd got too noisy, we'd get a summons for harboring a public nuisance. How do you quiet down a bunch of bellowing buffalo? And would the bulls get really nasty? We just didn't know.

According to Western histories, the bulls became very ferocious at this time, attacking anything that appeared to be a rival. They engaged in deadly fights, the victor winning many wives and the loser being left with his wounds and another year of celibacy.

We painted new signs reading, "Kahtanka's Honeymoon! Keep Away!" in readiness for the wild season of romance. Of course, we really didn't know if there was going to be a mating season. All our animals were so very young. The three oldest heifers were only teenagers by buffalo maturity standards and perhaps not old enough for motherhood. Kahtanka had filled out beautifully during the summer and appeared to be a fullfledged bull. Bull-in-the-Bush, although the same age, was not quite in the peach-fuzz stage yet. Still, he and Kahtanka scuffled, locked horns, and generally showed off their bulliness to the admiring young heifers.

One Sunday in mid-August, Bill, the children and I drove through the countryside looking for apple trees in the woods. We filled the trunk of our car with slightly

103

wormy apples which had fallen to the ground, and proudly took our treat to the ranch for the horses. We casually tossed a few apples to the buffalo, doubting if they'd even eat them, but our herd turned out to be real apple-lovers. We had such a good time pitching apples into the pasture that we got carried away and gave them more than was wise. Afterward we recalled all the tales we'd heard about cows and horses dying from getting into an orchard and eating too many apples.

The next day, when we fearfully checked on the herd, our worries were confirmed. Kahtanka seemed to have a tremendous tummyache. He stared at us accusingly while low rumbles and growls spewed out from deep inside him. He belched a couple of times, all the while glaring menacingly, and the basso rumbles continued vibrating through his chest. We went home feeling uneasy. He didn't appear desperately ill, but his digestive system sure seemed out of whack.

Two more days of deep growling passed before it occurred to us inexperienced greenhorns that Kahtanka didn't have a stomachache from eating apples. It was rutting season!

We viewed Kahtanka's new maturity with the same mixed emotions a mother feels upon her little son's first haircut. We were delighted that Kahtanka was really a man, or rather, a bull. But we dreaded the consequences. Quickly we put up the "Kahtanka's Honeymoon" signs and strung barbed wire across the paths where sightseers usually walked to get a closer look at the herd.

In his new-found bullhood, Kahtanka became a fierce, prancing monster who frightened even us. If we got within six feet of the fence, he would gallop toward us, threatening to come right through. Or he'd stand still, glaring and growling, and then suddenly jump toward us. Obviously, Kahtanka wanted to be alone with his harem. We cleared out and stayed away. Every few days Bill approached the fence to test him, but was always met with that mad glare and rumble.

The black Angus heifer given board and lodging within Superfence was with our buffalo herd for a purpose. We intended that she become a member of Kahtanka's harem and produce a half-buffalo, half-Angus calf. This hybrid calf would be the first tangible step toward our cherished project of developing a whole new breed of northern beef stock. The famous King Ranch in Texas developed a distinct breed of cattle, the Santa Gertrudis, about thirty years ago, making a tremendous contribution to the southern beef industry. They produced this breed after years of careful crossbreeding of the Shorthorn and the Brahman.

We intended to increase the hardiness of our northern beef breeds so they could comfortably withstand the rigors of our long, frigid winters. We believed the introduction of buffalo blood might be a major improvement.

This was not an original idea with us. As far back as the early nineteenth century, occasional breeders had been inspired by this challenge. This hybrid of the buffalo and domestic cattle is called a "cattalo." When we first started investigating the possibility of producing cattalo we met only discouraging words. "Cattalo have not proved satisfactory," was the pat answer we received to our inquiries. Or, "Hybridization of buffalo and cattle has not proved commercially practicable." They sounded very positive—approaching, but not quite saying those hated words, "It can't be done." But many a stubborn man has kept on trying, just because he was goaded with "It can't be done."

The difficulties of producing cattalo, we learned, were twofold. Male offspring of the first generation (an animal one-half buffalo and one-half domestic cow) were nearly always sterile. Not until a bull was only one-thirty-second buffalo could he be considered a reliably fertile bull. The other problem was the high death rate of domestic cows as they gave birth to their half-buffalo calves. At first, authorities said the mother cow died because the hump of the half-buffalo calf killed her. When they learned that even full-blooded buffalo calves have no hump at birth, the smart men studied some more.

Now they've decided it's a genetic problem which causes fifty gallons of fluid to build up around the unborn hybrid calf. When the domestic cow begins to give birth to the calf, the huge amount of fluid is expelled, causing the cow to go into shock and die. This discouraging conclusion is based upon cattalo-producing experiments conducted in Saskatchewan. However, in the past thirty years, vast progress has been made in the study of genetics, antibodies, and drugs, and Bill and I think it's time to try again.

Although our first feelers sent out to investigate the possibilities of cattalo resulted in squelches, we kept digging. Finally, in two out-of-print, nineteenth-century books obtained through the help of inter-library loans, we found encouraging words on the feasibility of cattalo.

The first book, *Buffalo Jones' Forty Years of Adventure,* compiled by Colonel Henry Inman,* covers the eventful life of C. J. Jones of Garden City, Kansas. Mr. Jones was better known as "Buffalo Jones" because of his consuming interest in the preservation of buffalo. At the time when the buffalo was in great danger of becoming extinct, Buffalo Jones initiated and supported a unique kind of buffalo hunt. He successfully roped and captured many dozen wild buffalo calves and transported them hundreds of miles to his ranch, where he protected them and encouraged their propagation. This

*Crane and Company, Topeka, Kansas, 1899.

would be a commendable achievement in itself, but we were fascinated by his interest and success with producing cattalo. His stated purpose: "to produce a race of cattle equal in hardiness to the buffalo, with robes much finer, and possessing all the advantages of the best bred cattle" was the same as our purpose. He said, "Only the first cross is difficult to secure; after that, they are unlike the mule, for they are as fertile as either the cattle or buffalo. They breed readily with either strain of the parent race—the females especially."

Many of his comments on his cattalo we found intriguing:

Size: "The half-breeds are much larger than their progenitors of either side; the cows weighing from twelve to fifteen hundred pounds."

Fur: "The fur of the three-quarter and seven-eighths buffalo makes the finest robes. This fur is perfectly compact, and when bred from the black strain of cattle, is as handsome as that of the black beaver."

Hardiness: "I have successfully wintered them on the range without any artificial food or shelter as far north as Lake Winnipeg. They withstood the cold when the mercury reached fifty degrees below zero, without artificial food or shelter."

He goes on to mention that buffalo characteristics seem to be dominant over domestic cattle characteristics. The cattalo display more buffalo traits than domestic cattle traits; for instance, they face into blizzards and are solid-colored.

The enthusiasm of Buffalo Jones for his cattalo and his faith that cattalo were "the coming thing" certainly contradicts the opinions of present-day animal husbandry experts. Mr. Jones' opinions weren't based on theory or research. He had produced cattalo, and his rancher's eye was impressed with them.

The other aging book which attracted our attention especially was a Smithsonian Institution Report from

107

House Miscellaneous Documents, 1st Session, 50th Congress, 1887–88, Volume 18. This was a report by William T. Hornaday on the extermination of the American Bison. In regard to cattalo, he said, "I fully believe that we will gradually see a great change wrought in the character of western cattle by the introduction of a strain of buffalo blood."

Later, he chastises cattlemen for their disinterest in cattalo: "Yet all this time the cattlemen have had it in their power, by the easiest and simplest method in the world, to introduce a strain of hardy native blood in their stock which would have made it capable of successfully resisting a much greater degree of hunger and cold. It is really surprising that the desirability of cross-breeding the buffalo and domestic cattle should for so long a time have been either overlooked or disregarded. While cattle-growers generally have shown the greatest enterprise in producing special breeds for milk, for butter, or for beef, cattle with short horns and cattle with no horns at all, only two or three men have had the enterprise to try to produce a breed particularly hardy and capable."

Wouldn't Hornaday be surprised to learn that now, eighty years later, cattlemen were still ignoring the opportunity to introduce buffalo blood into northern beef herds?

Since Hornaday's time there had been few cross-breeding attempts with a domestic bull and a buffalo cow because of the shortage of buffalo cows. However, the buffalo cow seems to have no ill effects while carrying or giving birth to her hybrid calf. Crossbreeding in this manner appears the logical course to follow; yet this course was impossible for us because of Kahtanka. Kahtanka would kill a domestic bull who approached his harem.

Our hope would have to remain with Angie, our black Angus heifer. Most of the time she lingered on the fringes of the buffalo herd, but periodically, she expressed great interest in Kahtanka. To our disappointment, Kahtanka showed only disdain for Angie, a mere raven-haired civilized female.

We talked cheerfully of producing "Herfalos" by crossing Herefords and buffalo, and of "Angelos," by crossing Angus and buffalo. We were so hopeful that our black Angus would give us an Angelo calf that we even had the future offspring named. "Michael" was to be its name—Michael Angelo.

Kahtanka's polygamous honeymoon lasted four weeks. At last one day Kahtanka allowed us to look at him again. Mating season was over. His growling ceased, and he returned to his old sweet self, although "sweet" doesn't seem the proper word. Once more he tolerated our coming up to the fence and disdainfully let spectators take his picture.

It was a real relief to have that period over. We felt like parents who had just reared a child safely through adolescence. The only trouble was that we knew this stage would recur annually, the next autumn, and the next. And we didn't even know if this year's bad behavior was productive. We wouldn't know for another two hundred and eighty days whether Kahtanka's behavior was just adolescent strutting, or whether he had been really serious. Would we have calves next spring?

Patients
Are Where
You Find
Them

8 That first summer with our newly-acquired buffalo herd, whenever time permitted, we studied them intently, learning their habits and planning for the future. Bill's busy practice kept him occupied ten to twelve hours daily, but during short lulls he managed to slip away to visit his herd. Even after six years, Bill did not find country practice dull. Strange and challenging patients seemed to stumble into Stanwood.

One sultry August day during the week of the county fair, an important annual event in Mecosta County, Bill received a telephone call that a doctor was urgently needed to see a member of the carnival troupe traveling with the fair.

Afternoon office hours had just begun. The waiting room was filled with hot, impatient patients. "Can't you get one of the doctors up there closer to the fairgrounds?" Bill asked. "I'm awfully busy with a lot of sick people to see."

The fair manager explained that he'd called all the other doctors, but they were tied up. Bill smiled ruefully at being the last choice. With a sigh he picked up his black bag and slipped out the back door, leaving his

111

office nurse to face the waiting room and its irritated occupants.

Bill parked his car at the fairgrounds gate where the manager met him. Together they walked down the midway. Curious faces turned to watch the doctor and his black bag, wondering who was sick. Bill noticed the manager was very restless, and his eyes twinkled impishly. Uneasy, Bill wondered what it could be about this patient that had prompted other doctors to be unavailable.

At the far end of the midway the manager led Bill into the sideshow tent. The sideshow seemed closed. It was empty except for three barking dogs and four small black children playing hopscotch. The dogs began snarling as Bill approached a bus parked at the rear of the tent. A middle-aged black man emerged from the bus and mumbled something incoherent to the bristling dogs, at which they crept away. The man glanced at the black bag and motioned them toward the door into the bus.

"I'll leave you with your patient," the manager said, patting Bill on the shoulder. He turned and walked away, but not quickly enough to conceal the wide grin on his face.

Bill knew he was in for something. He followed the man inside the bus and was led toward the back of the vehicle, which was screened off for a bedroom. The huge bed, made on a frame of rough four-by-four lumber, was not supported by legs, but by six automobile jacks. Sprawled on the bed, with one leg flowing over the edge, and propped up by a large number of pillows lay the patient, a very sick lady. Besides being sick, she had another claim for attention—she weighed eight hundred and twenty pounds. The patient was the carnival fat lady. Outside, on the sideshow marquee, she was billed as "Baby Flo."

As she lay ensconced on the huge bed, surrounded by

dozens of pillows, Bill thought she looked a bit like a sultan or shiek. There were no fine silks or brocades around Baby Flo, but there were three fawning attendants, waiting upon her attentively. Her husband fluttered about the enormous bed, asking where she hurt, and begging her to let him help in some way. Bill saw immediately that Baby Flo was their queen, and they, her servants. They depended upon her great volume for their livelihood, the income made up of the half-dollars people paid to gawk at Baby Flo's tremendous bulk.

Flo had a temperature of one hundred and three, and from her history and symptoms she obviously had a severe kidney infection with bleeding. Hospitalization was necessary—but how? Bill thought furiously.

It had been two years since Flo had borne her weight on her legs or walked, so Bill knew her leg bones would no longer support her great poundage. Since she couldn't get inside an automobile, the whole converted bus would have to take her to the hospital. Bill gave her husband directions and promised to meet him at the hospital with extra help. At the hospital Bill rounded up all the strong help he could find, then sent word to the village for additional help.

For a hospital bed they fastened together with steel straps two of the lowest beds they could find, then placed two layers of mattresses crossways of the tightly fastened beds. Two stretcher carts on wheels were strapped together and taken to the ambulance entrance where Flo's bus waited.

A dozen people helped, and with much nudging, grunting, and pulling, Flo was extricated from her bus and placed on the carts. The elevator transported her to the second floor, where the next job was moving her from the cart to the fastened hospital beds. Bill carefully instructed the help that if Flo ever slipped to the floor, they'd have a terrible time getting her up. The carts were nearly a foot higher than the hospital beds, so it was a matter of rolling her vast bulk downhill. Like a huge, water-filled balloon rolling down a flight of stairs, once the mass of fat started flowing downward toward the bed and the center of gravity passed, the rest of her flowed behind. Baby Flo was aptly named.

Along with the kidney infection, lab tests showed Flo had severe diabetes and very high blood pressure, and treatment was begun to get these conditions under control. After getting over their initial shock at her monstrous eight-hundred-and-twenty-pound bulk, hospital attendants found Flo a congenial, pleasant person, and they enjoyed caring for her, even though her volume was equal to that of six normal patients.

When Bill told me of his new corpulent patient, I burst into peals of laughter. It was just too ridiculous— Bill, of all doctors, caring for the carnival fat lady.

Bill always had fought obesity in his patients with great passion. He hated to see people shortening their lives by carrying around excess weight, and he preached zealously how much better and younger they would feel at a normal weight. Any obese person who wanted Bill for his doctor could expect to be placed upon a tea, broth, and jello regimen, accompanied by exercise, until his weight diminished. Thus it was ironic that Bill was caring for Baby Flo.

"How can anyone possibly get that huge?" I asked Bill. I constantly wage battle with midriff bulge, so I can easily sympathize with anyone fighting excess poundage of ten or even twenty pounds, but to be six hundred and fifty pounds overweight! It boggled my imagination.

Bill explained that obesity usually begins during childhood. The fatter the child becomes, the less active he is, and pounds collect even faster. By teen-age years the fat person is far beyond normal weight. He suffers from self-consciousness and retires from activities and social contacts. This stage is often a crucial one. If the

114

adolescent stays in high school, sometimes the weight gain slows, and we occasionally hear of the heartening "before and after" stories where a two-hundred-fifty pound individual works hard to shed weight down to normalcy and a happy life. Unfortunately, many fat young people leave school and drop out of life. They become recluses in their own homes. With no education or training, and suffering embarrassment over their unsightly appearance, they withdraw to the shadows even in their own family life. They eat more, move less, and the pounds accumulate steadily. When regular scales no longer will register their weight, they stop weighing themselves. Tent-like loose clothing, instead of the usual fitted clothing, allows another one hundred pounds to accumulate in concealment. Inwardly, the massively obese individual has been thinking of himself as freakish. Once the quarter-ton weight is reached, he becomes convinced he is a real freak, and decides to be a good one, by eating fabulously. To get a sideshow job, the fatter, the better.

Between a carnival fat person and the huge number of ordinary persons who are overweight, the difference is not only in pounds. Most obese individuals, even those one hundred pounds overweight, constantly battle the accumulating pounds. Occasionally making an effort to lose weight, they persistently try, at least, not to gain. They continue to lead normal lives, and though they acknowledge and even hate their fatness, they never consider themselves freakish.

Bill explained his theory on the cause of obesity. Fat people, he said, very seldom eat much breakfast. They eat an insignificant lunch or skip it entirely, but beginning in the afternoon and until they retire for the night, they take in huge quantities of food. Then, after they are asleep, this food is digested and presented to the body as nutrition. However, since the person is in bed and inactive, the nutrition is not used up, but stored in fat depots throughout the body. Eventually, the body gets wise to this cycle. The brain seems to realize subconsciously that every morning and early afternoon brings a starvation period of low blood sugar level. To ward off this daily low blood sugar level, the brain calls for a high caloric intake in the late afternoon and evening. It becomes a vicious cycle. And improbable as it may sound, a three-hundred-pound individual may be existing on a starvation-thought mechanism. The brain says, "Store up lots of food tonight, because tomorrow morning brings starvation."

Even when the obese individual decides to lose weight, he usually starts in the morning with the resolution not to eat. He tolerates the lack of food until late afternoon when hunger and habit of the old cycle break down his resistance, and he cleans out the refrigerator.

To break this feast and famine cycle, Bill requested his patients to start the day with a big breakfast—even the old-fashioned, meat-and-potatoes farm breakfast if possible. This would be burned off as energy during the active part of their day. They were instructed not to eat anything after four in the afternoon; thus they wouldn't stockpile calories which weren't going to be needed during their inactive night hours. Also, evening snacks are usually high-caloric foods. A box of chocolates can devastate a waistline.

Bill was considered a real martinet by his weight-battling patients. He refused to prescribe diet pills. Instead he encouraged them to get very busy with a consuming hobby, a new job, or community activities.

"Get active, think about others, and you'll forget about eating," he urged.

He praised, cajoled, and shamed them into shedding the unhealthy pounds. "That forty pounds of extra blubber you're carrying is just like lugging a forty-pound pack around all day," he would point out. "Don't kill yourself prematurely with such an unnecessary load."

Bill always warred against obesity with such verve, I wondered if he would tackle Flo. It seemed a lost cause, but lost causes don't discourage Bill.

Flo's condition improved and stabilized. Bill decided to talk to her about a weight-reducing regimen. Though she was only thirty-four years old, the combination of diabetes, kidney infection, and high blood pressure was a real death-threatening situation. Bill patiently explained to her that she was still a young woman who could have a long and active life if she would start on the project of losing weight slowly yet steadily until she reached one hundred and fifty pounds. Flo listened politely, but Bill sensed he wasn't reaching her at all. Losing weight would mean giving up her profession, the only profession she knew. Her family and retinue depended upon her bulk for their living. Encouraging Flo to reduce was asking her to forsake her role of family supporter.

On the fifth day of hospitalization Flo's condition was improved enough that she was dismissed. Bill didn't really expect her to diet herself down to a sylph-like creature, yet we often wondered how things went with her.

Less than two years later we learned the end of Flo's story: in the "Milestones" column of *Time* magazine was Flo's obituary. She had kept to her fat-lady profession, and Flo's proficiency at it meant her doom.

The ringing telephone summons the country doctor to strange patients.

When Bill isn't home, I have to face the demanding telephone. Patients always assume the doctor's wife is a nurse. Apparently they've read too many racy novels about doctors and nurses. After reeling off their symptoms to me, they'd ask for my diagnosis and advice.

I'd murmur sympathetically and say I didn't know.

Indignantly, they'd rebuke me, "Well, you're a nurse, aren't you?"

When I admitted that I was not, there was shocked silence. Perhaps they suspected me of living in sin with their doctor.

Finally I developed a stock answer to their medical questioning. I said simply, "Look, if you want to get well, don't ask *me*. Wait and ask the doctor."

There are many kinds of irritating phone calls, most of which come after bedtime, such as the man who whines, "I've been sick all day but I couldn't call the doctor before this because this evening was my night to bowl."

Another type of call which makes me grit my teeth is the caller who says she doesn't want to bother her regular doctor at this late hour because he's so tired and overworked.

Sometimes the ringing phone brought horror when only a rasping whisper of "Help!" came through the receiver. I'd desperately try to find out who it was, and where he lived, so an ambulance could be sent.

Early one evening I answered the phone. It was the woman who helped run one of the gas stations on the highway just outside of Stanwood. Her distraught voice cried, "We need the doctor! There's been a terrible car accident! A man's hanging in a tree!"

I started to tell her that Bill was still at the hospital when she interrupted. "Here comes Doc now!" she shouted into the phone and hung up.

I turned off the oven. At least that phone call had been productive. I'd learned Bill wouldn't be home for his supper for a while yet.

Two hours later when I heard the car door slam, I turned on the oven. Short order, warmed-over dinners are a specialty of doctors' wives.

118

"Hi!" I greeted Bill. "What's with the man in the tree?"

"Oh ho, the pipeline's been working already," Bill said, making a wry face. As he took off his coat, he told me about the strange accident.

"I like to think I save lives all the time," he said, "but it's usually a little intangible. This evening I definitely saved a life. The man in the tree is alive right now because I was driving home for supper."

As he approached the curve on the highway, Bill had seen the demolished car and the gathering crowd, so he was already slowing when they recognized his car and flagged him down.

"How many injured and where?" Bill asked, as he jumped from his car.

"Just one, but he's a goner! He's over there," an onlooker said, pointing toward the ditch on the far side of the bridge. A group of men stood near an old gnarled apple tree, staring upward into its branches. A limp figure was draped over a branch. Bill climbed over the fence and ran up to the apple tree. As he climbed up into the tree he saw the victim's face was already purple. Bill felt a weak pulse in the throat. The man had sailed into the tree with such force that the branch which stopped him had knocked the wind out of him. Suspended thus, the branch pressing on his midline, the unconscious victim couldn't get another breath. Hanging there like that, he was suffocating.

"Let's get him down! Give me a hand!" Bill ordered the nearby group of watchers.

The men looked at each other uneasily, but no one stepped forward.

"He's not dead yet, but he will be if someone doesn't help me right now," Bill shouted angrily.

Immediately several men climbed up into the tree to help. As soon as the victim was laid out on the ground,

Bill gave him artificial respiration. Soon the purple face turned an oxygenated pink.

The approaching wail of an ambulance siren was heard with relief.

Bill, following the ambulance, returned to the hospital, where the accident victim was X-rayed thoroughly. Though the man had gone through a bad accident and come close to suffocation, there was only one thing wrong with him. He was still roaringly drunk. The accident, the ambulance ride, the poking and prodding of doctors and nurses—nothing had sobered him in the slightest.

Bill laughed as he finished telling me about it. "The night shift will be busy tonight. That old boy is really swinging. You can hear him singing and laughing way down in the outpatient department."

I was still puzzled. "So you saved him by taking him out of the tree. If there were so many people there ahead of you, why didn't they take him down?" I asked.

"They thought he was dead," Bill said. "People shy away from the dead. It's a person if it's living, but if it's dead, it's a body. People who normally can't stand the sight of blood will come to the aid of a terribly mangled accident victim, if he's making noise and obviously alive. But just let the victim be declared dead and everyone moves back five paces. There seems to be a lot of unacknowledged emotion about spooks and ghosts— the old midnight-at-the-cemetery syndrome."

Before Bill finished his warmed-over supper, he had dealt with two more phone calls.

The first was from a woman who wanted to know how many aspirin she should take for a toothache.

The second was from the night nurse on the hospital's second floor. Unfortunately, the rommate of the evening's inebriated accident victim was a Baptist preacher. The songs of the tipsy patient were becoming progressively ribald, and just too much for the man of the cloth.

His blood pressure was soaring as he countered with loud Biblical quotations and hymns.

"Doctor," the distraught nurse begged, "someone has to be sedated—either the drunk, the preacher, or me."

As we prepared for bed, Bill began talking happily about the buffalo. The tired creases around his eyes smoothed away, and he became the happy farmer surveying his livestock prospects. I felt grateful affection for our herd of buffalo. The shaggy beasts provided a restful diversion from country practice.

As autumn progressed, the buffalos' fur began growing longer and thicker, with a dense wool next to the hide underneath the long outer hairs. On a frigid, below-zero day when you feel one of these animals, your fingers sink into three inches of dense fur. The skin feels warm to your fingertips, like touching the outside of a warm oven, and you understand why buffalo don't mind cold weather. Winter is, in fact, probably their favorite season since they aren't pestered by insects.

With the weather growing frostier, the buffalo grew more playful, cavorting about like a bunch of oversized puppies. They splashed through the icy creek water as if it were warm bath water. How they love cold weather!

We were beginning to feel like oldtimers in the buffalo business. With a good supply of hay on hand we were ready to face our first wintering of the herd.

We knew winter had arrived for sure when the sheriff laughingly told Bill one day, "Well, the calls have started."

"Already?" Bill grinned. "I didn't realize it was that cold yet."

By "calls," the sheriff meant complaint calls he received concerning our buffalo. It seems that a few animal devotees of the area feel we are inhumane because we don't keep our buffalo in a barn in the wintertime.

If, some frosty day, those animal lovers would watch

the buffalo rolling and cavorting in the snow, they might not be so vehement. And if they really were concerned about their welfare, I'd think they'd shudder at the danger of those sharp, swinging horns being shut into a barn together. Even if it were humanly possible to drive a buffalo herd into a barn, who would go into the barn to feed them? That is, assuming there was anything left of the barn after a few hours of confinement. With Kahtanka pitted against a barn door, I'd pick Kahtanka ten to one.

We seemed to have run into a case of differing regional customs. Here in our section of Michigan, farmers believe horses and cattle belong in barns—as the good Lord intended—not wandering loose in a pasture. Even on pleasant summer days many horses and cattle are kept in their stalls. We'd been reared in a region where fresh air and sunshine, winter or summer, was considered essential for both man and beast. Usually, shelter was provided for cattle and horses, but it was a voluntary shelter such as a three-sided windbreak, or an open-doored barn.

It took us a long time to get used to this "barn syndrome" of our neighbors. A clean barn seemed bad enough to us, but many barns weren't even kept clean. They were foul-smelling, dark, damp prisons. And these humane animal-lovers wanted us to sentence Kahtanka to such a fate!

We wished the well-meaning buffalo protectors would exert their energies toward really protecting our animals, such as helping deter the rock-throwers. We began finding huge stones in the pasture, and friends told us of seeing people throw rocks at the animals. The buffalo wised up fast and stayed far back in the pasture away from the mean arm of civilization. I suppose the rock-throwers thought the buffalo looked pretty serene and calm compared to the churning, running herds they'd seen in the movies. A well-placed rock might get a rise out of them, or even an excited stampede.

122

Buffalo had taken so much abuse from mankind that we really bristled at any mistreatment shown *our* animals. The wild herds had been subjected to many dangers in nature. The main predators of the herds were wolves and grizzly bears, of which grizzlies were the most dangerous, although they were able to take only the weak, sick, and old buffalo.

Prairie fires roaring over miles and miles of dry plains killed, maimed, and blinded thousands. There are reports of whole herds being roasted in a prairie fire, but fire can't be blamed for the ruination of the great herds, for the other prairie animals were subjected to the same danger.

Drowning destroyed huge numbers of buffalo, especially in the spring. Although buffalo are strong swimmers who unhesitatingly swim wide rivers, this often was their undoing during the heavy spring run-off. They would enter a river flooded by the melting snows and swim across easily, but at the other side, if they encountered a steep embankment with no place to climb out, many of them perished. Also, when crossing mushy ice, many fell through and drowned. With the swift floodwaters of springtime, historical accounts describe huge numbers of bloated buffalo carcasses being swept downstream, especially in the Missouri River.

As for sicknesses, the buffalo are a breed remarkably free of parasites and diseases when living in their natural environment.

Some authorities tried to prove that Indians and bad winters had naturally led to the decline of the herds. Most students of history disagree, however, and believe the buffalo multiplied so extensively at first because of its lack of natural enemies. Blizzards and Indian hunts took their toll, but this force of natural selection had gone on for generations and could certainly not be blamed for the buffalo's quick disappearance after the Civil War.

Their main enemy, of course, turned out to be the man with the rifle. With so many groups promoting their destruction, the buffalo herds didn't have a chance.

Sportsmen and big-game hunters from the East and England greatly enjoyed the sport of hunting buffalo. It was an adventure similar to going on safari in Africa.

The Army encouraged the complete annihilation of the buffalo, the Indians' main source of food. The military reasoned that the absence of buffalo would starve the Indians into surrendering and retreating to reservations.

Cattlemen urged their destruction because they wanted to save all the forage and grazing lands for their own livestock. This is on a par with our current policy of swinging the wrecking ball at a fine, historic mansion to make room for a new hotdog stand.

Railroads saw a big profit in the increased freight they would carry with shipment of the meat, hides, and bones.

Professional hunters and their retinue of skinners and drivers wanted to continue their exciting and profitable hunting.

Advancing civilization itself, with its small towns and fenced farms, could hardly be expected to appreciate a wandering herd of buffalo. Today's farmers know what even a few small deer can do to a cornfield.

It seems everyone wanted to destroy the buffalo; everyone, that is, but the Plains Indian. The Indian was bewildered and enraged at this rustling of his herds. Buffalo-stealing and killing was regarded by the western Indian as a serious crime, just as cattlemen considered rustling of their cattle as a crime calling for a necktie party at the nearest cottonwood tree.

To understand the Indian's concept of ownership of the buffalo, it has to be remembered that the Indian did not understand ownership of land. He could not believe that land could be bought, sold, or transferred.

Tecumseh said, "Sell a country! Why not sell the air, the clouds, the great sea as well as the land?" The Indians felt that everything which grows out of the earth, in the rivers and waters, was given jointly to all, and that everyone should share nature's products according to designated hunting areas. The wanton destruction of his buffalo herds was a serious crime to him. The Indian complained that if he stole a farmer's cow to feed his starving papoose, the white man considered this a terrible crime, yet the white man slaughtered the Indians' buffalo just for kicks.

Although buffalo once occupied most of the continental United States, they were never very numerous east of the Mississippi River, and by 1850, few, if any, still existed in that section. Historians and anthropologists believe the buffalo was a relative newcomer east of the Mississippi, probably not spreading there until about 1000 A.D. and perhaps even later.

West of the Mississippi the herds seemed endless, and we'll never know actually how many buffalo there were. Dr. Hornaday of the National Museum said we might as well estimate the number of leaves in a forest.

The Union Pacific and Kansas Pacific railroads apparently hastened the disappearance of the buffalo by bringing in civilization and by splitting up the huge grazing territory. The herds soon learned to stay several miles away from the steel rails bisecting the continent, for these meant the presence of man, and death for the buffalo. By 1875 there were two distinct groups of buffalo, the northern and southern herds, permanently separated now by this steel line of civilization. By 1878 the southern herd had been annihilated. And no wonder, as in 1873, the *New Mexican,* a paper published in Santa Fe, had reported that there were two thousand hunters on the southern plains. One party of sixteen hunters was said to have killed twenty-eight thousand buffalo during the summer of 1873.

With the destruction of buffalo in the southern plains,

plains, attention was turned to the job of destroying the northern herd.

By 1870 and continuing for fifteen years, trading in buffalo hides was the chief industry of the plains. A single firm in St. Louis bought two hundred and fifty thousand hides in 1871. In 1873–74, auctions in Ft. Worth, Texas, were moving two hundred thousand hides in a day or two.

Hunting from train windows was advertised widely, and in 1882 there were five thousand hunters and skinners on the northern range. The buffalo made their last stand along the Little Missouri River in Dakota Territory. By 1885 the northern herd was nearly exterminated.

By 1886 Dr. William Hornaday pointed out the disappearance of the buffalo, and in that same year he made a frantic search for specimens. He and his hunting party finally found some stragglers between the Yellowstone and Missouri rivers, where they managed to hunt down two dozen buffalo of various ages. These animals, he said, were extremely wary and hard to hunt, as they represented the survival of the fittest. Each animal was found to harbor several imbedded bullets, showing their survival of many hunts. These animals were mounted for display at the Smithsonian Institution, so people of the future could see what the great American bison had looked like. At this time it appeared the species would soon be extinct.

Two groups, the Flathead Indians and the American Bison Society, probably saved buffalo from extinction. In 1873 the Pend d'Oreille Indians went from the Flathead Valley for meat. A young brave, Walking Coyote, brought back four young bison calves: two bulls and two heifers. The descendants of these four animals became the famous Pablo-Allard herd, part of which became the Conrad herd at Kalispell, Montana. The American Bison Society, formed for the preservation of the American bison, bought thirty-four bison from the Conrad estate, and these, plus seven others, formed the Montana Bison Range herd, which was turned onto the range on October 17, 1909. These animals were the ancestors of our Kahtanka and his harem of hefty heifers.

Goats
in the
Basement

9 One chilly November morning, Bill and I left Stanwood to catch a plane for New York. Just at dawn we drove past the ranch, making our farewell check on the buffalo. They were just beginning to stir, the weak winter sun rousing them to feed. What a parting sight! The head and back of each of the dark animals was covered with a silver layer of frost. Each separate hair on their manes had been individually stroked with frost. In the pale yellow of winter daybreak the scene seemed ghostly and unreal, but a magic moment to enjoy recalling.

This was our first visit to New York, and we were very excited. Bill was attending a surgeons' meeting, but in his free time we took in all the proper tourist sights of the great city. When we'd been in New York City only one day, we too recognized "You can take the boy out of the farm, but you can't take the farm out of the boy." Already we were restless, needing to see grass and trees, so we headed for Central Park. We strolled there aimlessly for a while until we saw the zoo. Then we felt more at home.

A pair of yaks attracted our interest. An Asian animal from the Himalayan mountain area, they reminded us of buffalo. Their long, black, silky coats hung nearly to the ground, and the horn span of the bull was truly impressive. What really moved us, though, were their affectionate and companionable ways. Oblivious to our intruding stares, they concentrated upon each other. With nuzzles and rubbing, they conveyed their mutual love. True affection like this was rarely seen in the animal world. In the future, we agreed, we must look into the yak business.

We sauntered along, politely looking at the animals in their huge cage jails, until we came to the buffalo cage. The bull was really huge. Compared to him in size, Kahtanka was still a gangling boy. But in spirit, Kahtanka was definitely the better bull. The poor Central Park bull had no horns, and he stood listlessly, no spunk left in him. He was just a big hunk of bull, not deserving the title of Great American Bison. His companion, a medium-sized buffalo cow, seemed to have taken her captivity better. The big bull lumbered about his pen, unable to work up to a gallop. There just wasn't room, even if he had the inclination.

When we returned to our hotel room we wrote enthusiastic postcards to our children and friends, describing the sights of New York—namely, the buffalo in Central Park Zoo. How our friends kidded us about that when we got home!

Christmas neared and still no snow, unusual for our section of Michigan. Although we prefer a white Christmas as much as the children do, every day that passed without snowfall was saving us money. The buffalo were still foraging for themselves, and Bill only fed them once or twice a week to keep himself in their good graces.

Though the buffalo weren't giving us much trouble at this time, the goats became a real nuisance and a trial. Their original purpose (testing Superfence) had ended with the arrival of the buffalo. The buffalo were quite capable of doing their own fence-testing. However, the goats were kept on for another purpose: to eat the brush out of the swamps and clean up the elder thickets. Every time I saw the goats, though, they weren't eating brush, but nice grass or hay, and I suspected they were being kept on for two reasons: 1) Bill was fond of goats, and 2) he couldn't place them for adoption.

Something terrible had upset the romance timetable of the goats, and all the nannies obviously were going to have kids in December and January, instead of the proper warm months of spring. Since we had no barn at the ranch, we knew the babies would freeze when born. The expectant mothers had to be sheltered somewhere.

A few days before Christmas I found out where they were to be sheltered. The buffalo car chugged down our driveway, Nannie sitting beside Bill in the front seat. Two bales of straw filled the trunk. Ecstatically, the children ran out to meet our new boarder while I debated whether tears, fishwife screaming, or a nervous breakdown would be the proper response.

In no time a nice straw bed was prepared for Nannie in our garage. Many garages are a good distance from the house, but as my luck would have it, our garage is one of those sunken things under the house, actually just a continuation of the basement.

For some time our underground garage hadn't been used to house Bill's car. At the time of the the Cuban missile crisis, going along with the hysteria of the times, we'd decided we should have a fallout shelter. The concrete sunken garage seemed the proper site. We'd filled gunny sacks with sand and sand-bagged in the swinging entrance doors to the garage until we had a tight hole-in-the-ground. We'd stocked it with water, canned goods, and medicines. Though Bill's car had to face the wintry blasts outside, we congratulated ourselves that we had a fallout shelter.

Now the fallout shelter was to become a goat shelter. We moved out all the supplies which were to insure our survival, and moved in the straw and hay.

The children were thrilled to be sharing their roof with a goat. They did all the work for her, performing their chores of feeding and watering her every morning before school, and again before bedtime. Bruce and Beth worked out a division of labor on the chores. What with her long hair to be unsnarled and braided, Beth needed more time in the morning to get ready for school, so Bruce took over the morning chores, and Beth, the evening ones. Every morning, Bruce brought the water buckets to our bathroom, filling them in the shower stall. Frequently, this occurred during Bill's morning shower, causing bellows and groans; but with one goat and one bathroom, what could be done?

I, too, did my share of grumbling and threatening, but it was all noise. I'm not so mean as to throw a mother-to-be out in the cold. It was embarrassing, though. There were times when I suspected neighbors of looking at me strangely. I thought I heard whispers of "She's got goats in her basement."

On Christmas morning when the children went down to feed Nannie, we heard great shouts and screams, and we rushed down the basement steps. There, in our straw-filled garage, were two damp, just-born goats. We carried them upstairs to the bathroom where we dried their curly black-and-white coats. The children were enraptured. Baby goats born in the hay on Christmas morning made the manger scene of Bethlehem very real. That was one Christmas where Santa Claus took a back seat. A stable birth was very much in the children's minds all that day, and their Christmas toys lay neglected under the tree. The baby goats in the garage drew them like a magnet. The twins, a boy and a girl, were named Nick and Noel, and no baby goats ever got more cuddling and care.

As soon as Nick and Noel were frisky enough to brave the cold, they and their mother were returned to the ranch, and another expectant nanny brought home. At

132

first, the children protested losing Nick and Noel, but after the next babies were born, they became just as devoted to them. The goat maternity season continued until the end of March.

To me, the goats were an embarrassment and an inconvenience, but I'd been practicing over the years, and I could now face such things with more equanimity. Bill was so soft-hearted toward crippled and downtrodden animals that I'd faced a horde of healing beasts. Even in those first years of marriage when we lived in a near-downtown city apartment, Bill had brought home a succession of ailing pigeons. I remember especially a one-eyed pigeon, several pigeons with broken wings, and three squabs who were too young to feed themselves. They had to be force-fed for days.

After moving to the country, the range of unfortunate animals brought home widened considerably.

One day, after attending a farm auction, Bill trotted up the back steps jauntily. "Pinkie!" he called, "come see the garbage disposer I got you."

Eagerly I ran out to the car to see the bargain, wondering how soon I could get a plumber to install it.

I needed no plumber. In a shoe box on the back seat was my garbage disposer—a two-day-old, motherless pig.

While I sputtered my disappointment Bill cooed to the little pink orphan. Bill had brought home a lot of strange things from auctions, but up until then the purchases had all been inanimate. I informed Bill that, for my own protection, I would accompany him to any future auctions. That occasion arose sooner than I'd anticipated, and it was a most animate auction—a horse auction.

For some time the children had been pestering Bill for a horse. An ardent horse lover, Beth's bookshelves were filled with horse books and horse figurines. Her grandest dream was that someday she might have a horse of her own. Bruce agreed that it would be fun to ride a horse, and he added his voice to Beth's persuasive pleading.

At last Bill promised to take the children to a horse auction where they could look over the possibilities. I insisted upon accompanying them, "for my protection," I said.

The horse auctions were held every other Saturday night in a large, drafty barn, with wooden bleachers set up on one side for spectators. We'd dressed in our warmest outdoor clothing and boots, as Bill had warned us it would be cold, and it was—so cold we could see our breath. The children and I huddled together under a blanket on a lower section of the bleachers. Bill sat behind us and higher, with a friend who had saved him a choice spot.

The auction was well underway when we arrived, but for the first several hours of a horse auction, no horses are to be seen. First must be sold a large collection of junk items having absolutely nothing to do with the equine world, such as ornate clocks, off-brand watches, and lamps with Venus de Milo bases. When we arrived they were just finishing with neatsfoot oil, halters, bridles, cinches, bits, and quirts, and were ready to go on to saddles.

The crowd was composed of mostly straw-hatted farmers or younger cowboy-types with high-heeled boots and rolled-brim Western hats. There were three bidders present who were obviously "gentleman farmers." I spotted them first by their well-tailored Western-cut jackets, and soft, narrower brim Stetsons, and then I noticed the deference with which they were treated. The auctioneer droned steadily in a nasal cadence, his eyes darting about the barn, missing nothing. I couldn't understand a word he said, but apparently the bidders could. Bids were made by blinks, grunts, nods, motions of the hand, or occasionally, a loud enthusiastic "Yeah!"

The children were leaning heavily on my shoulders, nearly asleep, by the time the horse auctioning began. Instantly, they became alert and watchful.

Two adolescent cowboys took turns riding the horses in. They roared through the gate at a dead gallop, then raced back and forth on the narrow runway before the bleachers. Each rider wore wicked-looking spurs and used them freely to keep their horse prancing and looking lively to bring a higher price. When they halted the horse, the auctioneer looked into its mouth, peered at its teeth, and announced its age, whether two or three or five years old. If older than five, the auctioneer said, "She's old enough to sleep alone."

Two dozen horses had been run through the chutes and sold, and the children and I were stamping our numbed feet. I turned around and waved at Bill until I caught his eye, and mouthed out the question, "When are you going to buy one so we can go?"

With signs and motions he conveyed the idea that so far all the horses had been too spirited and unpredictable for our inexperienced children.

The next two horses which galloped out were even more flighty, and one put on quite a bucking show, nearly unseating the plucky rider. Just as that horse was sold and being led off, the other demonstrating cowboy rounded the end of the incoming chute tugging at a lead rope. When the crowd saw what was at the end of that lead rope, it broke into a roar of laughter. The other horses had been ridden in, galloping up a cloud of sawdust. This poor dapple-gray bag-of-bones was pulled in, one step at a time. Her loose hide seemed draped over the boney prominences, and you could count every rib. She carried her head very low and, as she slowly stepped into the brighter lights, you could see large bare spots on her hide, probably from mange. One-third of the way across the ramp, she stopped, exhausted. The crowd jeered and howled. It was the saddest-looking horse I'd ever seen!

Embarrassed at being unable to tug her farther on, the young cowboy motioned to the auctioneer to sell her—quick!

The crowd continued hooting until she was sold for thirty dollars. They pulled her away, a heavy quirt urging her out.

"Who on earth would buy her?" I asked the lady sitting in front of me.

"Oh, there's usually somebody here from the rendering works to buy up the real dogs," she explained.

The auction finally ended. The children began tugging at me, whining that Daddy hadn't bought them a horse.

I was trying to explain that Daddy hadn't seen a horse they would be able to ride, when Bill climbed down to meet us.

"What's all the fuss about?" Bill boomed happily. "Don't you want to go see our horse?"

The children were ecstatic as we picked our way to the horse stalls. We followed Bill to the farthest out-of-the-way stall, where he pointed proudly at his purchase: the scrawny, sway-backed, saddest horse at the auction.

The children squealed with delight and ran up to pet their new horse. "What's her name?" they asked.

"Minnie Bones," I growled, giving Bill a piercing look. Sympathy can go too far, especially when it costs thirty dollars, plus trucking fee.

Minnie Bones didn't last long. After getting her stabled in a friend's barn where we hoped to fatten her up, we found out why she was so thin. She couldn't eat because she had no teeth. The friend loaded her in his truck and delivered her to the fox farm, which bought decrepit horses for fox food.

A few days later, when the friend delivered a thirty-dollar check to Bill, the nickel-a-pound payment for Minnie Bones, he mentioned he was enroute to pick up another mare destined for the fox farm. Bill's sympathy antenna picked up this signal of distress.

"What's the matter with her?" Bill asked.

"She broke her stifle bone a couple years ago and is crippled pretty bad. The owner just doesn't want to feed her anymore," he answered.

Bill set off to see the doomed horse, where he promptly paid the owner a nickel a pound for her in lieu of the fox-farm payment. Though a small horse, she was well-fed and healthy, and the bail price was forty dollars.

When Bill broke the news to me that he'd bought a crippled horse, I was pretty grouchy, but after seeing her, I rallied. She dragged one hind leg in a severe limp, but after Minnie Bones, she was beautiful. Princess was her name, and her chestnut coat was shiny, and her soft eyes showed an easy-going, patient disposition. Bill explained that a three-legged horse would be safe for children learning to ride, since she couldn't gallop or rear. Maybe at last Bill's sympathy for the downtrodden would be of some use.

The buffalo never bothered Princess. They seemed to sense by her slow-moving gait that she was no threat to them.

Bill had two different horse breeders check Princess to see if she could possibly become a mother. After prodding and punching, each of them agreed her deformity was too great to allow pregnancy.

One cold morning exactly one week after the last horse authority had declared Princess unable to ever become pregnant, Bill began his daily animal feeding chores. He noticed Princess far out in the middle of the snow-covered hay field. He squinted, looking harder. There seemed to be a deer standing beside her. Bill

137

pulled the binoculars out from under the car seat and focused them upon Princess. Her companion wasn't a deer, but a newborn foal.

Quickly, Bill shouldered a bale of hay and waded out through the snow toward Princess, taking her rations. Though born in six inches of snow, the foal was a vigorous little chestnut colt, who grew up with his mother's same quiet and affectionate temperament. Bill's Good Samaritan projects with unfortunate animals had finally provided dividends. Princess continued to present us annually with a new foal, and each one, as soon as it was weaned, was worth three times the nickel a pound we'd paid for Princess.

With all those animal mouths to feed in the wintertime, we hoped for a mild, snow-free winter so the buffalo, goats, and horses could forage for themselves. Our snowless good fortune lasted only until after Christmas. Then snow began falling, and went on and on. What little bit of grass remained after their intense foraging was now covered under deep snow, and the hay feeding season began. We started with four hundred thirty-three bales of hay.

Feeding the buffalo daily involved a certain procedure. First Bill had to find a stretch of clean ground not too far from a haystack. Then he'd toss a few bales of hay over the fence. I shouldn't say "toss," for that makes it sound so easy, and you don't easily toss a bale of hay. I can hardly lift one. Then Bill had to climb over the fence and break up the bales, pulling off the binding twine and spreading the hay in separate feeding stations so everyone would get something to eat.

By this time the buffalo usually sensed it was dinnertime and came crashing through the brush, while Bill leaped for the fence and safety. After several days of dependency upon Bill's feeding them, the buffalo became very wily. They learned to recognize the sound of his car passing on the road, and came thundering after

138

him. They continued to forage for grass when they could find it, and delighted in eating dead willow leaves and twigs. We understood that buffalo ate a wider variety of forage than domestic cattle, and this seemed to be so. They kept growing fatter, so we assumed they were getting enough food with our daily supplement of hay and occasional grain. Some days they relished the hay; other days, they practically ignored it.

As they were being fed, the buffalo milled around and cavorted in wild excitement. It was play to them, but it looked rough and very close to vicious. They would attack each other, digging their horns into the other's ribs. Bill knew what those horns would do to his human hide, and he tried to be cautious. Several nights that first winter, he awakened from dreadful nightmares in which he dreamed a buffalo charged him, and to save himself, he threw himself on the head between the horns, and was carried helpless around the pasture, hoping to get out of this lethal position somehow.

One night his nightmare almost came true. It was nine o'clock at night before he got away from the hospital to feed the animals. He had bundled up well against the below-zero cold and blowing snow. In the darkness he threw a decoy batch of hay into the far end of the pasture to attract the buffalo there. Then he hurried back to the other end of the pasture to spread out the major supply of hay while the animals were gone. Bill had carried two bales across the creek and was heading back to the fence for more. With the wind howling and protecting earflaps over his ears, he didn't hear the tearing trees and breaking ice that warned of the prematurely approaching buffalo. With terror, he saw the rambunctious herd thundering down upon him. Already they were nearly between him and the fence. There were no trees high enough to climb.

In the lead was Old Cow with an angry look, her eyes showing white. Bill's only hope was to out-buffalo them.

Shouting as loud as he could, Bill crashed through the snow and ice directly at Old Cow. He waved, screamed, and whistled. Just ten feet short of impact, Old Cow stopped and stared. The fence was now only fifteen feet away, and immediately Bill changed course and tore for it. With a flying jump, Bill's hand and foot caught the woven wire, and just as he brought his boot over the top of the wire, Old Cow hit the post. Though ten inches thick, the post creaked as it loosened. Fortunately, the post held, and Bill was safe. The herd gathered at the fence, roaring, then turned their irritation on the brushy elder trees, crashing into them and tearing them up. Bill understood. They were showing him symbolically what they'd do to him if he got too bold again.

Grateful, he came home, and, over soothing, whiskey-laced hot coffee, he told me how the buffalo had nearly become widow-makers.

I promptly insisted that we get rid of the monsters. "Let's try chinchillas or poodles, or something," I pleaded, trying to think of interesting animals without horns.

As I harped away, Bill just smiled and promised he'd be more wary from now on, and that he'd try to find a safer method of feeding them.

Our incipient crossbreeding project was not going well. The Angus heifer usually remained on the outskirts of the herd with Ringo. Kahtanka's indifference to Angie puzzled us. Because she was a domestic bovine, Angie's fertility cycle repeated itself every twenty-one days. This was in marked contrast to the once-a-year fertility period of buffalo cows. While buffalo cows could mate only once during the year, Angie had frequent opportunities to seek motherhood by enticing Kahtanka's attention. In spite of these many chances for pregnancy, Angie remained barren.

One wintry morning Bill discovered why. As he watched the herd moving about, grazing at the stubble peeking through the snow, he noticed that Kahtanka

140

was following Angie wherever she went. Bill kept a close watch on the progress of this romance and discovered that the foolish young Angie was playing the mating game all wrong.

Playing coy and hard-to-get, Angie promised much and delivered nothing. Her flirtatious ways bored Kahtanka, who was accustomed to the plain, no-nonsense kowtowing of his buffalo heifers. Finally, Kahtanka gave two disgusted grunts at the silly, cavorting heifer and walked off. Our hopes for an Angelo calf dimmed considerably.

We began thinking of getting an older, more experienced cow—one who had "been around." Perhaps a cow with a shady past would be more intriguing to the mighty Kahtanka.

Irritated with the foolish and unproductive Angie, I suggested that we call the butcher. Neatly packed in our freezer, her round carcass would feed us for months. But Bill would have none of such bloodthirsty talk. Twice, he had dreamed that the ebony-coated Angie gave birth to a white calf. If bedtime snacks had caused these strange dreams, Angie should give thanks to dill pickles and sardines for furnishing a stay of execution.

Entertaining the possibility that a white calf might be born to a black Angus heifer might strike many as being outlandish and impossible. But Bill's enthusiastic optimism and positive thinking is so infectious that sometimes I find myself believing these will-o'-the-wisps. I didn't anticipate Angie's producing anything startling, but, along with Bill, I let my fancy wander to the possibility of the birth of a white buffalo calf to our herd.

The legend of the white buffalo has long been one of mystery and awe. Many Indian tribes revered the white buffalo above all else and believed the white buffalo was The Great Spirit. According to the practices of the Sioux, if a brave was out hunting and glimpsed a white buffalo, he would hurry back to tell his tribe. Because he had seen The Great Spirit, he would be made chief. In those days before white civilization's corrupting influences, it would never have occurred to a Sioux to lie about seeing the white buffalo. Each brave's personal integrity was a part of his spirit, and he would never have polluted his spirit by speaking falsely.

Later, after association with civilization, the Indians were to learn very well how to lie to the white man. Poor interpreters and cultural differences led to frequent misunderstandings and false tales. Many Indians found it best to tell the white man whatever he wanted to hear; and finally, the practice evolved into nearly always lying to the white man.

The white buffalo was rare, indeed; most buffalo were of the usual brown color. However, in the days of buffalo hide hunting, five distinct colors of buffalo robes were recognized:

1) The common, brown robe.
2) "Buckskin" robes, of a dirty cream color.
3) "Blue" robes, mouse-colored.
4) "Beaver" robes, silky and glossy-smooth.
5) The extremely rare white robe.

The plainsmen believed that the "beaver" robe on a buffalo was from an animal who had been orphaned as a calf. Buffalo cows adopt any motherless calves, and the constant licking and grooming of the sympathetic foster mothers was supposed to have caused the silky "beaver" coat.

In 1882 in Miles City, out of one hundred and eighty thousand hides gathered for shipment, there was only one "buckskin" robe. One percent of the hides were "blue" robes, which brought sixteen dollars each, instead of the usual three and one-half dollars for an ordinary brown robe. One hide was considered a white buffalo robe, though it was really a dirty cream color. It

142

was the only one of its kind taken on the northern range that year and sold for two hundred dollars.

At the New Orleans Exposition in 1884–85 the Territory of Dakota exhibited the skin of a two-year-old buffalo which was a uniform dirty cream color.

Dr. Hornaday, the National Museum curator and conservationist of the last century, believed that not over ten or eleven white buffalo or their skins had ever been seen by white man.

It is possible that white buffalo were not always so scarce. Reports from Indians in the early part of the nineteenth century and a study of their winter counts of outstanding happenings indicate that, at one time, white buffalo, though not common, were not so rare as later in the century. In one Mandan village, anyone-who-pretended-to-be-anyone had to possess a white buffalo robe. It seems likely that as the Indians became mounted on horses, brought to this continent by the Spanish conquistadors, they were aided in hunting down the herds and choosing their specimens. A white buffalo stood out conspicuously in a herd of dark brown animals. Probably few white buffalo survived beyond their second year of life; thus over the years, the strain would become more and more scarce, since white buffalo could not survive even to breeding age to pass on their characteristics.

Three white calves have been recorded in federal herds in the past sixty years. One white buffalo bull named Big Medicine was born in May of 1933 on the Montana buffalo range. He had pure silky white hair, except for the woolly crown between his horns, which was of long, dark brown hair. He died at age twenty-six, in August of 1959.

Since the ancestors of our herd were purchased from the Montana buffalo range in the late 1940's, we cherish the hope that some of our animals may carry the sleeping genes of Big Medicine. Someday, one of our brown cows may give us a white buffalo calf. Then, according to Indian legend, the sun always should shine down upon us, and good fortune would be ours forever.

A zoo supply company persuaded us to try their concentrated bison food which they supply to zoos. It was shipped in big square cartons imprinted with the head of a buffalo, and was made from concentrated nourishing grasses. Surprisingly, it was formed in small pellets, looking exactly like rabbit food.

Bill began sprinkling a few handfuls of the buffalo pellets on each pile of hay. Kahtanka really got hooked on those pellets. His big purple tongue could seek out the tiny pellets scattered in each pile of hay. It was like finding a needle in a haystack—but that's what he did. After licking the pellets out of his bunch of hay, he'd look at Bill with an expectant, but warning glare. If Bill didn't pour on another handful of pellets, Kahtanka's temper often got the better of him. He'd lower his huge dark head to the ground and gore that poor bundle of hay to pieces. He'd swing his head, scattering hay all about. Then with bunches of hay still impaled upon his horns, he'd glare some more, as if to say, "That's just a sample. Must I get tough?"

The animals matured a lot that winter, growing taller and heavier. The yearling heifers, who were still quite straight-backed when we got them, now had respectable hump-backs. Their horns began to curve upward and they lost their calf-like, spike-horn appearance. Buffalo's horns are hollow and become larger and more curved with age. You can come pretty close to guessing the age of a buffalo by looking at his horns. They aren't shed annually as are the antlers of deer. Yet the horns do seem to have a capacity to grow back if the base isn't injured. Bleeding Horn, who suffered the broken horn in shipment, has shown us this. Her horn was snapped off very near the base, yet in just one year's

144

time it had grown back at least two inches.

One frigid sub-zero day, our whole family went to the ranch to help Bill throw hay to the buffalo. As the buffalo loped toward us they made a fascinating sight. From each animal's beard hung huge baubles of ice. The ice chunks looked like cut glass, resembling the flashing prisms hanging from chandeliers. As the animals walked, the icy baubles clinked together, making a weird and ghostly music. These sparkling nuggets were formed when the animals drank the icy creek water; as it dribbled down their beards, it froze there. Having their beards weighed down by extra pounds of ice prisms didn't bother them at all. They seemed completely unaware of their strange frozen necklaces.

As children, we used to chant, "When the days begin to lengthen, the cold begins to strengthen." That's exactly what happened in February and March. School was cancelled for days at a time because of blizzards, and the snow piled deeper and deeper. As the snow gets deeper, of course, the fences get shorter. Our big worry was that the snow would pile up against a fence and allow the buffalo to walk over the fence and out. Mr. Sherman had warned us about that. His buffalo had gotten out once when the fence became buried in snow. Bill walked our fence line often that winter, plunging through hip-deep snow. About then we began having second thoughts about buffalo-breeding as a hobby. Stamp-collecting sounded temptingly warm and cozy.

By March our four hundred thirty-three bales of hay were nearly gone, but the blizzards continued. On St. Patrick's Day morning, a howling snowstorm began, and the school busses were sent home. That blizzard continued four days, but we still had to feed the animals.

We bought hay three more times before spring finally decided to return to Michigan. How we welcomed each little blade of grass that peeked up in the pasture!

It's
a Heifer!

10 Now that spring was smiling upon us, the animals could graze for themselves. No more buying feed—we could balance our budget once again.

Our thirteen buffalo had become blonds. Buffalo hair is dark brown when it is prime in the early winter months, but then fades to a light seal brown by spring. Patches of this pale fur were beginning to loosen, and this was as much a harbinger of spring as the appearance of robins and jump ropes.

I dusted off my golf clubs. Superfence was done, and I anticipated a summer of golf, gardening, and swimming. But it didn't quite work out that way.

I had begun to suspect that raising buffalo was more than a hobby. It was a job, and threatened to become a way of life. It was interesting, even fascinating at times, but I sometimes worried that the buffalo were running us. They dominated our spare time, our family activities, our mealtime conversations.

They seemed even to dominate our relationships with other people. Every time I met someone on the street, they didn't give the conventional greeting, "How are you?" It was, "How are the buffalo?" I dreaded becoming known as "the buffalo lady." A raving beauty might not mind, but my self-esteem is sensitive. From a girlhood spent towering over all my girl classmates and three-quarters of the boys, I'd never enjoyed feelings of daintiness. Now, when someone said, "Oh, you're the buffalo lady!" I cringed, remembering my adolescent gawkiness.

Bill ran into the same thing. Some of his young patients had always called him "Doctor Bill," which we felt had unpleasant monetary implications. Slowly the change crept in, and he became known as "The Buffalo Doctor." It sounded like a cross between a witch doctor and a veterinarian. The title served a good purpose for many elderly patients who had difficulty remembering names. They could remember "Buffalo Doctor" and thus were assured they had the right physician.

Of course, who could resist calling him Buffalo Bill? We didn't seem to be individuals any more. We were the owners of a buffalo herd.

With the arrival of spring, the sidewalk greetings changed. "Any calves yet?" everyone asked.

"Not yet," I'd sigh, shaking my head in the negative at each questioning passer-by.

We really didn't know if, or when, a calf could be expected. Carefully, we studied each heifer, debating whether she looked motherly and about to present us with a calf.

Our children listened intently to our mumbled conversations and soon began watching the heifers with knowing looks. Children raised around farm animals learn the facts of life young, and easily. Since ours were only eleven, nine, and four years old at the time, we gulped the first few times these animal-husbandry expressions came out of the mouths of such babes. However, we consoled ourselves with the hope they were getting a normal, healthy, and wholesome sex education. When the children had absorbed the whole birds-and-bees bit, we breathed a sigh of relief. Then the guppies fouled everything up.

In the fall the children had bought three guppies, one

148

female and two males. One male met an untimely end by jumping into my dishwater. That left a cozy family group of mother and father, soon joined by nine pinhead-size babies. Our children transferred the little dust-speck babies to a separate bowl to thwart the parents' cannibalistic tendencies. Then tragedy struck. Father guppie got squished by the china deep-sea diver decorating the aquarium. That left mother guppie all alone in her bowl. When another litter of guppies were born to the widow six weeks later, we were puzzled, but the children decided that mama guppie had been pregnant at the time of papa guppie's demise. However, a month later another posthumous litter arrived, and a month later still a third batch. The children were hopelessly confused. They had just reached the stage of "By George, I've got it!" when the widow guppie pulled that stunt and left them bewildered. They finally decided they'd forget about guppie-husbandry and concentrate on buffalo.

As soon as it became warm enough we started picnicking beside the buffalo pasture on Sunday afternoons in order to watch for tell-tale maternity signs. We thought surely the pregnant animals would look heavier and bulkier than the others, but their long, shaggy fur coats served as modest maternity smocks. We just couldn't tell.

We counted on our fingers and consulted veterinary books. Of course, these books were geared for domestic cattle, and we didn't know how closely buffalo would imitate cattle in the various biological functions. The gestation period, or length of pregnancy, was supposed to be the same as that of cattle, approximately two hundred and eighty days. (Deflating thought that it is, two hundred and eighty days also happens to be the gestation period for humans.)

Finally, Old Cow gave us a sign. Her udder began to enlarge in preparation for nursing her calf. The children and I learned this was called "bagging" or "making bag." Beth announced the new symptoms the next day in school during Show-and-Tell. Teachers have to be prepared for anything.

One Sunday late in April we were sure Old Cow was about to bear a calf. She kept going off by herself, lying down and panting strangely. Only when darkness fell did we leave, and we were certain we'd find a newborn calf beside her the next day. At midnight Bill armed himself with a flashlight and drove to the ranch to check on Old Cow. The herd was bedded down in the elder thicket, and he couldn't get close enough to see what was happening.

The next morning there was no calf, and we realized we weren't buffalo experts yet.

A week later, still no calf, but the herd did give us a new thrill. They performed their first buffalo dance. The maneuver is performed by the whole herd, and is both fascinating and frightening.

Bill had slipped into a deserted section of the pasture and poured out thirteen pyramids of golden grain. After retreating to the fence, he called the dinner call, "Kahtanka!"

Soon, in the distance, we glimpsed the brown heads of the herd bobbing up a shallow valley. They galloped fast, straight toward us and the mounds of food. But, strangely, they tore on past and headed out into the pasture. They'd never passed up an offering of sweet ground feed before, which was odd in itself, but the strange, stiff-legged way they were running was downright weird.

The buffalo bounced past, propelling themselves with their ankles, growling and belching all the way. Circling the solitary tree in the field, they ignored the surprised and ogling horses, and headed back toward us. With tongues dangling, plopping back and forth, they ran, thrusting their stiff front legs forward as if they were

150

striking out at something. As the herd bore down at us, Superfence looked awfully frail, and we scurried into the woods behind some huge oak trees. The buffalo stopped, thank goodness, and began digging furrows in the earth with their horns, pawing and panting. After a while they calmed down, began to eat, and the buffalo dance was over.

Since then we've seen several buffalo dances. They are frightening, yet funny. The animals manage to look both threatening and ridiculous. We can't determine what sets them off into one of these bizarre tribal jogs. It seems if one animal gets the urge to dance, the whole herd joins in. Not a nonconformist in the bunch. Then they go pogo-sticking across the fields, looking like something out of an animated cartoon.

Even at their normal gallop, the speed of buffalo is amazing. They look slow and clumsy, but don't let that fool you. Despite their bulkiness, they can wheel instantly, and gallop at great speed.

Maybe they're just showing off, or trying to start a new dance craze. If young people were willing to do the Monkey, why not the Buffalo?

By late May we began to despair of getting any calves that year. Perhaps our teen-age herd was just too immature. Maybe Old Cow's symptoms were just false pregnancy.

One warm Saturday afternoon I drove the two older children, Bruce and Beth, to the pasture to check on War Cloud, the yearling son of crippled Princess. I left them there while I made a quick trip to the grocery store. When I returned half an hour later, I met the two of them, red-faced and out of breath, running to meet me.

"A calf, a calf!" they shouted.

I tried to quiz them. "Are you sure it wasn't one of the goats?"

Bruce's sky-blue eyes gave me that mothers-don't-know-anything look. Very haughtily, he drew himself up to his whole four feet, ten inches. "Don't you think that by now I know the difference between a goat and a baby buffalo?"

Well, I knew he'd never seen a baby buffalo before, but then, neither had I. "Show me," I said.

Old Cow couldn't have picked a more distant place to have her calf. It was fine for her, offering maximum seclusion, but from our point of view, it made a long tramp. It was a three-quarter mile walk, up and down hills, and at the very end, a squishy walk through ankle-deep black mud. My brand-new white tennis shoes were never white again.

At the far east end of the pasture the herd lay, contentedly sunning themselves. There beside Old Cow was a bright auburn calf, wobbling about on his tiny legs. We said "his" until Bill got there and informed us that he was a she. The calf was nearly the same color as an Irish setter, and her silky hair had a suggestion of curliness. Contrary to popular opinion, buffalo calves don't have a hump. They look much like newborn domestic calves, especially a Jersey calf. Buffalo are one of the few species whose young are of a strikingly different color from the mature animals. The calves shed this reddish natal coat at four months of age.

The little heifer calf was named Wanji Sidga, meaning "first calf" in Sioux. On the very day of her birth she managed to follow her mother all the way across the pasture, a distance of half a mile.

Within a few days, her legs became surprisingly stable and strong, and she romped along with the herd. She often stood or lay resting directly under her mother, enjoying the shade. A protective mother, Old Cow was very possessive and allowed only Kahtanka to sniff and inspect her child.

After waiting and hoping for a calf for so long, we were like excited new parents. We decided to send out birth announcements to friends and relatives in other

152

states. We made a list of families who would get a kick out of receiving a "buffalo birth announcement," and went to work making them. We cut the shape of a buffalo out of some thin leather. With their wood-burning outfit, the children burned the information onto the leather. On one side of the leather buffalo shape were burned the words:

"IT'S A HEIFER!"

On the other side were the vital statistics:

"WANJI SIDGA
Weight: 40 Pounds
Arrived: May 22, 1965, Rx Ranch
Parents: Kahtanka and Old Cow"

We were quite sure Good Cow was also going to have a calf. Her udder was enlarged, a positive sign, and in late April she showed a marked personality change.

Worms had always been the tamest member of the herd. She was still a wild, unpredictable buffalo, but she had one trait peculiar only to her. She liked being scratched. Worms enjoyed standing placidly by the fence while Bill sought her itchy spots.

One day Bill was reaching through the fence to scratch Worms when Good Cow suddenly sidled up to the fence, chasing Worms away. Hesitantly, Bill reached through and scratched her, and she loved it. From then on Good Cow followed Bill around, pleading with her doleful brown eyes to be scratched. This, along with the enlargement of her udder, made us suspect she, too, would soon be a mother.

Eight days after Wanji's birth, Bill discovered the second calf, still moist from birth. Evidently in her need for human sympathy and affection, Good Cow temporarily forgot her wild instincts. Instead of searching out a secluded spot in which to bear her calf, she gave birth not eight feet from the fence, at the place where spectators congregated to see the buffalo.

By the time the children and I arrived to see this second calf, a large crowd had gathered. Bill was asking people to stay back, for the herd appeared nervous. With the coming of the crowd, Good Cow had regained her animal instincts and was trying to get her calf to stand up so she could lead it away. The calf, another little heifer, was just too worn out to budge. No amount of nuzzling or pushing would bring her to her feet.

Deciding she was thirsty, Good Cow sauntered forty feet to the creek for a cool drink. She drank deeply for nearly a minute. Then she jerked nervously. You could see her thinking, "Oh, my gosh, the baby!" and she tore back to her calf at full gallop.

The rest of the herd began to move off. Good Cow desperately wanted to follow, but the calf still wouldn't rise. As the herd moved farther, she stared forlornly after them and began to grunt. Kahtanka and Old Cow stopped, glancing back. When they sensed Good Cow's predicament, they walked back to stay near her.

It was another hour before Good Cow coaxed the newborn calf up on her legs and led her away from all those peering eyes to a more secluded section of the pasture.

This calf we named Nopa Sidga, meaning "second calf." Her auburn coat was somewhat different from the first calf's. It was curlier and the hair had a roughened appearance, as if it had been rubbed against the nap.

A few days later we discovered that Good Cow had been appointed official baby-sitter for both new calves. Apparently, Old Cow's many responsibilities as leader made it necessary for her to use Good Cow as baby-sitter for the playful calves. When the herd was resting, each calf could be found beside its own mother, but when

154

Old Cow was leading the herd, the calf was relegated to Good Cow, who kept both calves at the rear of the herd in safety.

Though we were delighted to have two buffalo calves, we were disappointed that Angie had made no progress toward producing a cattalo calf. As we learned more about buffalo, we valued their many fine traits even more, and were anxious to introduce these excellent qualities into domestic beef.

Our virginal Angus heifer flirted with Kahtanka off and on all summer, but her coy, teasing ways continued to disgust Kahtanka. He had plenty of girl friends without bothering with a hard-to-get fat female. We decided to get a more experienced cow.

Several local farmers had cows they were willing to sell. The qualifications of one particular cow stood out from all other contenders. A middle-aged, red Durham named Mabel was known as a most passionate cow. Mr. Gardner, her owner, said he'd often remarked to his wife, "Honey, if you were just a little more like that old red cow." It seems that whenever a bull was placed in the pasture, Mabel was always the first to strike up a romance with him. A very forward and brazen cow, Mabel was also extremely maternal. She frequently stole calves from other cows.

Mabel sounded like just what we needed: passionate and maternal. Kahtanka should appreciate her kind of cow.

Mr. Gardner promised to dry up Mabel's milk supply before delivering her to our buffalo pasture. Neither Bill nor I wanted to enter the buffalo herd twice daily to milk Mabel.

One warm afternoon Mr. Gardner brought Mabel to her new home. We were concerned about her confrontation with her new pasture-mates, the buffalo, for Mabel had another distinctive trait. She had been boss-

155

cow in her dairy herd, which means she was used to giving orders and getting her own way in the herd. Would she try to be boss-cow with the buffalo?

The buffalo were out of sight when Mabel was released into the confines of Superfence. She ran back and forth through the grass, mooing and bellowing in confusion.

Worried, Mr. Gardner bit his lip as she bounced around. "She was born and raised in my pasture," he said sadly. "She's never been off the farm before."

Bill spread feed out on the ground and called the buffalo. There seemed no point in delaying the meeting. When the buffalo came into sight, Mabel stopped her mooing and stood motionless, staring. We wondered what her cow-brain was thinking; maybe, "Dig those crazy humps!"

When the buffalo caught sight of her they advanced faster. She held her ground, still unmoving. Then Angie spotted Mabel and let out an ecstatic bellow. Her moo seemed to say, "Oh, boy, another one like me!" Angie loped toward Mabel as fast as her fat body would allow. Mabel stood fast another moment, then turned and fled from all the approaching strangers. This was the buffalos' cue to charge. They spread out in a phalanx and, heads down, started for Mabel.

Poor hornless Angie, so timid and shy, suddenly became a brave heroine. She circled the buffalo herd running faster than one would believe possible and got between the charging herd and Mable. Her action seemed to say, "Please spare this one—for my sake?"

At least, that's how the buffalo seemed to interpret her behavior, for they stopped immediately, with an "Oh, all right" toss of their heads and turned back to the waiting piles of grain. Mabel had been spared, and we hoped she'd been taught an important lesson—that she wasn't boss in her new home.

Angie tried hard to make up with the newcomer,

grazing close by her, but Mabel kept aloof from all the four-footed creatures. Moving had been a traumatic experience for the bossy red cow.

We were prepared to be patient. It would surely take a few months for Mabel and Kahtanka to realize they could be compatible. Mating season of the buffalo would soon be beginning, and Kahtanka would be busy taking care of his shaggy harem. We just hoped that by wintertime Mabel's passionate nature and Kahtanka's roving eye would find each other.

Following the birth of the two calves we had fifteen buffalo, but only for a week. Shortly after the second calf was born, we realized that Sitting Bull, the youngest of our three bulls, was sick.

He'd always been small, almost runty, but now his ribs began to show, and he lacked interest in food. He'd make an effort to eat grain, but he seemed to have difficulty in chewing and swallowing.

Several local cattle raisers stopped by to give a road-side diagnosis of Sitting Bull's difficulty. Most of them watched him for a moment, then announced, "He's got hardware."

This seemed a strange name for a disease. Most diseases, both animal and human, are dignified by being unpronounceable.

It seems that "hardware" means the animal has swallowed some small metal objects which irritate and pierce the stomach. These bits of metal are usually pieces of barbed wire or staples. Cattle (and buffalo) can't separate bits of metal from their food, or mouthful of grass, so they just swallow the whole mouthful. Often ten percent of the cattle in a herd will have enough internal hardware to cause trouble.

The prevention of this condition is so simple it's ridiculous. The farmer merely pushes a small plastic-coated magnet down a cow's throat until she swallows it. The magnet rests permanently in the forward part of the second stomach, attracting all pieces of metal swallowed thereafter, making them harmless. So simple! But who ever tried to get a buffalo to swallow a magnet?

We called the veterinarian, and he came for a look. I say a "look" because that's all he could do. The same veterinarian who had been so brave with our sick dogs now seemed a different man. He didn't climb over the fence, pat Sitting Bull, and say, "It's all right, old man, I won't hurt you."

He stayed outside the fence and studied his patient from a distance. Finally, he offered three possible diagnoses: it was either hardware, barbed wire caught in the mouth, or a broken jaw. Now we had a general idea what was wrong with Sitting Bull. Now what?

The vet walked to his car and brought out a long piece of very heavy, thick rope. Handing it to Bill, he said, "Use this. Get him tied to a sturdy post and then call me."

Bill and I stared dismally at each other as the vet's car disappeared down the dusty road. I thought of all the self-improvement correspondence courses I'd taken— Ceramics, American government, The Works of Camus. They were all so useless. Why hadn't I taken a course in roping?

What made the job of catching Sitting Bull almost impossible was trying to isolate him from the herd. Once we got him temporarily separated from the other animals and succeeded in getting the lasso partly over his head and one horn, but he pulled away and the loop slipped off. Now we had tipped our hand, and Sitting Bull and the rest of the herd seemed to know we were trying to catch him. The herd stayed protectively around him.

We spent the next two days trying to catch Sitting Bull. Once Bill got inside the fence with a bucket of grain, trying to entice Sitting Bull off alone. I turned away for a moment, and when I looked back, my heart

158

jumped. Sitting Bull and Bill were running around in a big circle. To this day Bill insists *he* was chasing Sitting Bull, but it didn't look that way to me.

What we needed was a tranquilizing gun, a device that shoots a tranquilizing drug into an animal from a distance. Their main use is in subduing wild animals to be captured alive. Upon contacting the Conservation Department, we learned there was only one such gun available, and it was hundreds of miles away in the wilds of the Upper Peninsula. They could have it to us in three days. We feared Sitting Bull wouldn't last another three days.

And we were right. We found him in the morning, but he had been dead several hours. We felt genuinely sad, and not just from the loss of a costly animal. Sitting Bull had always been the smallest animal in the herd, an ugly, scrawny creature. This roused our sympathy, and our feelings of helplessness the past few days made the sight of him lying dead especially pathetic.

We had to get the carcass out of the pasture and hoped to save the hide. Several times we tried to get inside the pasture with the car to drag him out, but the herd always spotted us and came running, still protecting the departed Sitting Bull. Finally, late in the afternoon, we sneaked in undetected by the buffalo, and brought out the carcass in a borrowed truck. Several men, all seasoned deer hunters, volunteered to help in the skinning. Throwing a heavy rope over a high tree limb, they tied one end to the truck's bumper and the other end to Sitting Bull's hind legs. By pulling the truck forward, Sitting Bull was lifted to a workable height for skinning, suspended head down.

The hot June evening had not a hint of a breeze. The flies and mosquitos gathered in a huge convention. Those hide hunters of the last century were smart to do most of their slaughtering in winter months. The stench, flies, and mosquitos made it a miserable job. At

159

last, when the furry hide was off, I rubbed a thick layer of salt into the fleshy side while the men began digging the grave. By this time it was dark, and as I watched them working in the glare of the truck's headlights, it seemed like something out of a horror movie.

Suppose a state trooper happened by? I could imagine him saying, "What are you doing, fellows?"

And they, answering, "Digging a grave for a buffalo."

If there's anything that riles a state trooper, it's a smart-aleck response.

Bill performed a quick autopsy on Sitting Bull's head and discovered the cause of the trouble: a broken jaw. Evidently poor Sitting Bull had been struck by a lunging horn or a kicking hoof.

I guess the grave-diggers got weary, for the grave was mighty shallow. When they finally packed the last loose earth over Sitting Bull, his four hoofs and forelegs all stuck mournfully out of the ground. They remained like that for a month, and I sometimes wondered what people thought as they were casually sauntering along a path and came suddenly upon four cloven hoofs growing out of the ground.

The reason for the shallow grave was that Sitting Bull was not to rest in peace for all eternity. We intended to save his skull and some of the bones. After all, a few buffalo bones scattered about on knicknack shelves ought to be conversation pieces, if not exactly status symbols. A buffalo skull might blend nicely with our Early American furniture. We buried Sitting Bull near a large ant hill and knew before the maples reddened we would have a clean, flesh-free, buffalo skeleton.

With school out, summer was in full bloom. I managed a once-a-week fling at golf, but somehow I never did get any petunias planted that summer. There was always something needing to be done at the ranch.

Since Bill's office was only a loud shout from the buffalo pasture, he devised a clever system of changing from doctor to farmer in a hurry. He kept a set of very ragged jeans and torn work shirt at the office. If his appointment book showed a free half-hour before the next patient, he'd hurriedly don his farming clothes and slip out the back door. He frequently forgot to watch the time, and then Wilma, his long-suffering office nurse, had to trudge across the fields—white nylons, uniform, and all—calling, "Doctor, oh Doctor!"

His Dr. Jekyll-Mr. Hyde transformation of clothing sometimes confused his patients. One afternoon after seeing his last patient, an elderly gentleman, Bill slipped into his tattered buffalo-watching clothes and went out the back door.

A few minutes later Bill was kneeling beside the yellow No-Sag gate, tightening a hinge, when the same elderly gentleman drove up and got out of his car. After watching the buffalo a few minutes, he commented to Bill, "Quite a herd The Buffalo Doctor has there."

Bill looked up at the man and smiled, to be recognized.

The man went on, "He's gonna cross them with Angus and Herefords."

"Yeah," Bill mumbled, realizing the man didn't know he was speaking to his doctor who, just a few minutes before, had been poking and prodding him while conducting an examination. Bill made an excuse and quickly left the old gentleman so not to embarrass him if someone drove by and called out, "Hi, Doc!"

For a while Bill-the-doctor and Bill-the-farmer were two separate personalities and appearances, but the buffalo soon began to invade even the office. I don't remember which was the first little buffalo figurine a patient brought in, but buffalo souvenirs began arriving in avalanche proportions. Where people find them, I don't know. I've spent years looking for them in all kinds of souvenir shops, and the only buffalo I've ever found was a stuffed toy. The buffalo figurines came in all shapes and sizes. Some patients who were adept in ceramic work even made some beautiful originals. Those who had trouble, as I did, in finding buffalo figurines, brought in related objects such as totem poles and Indian statues.In the waiting room buffalo nickels began to collect under the glass top of the coffee table. The hugh L-shaped desk in Bill's consultation room soon was covered with souvenirs, and the buffalo and Indians began to creep onto the bookshelves, threatening to evict the medical library. Bill was delighted with every gift and remembered faithfully who gave him what. I suspect he has the world's largest collection of buffalo figurines.

When a new patient arrives at the office, it doesn't take long for him to get the picture. After staring about for a few minutes he'll soon comment dazedly to the others in the waiting room, "I guess Dr. Cummings likes buffalo?"

Those who couldn't find buffalo figures resorted to strange substitutes. One day a large package arrived from Canada. It contained a colorful witch-doctor mask, three feet in diameter. Now what do you do with something like that? It'd be all right in a rumpus room, but we don't have a rumpus room.

Bill dutifully mounted it on the wall of his consultation room, and to say it overpowered the small room is an understatement. Shuddering over the monstrous thing, Bill's office nurse and I held several whispered conferences, debating how we tactfully could suggest it be taken down. I was elected to broach the subject to Bill.

I couldn't think of a tactful way, so one evening I just flatly stated I thought the mask was an unsuitable decoration for a doctor's office.

"How can you expect your patients to keep their confidence in you as a specialist?" I protested. "It's bad enough the way you work on the ranch in torn, dirty

162

clothes and spend your leisure mingling with buffalo. If you keep that witch-doctor mask on your office wall, it will emphasize your reservation background. Before you know it, your patients will be asking for Indian herbs and root potions. They'll think you're a medicine man!"

"Nonsense!" snorted Bill, never one to be swayed by feminine logic. "Now look, Pinkie, I never objected to your putting up your Scottish family crest on our living room wall. This sun-god face mask is the best a poor old Indian can do for a coat-of-arms."

Having lost that line of argument, I dropped it and began anew. "That leering mask must terrify small children."

"No," Bill smiled patiently, but firmly. "The little children love it. They're so fascinated looking at it they forget to worry about the shot they're going to get."

That ended my campaign. The witch-doctor mask reigned victorious.

Make Hay
While the
Sun Shines

11 All spring, Kahtanka and Bull-in-the-Bush rough-housed and skirmished, scuffling like a couple of ten-year-old boys. As summer ripened, their playfulness grew rougher, more like two jealous swains battling over the hand of milady. Only they were playing for high stakes—they were battling over ten miladies.

Kahtanka always seemed faintly bored when Bull-in-the-Bush charged him, easily rebuffing the lesser bull. Yet we worried that Bull-in-the-Bush might get in a lucky jab, and Kahtanka was the bull we wanted to save.

It is normal buffalo behavior for bulls to become rambunctious and fight among themselves. In buffalo herds the strongest bull is the "herd bull," the king of the herd. He wins his throne by defeating the incumbent herd bull in a violent, snorting duel. As the herd bull grows older, he is challenged more and more often by ambitious young bulls, and eventually the day comes when his aging strength is not equal to a more vigorous challenger.

In the days when the herds wandered unfenced and free, the deposed monarch frequently was allowed to live. Exiled from the herd, he wandered alone over the prairies, or sometimes was allowed to remain on the fringes of the herd.

Today's fenced pastures have made this fight to the top become a duel to the death. Because of the fences, the winning bull cannot drive the has-been leader into impotent exile, and the aging monarch is usually killed.

In a large herd the herd bull is not the only bull who fathers calves. He is the Big Boss, taking first choice of the most attractive cows, but he does have limitations. The younger bulls compete for the affections of the remaining wallflowers. One bull for every ten cows is considered the best proportion in a herd. If there are too many bulls, they spend all their time fighting each other, and neglect their romancing duties. Then there is no calf crop in the spring.

A certain amount of cooperation seems to exist between the bulls in a herd larger than ours. Francis Sherman's Iowa buffalo herd, the parent animals of our herd, was ruled over by two huge bulls, a father and his son. They had developed sort of a king-prime minister relationship. The father was larger than the son, but in their dual alliance they ruled cooperatively. Bill remembered the older herd bull well. He was the angry monster who fought off the tractor when Bill tried to help the Shermans round up our buffalo.

Francis called us one day to tell us the fate of the old monarch. Francis had sold the younger bull to a rancher who planned to establish him as herd bull of a new buffalo herd. As soon as the younger leader was shipped away, the adolescent bulls sensed that the old herd bull was now vulnerable without the support of his crown prince. Four young bulls ganged up on the stately old ruler and slowly wore him down. In brutal gangland manner, they drove their horns into his thick hide and finally hurled him through the fence, tearing out nine rods of heavy fencing. Francis found the old bull lying outside the broken fence, still alive, but so savagely gored he had to be destroyed. The bull was butchered,

166

packaged, and frozen, and Francis stocked up his home freezer.

"You know," admitted Francis ruefully, "I can't eat that meat."

"Why not?" we wondered. "Is it tough?"

"No," he answered, "it's very tender. It's just that I've had him for so long, sixteen years. I can't eat him."

As the battling between Bull-in-the-Bush and Kahtanka became more violent, we knew something must be done. It was a hard decision, but we didn't dare carry Bull-in-the-Bush into mating season, where their fighting might become deadly. Bull-in-the-Bush had to go.

The hospital guilds were planning a day-long celebration for early August as a money-making venture for the benefit of the hospital. The previous year they'd held the first such celebration, which featured an auction, a midway of carnival booths and professional skydivers who dropped in from above. The benefit dinner had featured barbecued chicken, and over three hundred people had attended the chicken barbecue.

When we offered Bull-in-the-Bush as the main dish for this year's event, we didn't have to offer twice. The guild ladies immediately began planning the menu around Bull-in-the-Bush as if they were old hands at planning buffalo roasts. The date for the buffalo barbecue was set for August 14. That meant Bull-in-the-Bush must be killed August 7, as buffalo meat needs to age only one week.

The guild ladies enthusiastically threw themselves into preparations. They engaged a carnival for the affair. Donated items ranging from butter churns to electric stoves began accumulating in the barn behind the hospital for an auction sale. The guilds secured a well-known country music group to play for an evening street-dance following the buffalo barbecue. A huge circus tent was rented to use as a shelter on the big day.

167

It would form a huge canopy over the eating area, giving shade from the sun, or shelter from any unwelcome rain.

Half the auto bumpers in our county were festooned with orange bumper stickers advertising the coming buffalo feast. Posters decorated every store window and telephone pole for miles around Stanwood.

As the time crept nearer, Bill and I began to feel depressed and guilty when we watched Bull-in-the-Bush peacefully grazing. He had to be sacrificed for the welfare of the herd, but it seemed a shame. He was such a handsome animal. It was just his hard luck to be a herd-mate of the outstanding Kahtanka.

On the morning of the buffalo shoot, Bill sighted his gun. He chose to do the shooting himself since all the other volunteer gunmen readily admitted the thirteen buffalo all looked alike to them. We certainly didn't want the wrong buffalo shot.

Word of the buffalo shoot had spread afar. When Bill arrived at the ranch he found the gravel road bordering the buffalo pasture lined with cars. With difficulty he maneuvered his car through the clogged traffic and up to the pasture gate. There he was stopped by a deputy sheriff who had the buffalo pasture cordoned off. He waved Bill away.

Defiantly, Bill approached the gate.

"Oh, it's you, Doc," the deputy said. "I have men posted on all the side roads to stop traffic during the shooting."

As Bill looked around, he discovered fifteen armed gunmen gathered along the buffalo fence. Evidently the deputy expected the buffalo to stampede out of their pasture and through the fences. To protect Stanwood from demolition, the militia had assembled. During the deputy's five-year tenure of office this was the first event that could hint of an emergency, and he was making the most of it.

Bill said nothing, but drove through the gate, the deputy following close behind.

Bill dared not let those men keep their guns. We didn t know how the herd would react once the shot was fired. Just one bit of unusual herd behavior might set off a barrage of gunfire. These men were all avid hunters, and with the safety of their village in mind, they would be trigger-happy. Too easily Bill could imagine his herd decimated, their brown carcasses littering the meadow.

"I'm collecting the guns," Bill announced, moving around among the men. When the confiscated rifles were all laid out in the station wagon, it looked like an arsenal.

Then Bill turned to the deputy. "I'll have to have yours, too," he said, motioning to the high-powered deer rifle. The deputy's community defense program had been collapsing before his eyes; now this request was the crowning blow. Visions of heroism and glory crumbled, he complied, laying his rifle beside the others. The deputy comforted himself by patting his ever-present holstered sidearm. This face-saving weapon made him the only armed man beside Bill.

Two local meat processors who would prepare the carcass for the big festival were on hand to take charge as soon as Bull-in-the-Bush breathed his last.

Bill waited until Bull-in-the-Bush wandered to a safe position for shooting; then he pulled the trigger. The target was the small vital spot an inch below the ear, unprotected by the heavy matted mane and thick bone structure of the skull. Bull-in-the-Bush dropped to his knees. There he lay wheezing, blood pouring from his nose and mouth, but not yet dead. After their first startled jump, the herd milled around uneasily. Bill feared once Kahtanka sensed his long-time adversary was wounded, he might attack and finish him off, ruining the carcass.

169

We all held our breath to see what would happen. Kahtanka didn't attack the fatally wounded Bull-in-the-Bush. Instead, a pathetic scene followed. Kahtanka approached the fallen bull and very gently nuzzled him, trying to coax him to his feet. When nudging failed, Kahtanka lay down beside Bull-in-the-Bush in sympathy. Bill kept hoping to get a *coup de grace* shot to finish off the wounded animal, but Kahtanka stayed so close he dared not shoot. The other buffalo grouped around their fallen member in a large, protective circle.

When all his nuzzling and sympathy failed, Kahtanka got his nose under the wounded animal's head to help him stand. Bull-in-the-Bush struggled to his feet and staggered in circles, Kahtanka staying always against him, lending support.

Bull-in-the-Bush finally dropped, breathing no more. We were saddened, but relieved it was over. We'd known the herd-survival instincts were great, but never suspected that one bull would try to help an adversary bull, a competitor.

Bill spread feed at a distant end of the pasture to entice the buffalo away from the carcass. The thirteen remaining animals answered his feed call and disappeared over the hill toward the east end of the pasture. The meat processors moved in with two tractors, a winch, and flatbed rack to haul Bull-in-the-Bush to the locker plant.

A week later, the day of the buffalo barbecue, the streets of Stanwood began filling early. It doesn't take much to fill a block-long village—twenty cars cause a traffic jam—but this day hundreds of cars poured through Stanwood. Handmade signs pointed the way to the hospital grounds, but they were unnecessary. The carousel music from the merry-go-round and the loudspeaker broadcasting the auctioneer's droning lingo told where the excitement was located.

The mounted sheriff's posse in their western uniforms, cowboy hats, and boots, added a colorful touch as they directed traffic and organized the parking of cars.

The hospital guilds had set up several food stands furnishing hot dogs, homemade desserts, and beverages, and they did a brisk business. However, everyone eagerly awaited four o'clock, when the serving of the buffalo was scheduled to begin. An hour early a long line formed beside the big tent where the serving tables were being assembled. I had no intention of standing under the hot sun in a long line. I decided to try later. At five o'clock the line snaked back and forth in three long loops, constantly getting longer as the supper hour approached, so the children and I took our place in line. Eventually we reached the serving tables, where a stout, smiling woman placed two slices of Bull-in-the-Bush on my paper plate.

We found a place at one of the long folding tables under the big tent, and I stared at my plate. How could I possibly eat something I knew personally? I ate my mashed potatoes and shoved the meat around the plate. As I looked about, I saw everyone else relishing Bull-in-the-Bush.

An elderly woman seated across from me asked her companion, "Do you think it's really buffalo meat? It tastes just like roast beef to me."

Her companion just shrugged. "Whatever it is, it's good."

Offended by their suspicious minds, I was about to protest when a man down the table spoke up.

"Oh, this is genuine buffalo meat," he assured them. "Can't you taste how it's sweeter than beef?"

According to what we'd read, the man was correct. Buffalo meat was supposed to be sweeter than beef. I told myself sternly that I really should taste it rather than take someone else's word for it. With great difficulty I managed to eat two bites, silently begging the

171

forgiveness of Bull-in-the-Bush in his Happy Hunting Ground with all his slaughtered ancestors.

It was as tender as any roast beef I've ever had. I heartily dislike venison because I don't care for the wild flavor. Although buffalo meat is sometimes referred to as venison rather than beef, I tasted no similarity between it and deer meat. Bull-in-the-Bush tasted like tender, choice domestic beef.

Buffalo meat has a lower fat content and a lower cholesterol content than domestic beef. To be tender, domestic beef has to have marbling or distribution of fat throughout the meat. This isn't true with buffalo meat, which can be very tender even without the saturated fatty acids. Buffalo meat has just a little more flavor than domestic beef, but never the offensive flavor sometimes found in venison. Buffalo meat doesn't require a long period of cooking to make it tender. A cut of buffalo meat should be cooked for a shorter period of time than the same cut of domestic beef. The shorter cooking period means you don't cook out the flavor in the meat, or destroy its spirit.

Perhaps believing there is spirit in meat is a fanciful thought, but Bill and I often discuss the possibility. Back on the reservation, Bill tells me his people said, "You are what you eat."

Over a century ago both the fur-trapping mountain men and the wild, hunting Indians had a disdainful name for the encroaching white settlers. They called them "pork eaters," and felt disgust toward those eaters of salted pig meat. The Indians believed you took on some of the characteristics of the animal you ate. Though they had no knowledge of science, perhaps those savage Indians knew something we're just beginning to speculate about.

Present-day researchers have found that the characteristics of an animal are perpetuated and preserved in a

172

coding of the DNA nuclei in the protein molecules of the animal. When we eat those protein molecules, we are ingesting some of the characteristics of that animal. What if the Indians were right? For several generations we have eaten a meat diet of sheep, highly domesticated hogs, feedlot-fed beef, and tame, confined chickens. All these domesticated animals are docile, colorless, and extremely dependent. Could ingesting meat containing these qualities make our civilization more and more domesticated, a society of followers with fewer men of originality and perseverence?

Just as feeding a potential queen bee the special diet of royal jelly makes her a queen, so might feeding our potential leaders DNA-coded protein from the self-reliant, virile buffalo make them natural leaders.

Being influenced by the food you eat isn't just a far-fetched idea that Bill brought off the reservation. There is considerable literature coming out now about the future possibilities of educating people with pills, a whole college education contained in a special diet, or capsule. Such futuristic projections come from various experiments, especially those of teaching worms a maze. After a group of worms has learned to run a maze, they are ground up and fed to a new group of worms which has never been in the maze. This new group learns the maze at a much quicker rate than the first group. Thus, the knowledge of the first group of worms is actually absorbed by the group which ate them.

Bill and I found our imaginations titillated by these ideas. We thought of the stupidity we might be ingesting with mutton and fowl, indolence and sluggishness in our pork, and gluttony in our feedlot-fattened beef. We could find few admirable characteristics in the animals which composed our present meat diet. As soon as our buffalo herd multiplied sufficiently, we vowed we would concentrate on eating buffalo meat. If characteristics

173

could be passed on in meat, we preferred the traits of buffalo: courage, bravery, self-reliance, determination, and protectiveness.

Bull-in-the-Bush had these fine traits, but eating him was just impossible. My second bite was my last. I'd satisfied my curiosity, and I refused to continue such cannibalism. I felt sure that once our herd enlarged, we wouldn't get so personally attached to each animal. I could eat "one of the herd," but not an animal with a name and personality.

While the other diners heartily enjoyed their roast buffalo, I kept thinking of all the buffalo meat wasted in the nineteenth century, when the buffalo were killed just for their hides. All that delicious meat was left to decay on the plains, while the tough, scrawny longhorn was trailed all the way from Texas to furnish the "good" meat for the palates of our forebears. Here was a case where Nature placed an abundant meat supply on the vast plains, a land that grew very few edibles, yet Nature's menu was scorned.

We have to remember that the destruction of our native beef—buffalo—took place during the Victorian age. America had just celebrated her centennial and was anxious to win a place as one of the important powers of the world. Beside Britain, we had always seemed an uncouth and barbaric new nation, sadly short on culture, taste, and tradition. Our national inferiority complex seemed to keep us in a position of constantly emulating the English. Since the English weren't eating buffalo meat, obviously we Americans would show our boorishness by eating our native beef. Buffalo tongues were considered respectable delicacies, probably because they were more scarce and could be considered exotic, like snails or tripe.

Almost certainly, the meat taken from the hump region of a buffalo cow was better meat than the best

174

beef raised to charm the taste buds of nineteenth-century gentlemen.

The hunting of buffalo cows in preference to bulls, by both whites and Indians, contributed to the near destruction of the species. Both the meat and the hide taken from cows was considered superior. Often a bull's meat was found to be tough and inedible, and the hides were too thick for use in anything but shields and boats.

The Texas longhorns brought in to restock the former buffalo ranges didn't last long. Their meat was too inferior. Stockmen had to breed up their herds with whitefaces and Shorthorns.

After feeding over two thousand people, Bull-in-the-Bush was gone, and late arrivals had to be turned away, disappointed. The sheriff's posse estimated seven thousand people had swarmed to Stanwood that day, the largest crowd in the village's history. When the guild ladies totaled up their profits from the day's activities, they discovered they'd cleared three thousand dollars, to be used in the remodeling of the hospital kitchen. Everyone agreed that Bull-in-the-Bush had been a real crowd-getter.

In a few days Stanwood settled back to its normal snoozing in the sultry summer sun. Kahtanka relished his new role as the only male in the company of a twelve-member harem. Mating season would be arriving soon, and we hoped the ten comely cows would kindle a romantic gleam in Kahtanka's eye.

Although the buffalo roast was the big local event of that summer, I'll always think of it as the summer I learned to drive a tractor.

All my life I've heard the expression, "Make hay while the sun shines." I thought it meant something like "grasp your opportunities when they're presented." I was wrong. I learned the expression means exactly what it says. When the hay is ripe, you have to cut it and bale

175

it quickly before a dark cloud crosses the sun, bringing rain. Rain wrecks the hay.

We had a small, twenty-acre hayfield, and inconveniently for me, right in the middle of golf tournament season, the hay became ripe. It was also an inconvenient time for Bill. Though he had planned to cut the hay himself, there were several seriously ill patients in the hospital needing his close attention. His hay work could be only sporadic.

Over breakfast, Bill broke the news to me. "You and Bruce will have to learn how to cut hay, so work can go on whenever I have to skip over to the hospital to check the patients."

Putting on my best long-suffering look, I sighed, "I'll get ready."

Bill laughed. "Sit down and finish your coffee. You don't cut hay this early. You have to wait until the sun dries off the dew."

As he left for the hospital, he called over his shoulder, "Meet me at the hayfield at ten, and I'll teach you how to make hay. Bring lots of drinking water. Making hay is a thirsty job."

When the children and I arrived at the hayfield, Bill wasn't there yet, so we proceeded to set up housekeeping in the shade of a large maple tree. We unloaded the many water-filled jugs and spread a blanket. Beth had been appointed baby-sitter for four-year-old Brenda, and she'd brought along a plentiful supply of books and games to keep her younger sister amused. Though it was yet early, the sun was already uncomfortably hot. I was about to stretch out in the shade when Bill arrived to give Bruce and me our first, and only, tractor-driving lesson.

As Bill began explaining, I listened in horror. I've always been terrified of noisy machinery, and the antique tractor he was demonstrating was nothing but

176

noisy, greasy, sharp machinery. As Bill described all the parts and functions of the tractor, Bruce listened carefully. Though he was only eleven, Bruce was beginning to suspect that in some things (such as tractor-driving) he was smarter than his mother. His bright blue eyes noted everything calmly, and his serious, grown-up look showed he felt master of the whole situation.

A crank at the front end was the "starter," and I watched in alarm as Bill swung the crank. I dimly recalled all the broken arms people used to get cranking the old cars. A surgeon with a broken arm would be worse than a barber with the hiccups. The horrible machine started with a smoking roar, but Bill escaped without injury.

"Don't *you* try to start it," he shouted at me over the clatter.

Great scott! Did he think I was a complete idiot?

"Who wants to try it first?" Bill asked.

My maternal protective instincts overcame my terror. "I will!" I cried. I tried to whisper to Bill that Bruce was too young to operate such a mechanism, but a whisper is useless around a running tractor.

Bill helped me up to the high seat with all the chivalry of a footman aiding a princess into her golden coach. I think he realized I was nearly at the foot-stamping, "I-won't-do-it!" stage. I sat down in the huge metal disc called the "seat," and immediately came to a screaming stand. Even through my blue jeans it had been like sitting in a bonfire. The sun-heated metal had reached the burning point.

After properly insulating the seat with an old sweatshirt, I was ready for my solo run. Just soloing on the tractor would have been challenge enough, but the mowing attachment, a row of sharp blades jutting seven feet sideways from the right rear wheel, had to be operated separately from the tractor. Since I can barely drive a car not having automatic transmission, I was way out of my element with all those gears and levers facing me.

I started off fearfully, waiting for the infernal thing to rear up and buck me off. I needed four feet, three arms, and nerves of steel. At the far corner of the field I stopped, amazed to be still alive. Behind me stretched a wobbly seven-foot swath of cut hay. Vowing to straighten out my driving, I went through the gear-shifting procedure to back up a few feet for a straight, fresh start. With so many gears to choose from, I somehow picked a high-speed forward gear instead of the slow backing one I expected. The tractor lurched forward like a charging buffalo, and if I hadn't been clutching the steering wheel in a frozen-terror grip, I'd have gone flying off. I looked back for Bill, but he had already returned to his hospital patients. The fate of hundreds of dollars' worth of hay was in my inept hands.

When I finally got the charging beast under control I concentrated on trying to cut nice, straight rows. Of course, it wasn't hard to concentrate. You couldn't hear anything over the roar of the tractor, and there was nothing to see but tall grass, which for some reason they call "hay."

My first turn around the field took forty-five minutes, and at the end of my round I gratefully dismounted and headed for the water jug. While I drank in thirsty gulps, Bruce ran over to the idling tractor and climbed on.

"He's only a little boy," I gasped, hurrying to stop him. But that little boy took off smoothly, slipping the clutch without a jerk, and roared away, leaving an expertly-cut, straight swath of new-mown hay.

The girls watched their brother maneuver down the field.

"Bruce drives the tractor better than you do, Mommy," Beth said, with a flick of her auburn ponytail.

Between gulps of lukewarm water, I growled, "He's a boy. They're better around noisy, dirty things than girls are."

I flopped down in the shade, watching the far-off shape of my only son on that fire-breathing dragon. I'd hardly caught my breath when the popping noise of the tractor told us Bruce was nearly finished with his turn around the square.

I relaxed some my second trip around the field, but I'm not sure being relaxed made things any more pleasant. Now I was aware of the burning sun, the flies and bees using my back for a landing strip, the dusty air, and my dry, thirsty lips.

At the end of that round I nearly staggered to the water jug. Beth and Brenda greeted me with frowning looks. "You look funny, Mama," Brenda giggled. Beth nodded, adding her disapproval.

"Funny?" I thought I was suitably dressed for cutting hay on a steamy summer day. I hadn't consulted Emily Post, but I had put some thought to it: blue jeans and sneakers because of the greasy tractor, a sun-top halter to get a nice tan on my back and shoulders, sunglasses against the sun's glare, and a big flowery straw hat to protect my hair from bleaching and drying out. I thought the whole get-up was very practical.

"Farmers just don't dress like that, Mama," Beth said. She looked disgusted. "You look like a city dude."

I felt like a city dude, too, but I couldn't admit that to Beth. She takes great pride in being a Country Girl, and has little patience with city folk and their ignorances. I was rapidly losing face with my elder daughter.

By noon I had made a new discovery. I'd often seen farmers working their fields on umbrella-shaded tractors. "What sissies! What softies!" I'd always thought. Now I took back all those churlish thoughts. Those farmers were sensible men, safeguarding their skin and health. Right then I'd have traded two buffalo for an umbrella on the tractor. My shoulders were beginning to turn a beefy red, and I suspected a new crop of freckles would be my reward for the day.

As the afternoon wore on, Bruce began taking three rounds to my one. Like many eldest children, Bruce has always been especially conscientious and responsible. He was thoroughly enjoying himself, doing an excellent, safe job, and the only reason he allowed me a turn at all was his suspicion that poor old Mom's feelings would be hurt if he declared me incompetent.

During one of my long rests in the shade while Bruce circled the field three times, I heard the approaching wail of an ambulance siren. The screaming, flashing ambulance tore into the hospital drive. I sighed in resignation. That probably meant Bill wouldn't get away to help us at all.

I was right. When Bruce finished and there was no more standing hay, Bill still hadn't joined us. We parked the tractor, gathered the now empty water jugs, and went home for supper. The weather forecasters promised no rain for three days. That would give us time to rake the cut hay into windrows and have it baled and stored for winter feeding. Though freckled and peeling, my life had been enriched. I had made hay while the sun was shining!

At dusk Bill came home. He took one look at my scarlet, sunburned face and chuckled. "Spent the day at the beach, I presume?"

I gave him a look that started out to be murderous, but we ended up laughing together.

"I'm really starved," Bill said. "We had a long, rough one this afternoon."

As he ate his supper Bill told the children and me about the strange and difficult case he'd been struggling over. It was the accident victim brought in by the ambulance I'd seen that afternoon.

180

When Bill had heard the wailing ambulance stop at the emergency entrance, he had hurried into the hallway toward the emergency room. Telltale drops of blood on the floor pointed the way to the patient. Bill heard rasping groans with each breath. Inside the emergency room, a perplexed nurse and ambulance driver stared helplessly at the victim, who lay face down on the table. The patient, a lad wearing only a swimming suit, had suffered strange injuries. Thirty-three parallel lacerations, each a foot long, ran crosswise up the boy's back. The skin was sliced evenly, like a package of sliced bacon, with each piece a uniform width of one-third inch. Midway down the back a sucking wound indicated the pleural cavity had been perforated, and the boy's right lung was in the process of collapsing.

Bill quickly instructed the nurses to put sterile wet packs over the entire spine and to press down over the area where the sucking wound was taking blood into the patient's chest with each inspiration. The switchboard operator had already summoned the surgical crew.

As Bill changed into his scrub suit and prepared for surgery, the ambulance driver briefed him on what had happened to the eighteen-year-old patient. The young man had been driving his motorboat and pulling his girl friend behind on water skis. While making a sharp turn, the boat hit a submerged stump, and the patient was thrown out of the boat. The boat's steering mechanism was stuck on the sharp turn, so the unmanned boat continued in a tight circle. As the boy rose toward the surface of the water, the boat had completed a tight circle and roared over him, the blades of the propeller crawling up his back. Bill shuddered at the thought of it. An avid water-skier and swimmer himself, Bill saw now what sharp, whirling propeller blades did to human flesh.

In the operating room, the anesthetist inserted an endotracheal tube and took the patient down to a deep plane of surgical anesthesia. The first necessity was to apply suction to the chest cavity to draw out the blood and air that had gotten in around the lung. Then the deeper portions of the wounds and chest wall layers were sutured. The loyal general practitioner, George, had offered to help Bill with the long, stitching process. George started at the top shoulder lacerations and Bill began on the waist. With thirty-three long lacerations, they knew it would be some time before they met. Fortunately, the ribs had not been pulverized, as one might fear, and though the spine had been nicked, the spinal cord was uninjured. For two and one-half hours George and Bill stitched away, bringing together the skin margins. Their backs ached, and the whole crew was getting tired.

Suddenly the red warning light flashed from the cardiac monitor, and the alarm buzzer sounded. The oscilloscope showed a straight line, indicating ventricular standstill.

Ignoring sterile technique and the fragile back wounds, Bill immediately rolled the patient over onto his back and began closed chest resuscitation. Dave, the anesthetist, poured straight oxygen to the patient. The chest wall directly over the heart must be compressed completely and rapidly, squeezing the heart against the backbone. This forces blood out of the heart and into circulation, providing the brain with the crucial oxygen-bearing blood. Closed-chest resuscitation is extremely hard physical work, and Bill and George traded off. An electrical tracing from the heart soon returned, but there was still no pulse. Finally, after much continued resuscitation, the pulse returned good and strong.

Once again, the patient was rolled over on his stomach, and the bleeding lacerations attended to. Some of the stitches had been torn loose during the resuscitative procedure, and these had to be repaired. As Bill and

George continued stitching up the boy's back, they discussed the worrisome question of whether brain damage had occurred during the heart stoppage. Would the boy have a greatly impaired mind, or be a semi-comatose vegetable? The cardiac tracing on the monitor looked good, with a normal complex. As the last stitch was taken, the circulating nurse announced that they had placed 623 stitches in the youth's back.

"And that was how I spent my afternoon," Bill said, as he finished telling us about it. "That's why I didn't get to help you with cutting hay." He stood up, stretching. "Now let's go to bed. Boy, will that bed feel good!"

Happily, the boy had not suffered any brain damage and over the next few days he made an astoundingly rapid recovery. On the third day following the accident, Bill removed one hundred sutures. Each day another one hundred stitches were tediously taken out. On the final day, the remaining twenty-three stitches were removed.

After ten days, electrocardiogram readings showed the boy's heart tracing normal at rest, but showed abnormal irritability and distortion upon slight exertion. The boy was sent home to rest quietly while his heart recovered.

Two months later, electrocardiograms showed completely normal tracings even with double amount of exercise. There was no heart strain and no brain damage. Bill was delighted.

The youth asked Bill if he could enlist in the armed forces. Bill told him he'd certainly be justified in using his cardiac arrest history to avoid service, but if he wanted to serve in the armed forces, he could try. Bill couldn't predict how the boy's heart would perform under severe strain.

Six months later Bill received an envelope with the boy's return address on it. Inside was a clipping from the youth's hometown newspaper headlined, "ONCE

183

'DEAD', NOW A PARATROOPER!" Illustrating the article were two pictures, one a snapshot of the boy's sutured back taken soon after his injury. The other picture showed a healthy, smiling youth in full paratrooper uniform. Bill felt richly rewarded.

Even through financial struggles Mecosta Memorial Hospital had managed to keep up-to-date in equipment such as the cardiac monitor. Because this small hospital had life-saving equipment, Uncle Sam had gained a willing and able paratrooper.

◼ Buffalo Breeders— Unite!

12 I've attended some pretty strange gatherings. From buying mops at Stanley parties to being the only Republican at a Jefferson–Jackson Day dinner, I've run the gauntlet. Yet when we received our invitation to attend the organizational meeting of the National Buffalo Breeders' Association, I faltered.

Denver, Colorado, was to be the gathering site, and two thousand miles seemed a long, expensive distance to travel for a meeting. Also, we had a dozen hungry buffalo needing their daily hay, as well as three children and three dogs to be cared for. These obstacles loomed so large that I immediately put the meeting out of mind.

I hadn't reckoned with Bill's eagerness to rub elbows with fellow buffalo-breeders. In no time he had arranged not only a baby-sitter for the children and dogs, but also a buffalo-sitter. Plane and hotel reservations completed the plans, and I had to face the prospect of going to a buffalo-breeders' meeting.

Over the years I'd finally mastered the proper mode of dress required of wives attending political conventions or doctors' meetings. A couple of suits, a couple of cocktail dresses, and a mink stole were the prescribed uniforms. But what on earth did buffalo-breeders expect of their ladies? Or didn't they believe in ladies? For two weeks I leaned heavily toward sporty, Calamity Jane-type clothes. Then Bill reminded me that many buffalo owners were millionaires. What a shattering thought! I might be walking into a pow-wow of diamond tiaras and Dior gowns.

A few days before our departure I had to quit fretting over my wardrobe and get on with my usual pre-flight procedures. They take the better part of two days and at least one sleepless night.

My Last Will and Testament was the first thing I checked. Everything seemed in order. Next, I cleaned under beds and behind heavy filing cabinets—all those places which get neglected for days, or weeks, I shamefully confess. No mourning relatives must find dust under my bed! Finally, my little notes giving posthumous advice and farewells must be hidden. The hiding-places have to be very clever. The longer the trip, the more concealed the note must be. I wouldn't want the children or the baby-sitter to find them if I should survive the trip. The notes must be hidden so they'll be found shortly after our tragic demise. A three-day trip meant the messages mustn't be too carefully hidden. Before stocking the refrigerator with a three-day milk supply, I carefully taped one of my notes to the rear wall of the refrigerator. So long as I returned on schedule to restock the milk supply, my sentimental farewell note would never be found.

On the morning of our flight, I lost my breakfast even before I had breakfast. I smiled bravely, mumbling, "The condemned man lost a hearty meal," but Bill looked worried. Assuring him that my symptoms weren't morning sickness took half an hour. I refused all tranquilizers, thank you. When traveling by plane I insist upon keeping all my wits about me. Who else will carefully watch the wings and warn the pilot of every wobble and variation of pitch?

In a fog of terror I was hurtled westward. As our taxi

186

delivered us to our Denver hotel entrance, I gaped happily at the high-heeled cowboy boots and creamy white Stetsons on the passersby. For me, a starry-eyed fan of the Old West, this was pure heaven. The awful thought crossed my mind that perhaps the plane hadn't made it safely after all. Maybe this *was* heaven.

Victorian in décor and lavishly decorated, the hotel was charming. Built ninety years ago, it radiated nineteenth-century Western atmosphere. Any moment I expected to bump into Buffalo Bill or General Custer. Bill looked indecently Eastern in his dark business suit and oxfords. Squinting eyes beneath cowboy hats looked Bill up and down and dismissed him as a city slicker.

While I unpacked our suitcases, Bill shed his Eastern clothes and Westernized with a suede sport jacket, slim pants, and his everpresent bronze buffalo lapel pin. Other men wear Lions Club buttons, or Masonic emblems, but Bill wears his little buffalo. In Denver it proved better than a name-bearing badge.

As we returned to the lobby I wondered how we ever were to find the other buffalo-raisers. They didn't know us, and we didn't know them. I needn't have worried. Buffalo-breeders are very proud of their buffalo. As the afternoon progressed, we buffalo buffs from all over the country found each other through various little symbols. Every breeder sported a lapel pin such as Bill's, a string tie with buffalo head clasp, buffalo-nickel cufflinks, or some sort of buffalo insignia.

By evening, twenty buffalo breeders had found each other. We congregated informally at a night-spot near the hotel. All evening I contentedly soaked up buffalo talk. I learned you don't *have* buffalo. You *run* buffalo.

"We run a dozen head at our spread," I soon learned to drawl in what I hoped wasn't a dude accent. I needed practice dropping my "G's" from runnin', eatin', and sleepin'.

Seated near me were Don and Adeline Hight, a

Dakota ranching couple. They explained their ranch was located on the White River near the South Dakota Badlands.

"How many acres do you have there?" I asked.

When the genial, ruddy-complexioned Don answered, the rock and roll band drowned out his reply. I heard only "Grmph-and."

With friendly interest I pursued getting acquainted. "How much livestock do you have on your ranch?"

My husband's heavy boot tapped me sharply on the ankle, and Bill whispered into my ear. "You don't ask a rancher how much land or livestock he has, Pinkie," he scolded. "That's like asking someone how much money he has in his savings account."

"Oh," I whispered, blushing at my stupid blunder.

Fortunately, my regional ignorance wasn't held against me by the Hights, and as the evening progressed, we began to feel like old friends.

Later on, Adeline said that they really should be going. They had to check on "Bill" and see if he was all right.

"Oh, did you bring your children along?" I asked, thinking Bill was their son.

"No," she answered. "Bill is a buffalo. We brought him with us."

She's got to be putting me on! I thought, but I hated to admit there was even the slightest possibility that I believed her.

Others around the long table solicitously asked Adeline about the buffalo's health and assured me that "Bill" ("Buffalo Bill," of course) was truly visiting Denver.

"Where is he?" I finally asked, suspiciously.

"Oh, down the street in the hotel parking lot, a block or two from here."

Aha! Now I had them! I'd show them I wasn't as gullible as I looked. I smiled sweetly to show them I wasn't offended at their dude-baiting.

188

"Can I go with you and see this buffalo?" I asked.

"Sure," they agreed readily.

We started off, a straggling group of twenty, through a back alley of downtown Denver. This must be some sort of Western gag, pulled out to use on greenhorns from the East—like snipe hunts, or searches for a left-handed bucket. I hoped it wasn't something violent like tossing ocean liner passengers overboard when they first crossed the equator.

At the parking lot, a blue pickup truck and large horse trailer stood out conspicuously from the parked cars. The trailer swayed slowly on its wheels. Obviously, something alive was inside.

As I stared, Don opened the tailgate of the trailer and led out a mammoth, shaggy buffalo bull. It wasn't a gag. He was for real. Only a small chain halter controlled the beast.

The men found some empty trash cans and an outdoor faucet and proceeded to give the thirsty animal a long drink.

It seemed so incongruous—that huge buffalo bull walking around the concrete parking lot in a canyon of tall buildings.

I learned that the twelve-year-old Buffalo Bill was a trained buffalo. *Trained,* that is, not tame. There's a difference; there's no such thing as a tame buffalo. The buffalo had been trained to restrain some of his ferocious instincts. His nose had been pierced so he could wear a restraining nose ring, but, "Bill doesn't like it," Don shrugged. It was clear that if Bill didn't like something, you might as well forget it.

Don explained that the buffalo wasn't a *bona fide* bull. He had been taken from his mother when only a half-hour old and castrated, becoming a steer. Technically, he was an "it," but because he looks like a bull, I'll call him "he." Besides, "It drank thirstily," sounds silly.

The buffalo calf was bottle-fed, reared, and trained as

189

a pet by the Hights. Now he prefers to stay near their house. When he's turned out with the rest of their buffalo, he's a loner. Not a bull, not a cow, he is rejected by the herd as inferior.

The shaggy beast was certainly real—not just a gag on me. To publicize our first National Buffalo Association meeting, the buffalo had been brought the hundreds of miles from his White River pad to Denver. Don explained that Buffalo Bill was scheduled to meet the press the next morning for pictures.

"Bill loves to travel," Adeline commented. "He really likes going places." She told us about his trips to Hollywood where he was used as a solitary buffalo. Twice, Bill has been painted white and thoroughly powdered to play the part of a white buffalo. Another time he had an extensive part in "The Rounders" television series. I recalled a television program in which the central theme of the plot was a buffalo galloping wildly up and down a western town's main street. Here was that buffalo in person. At last I was meeting a real celebrity, yet I couldn't even get an autograph.

As we admired the buffalo in the alley parking lot, curious onlookers gathered, forming a wide circle around Don and his mighty pet. A leather-jacketed hippie stepped out of the circle and walked bravely toward the buffalo. As he plied Don with questions, the hippie began testing the buffalo's reflexes by jumping toward him, gesturing, and grunting.

"Don't do that, boy," Don warned quietly.

The youth ignored Don's admonition, continuing to pester the animal.

Don faced the boy sternly, saying "Don't."

Anyone raised in the West knows that a quiet, short command must be heeded. When a Westerner says "don't," all activity ceases.

Still the overbearing young gadfly paid no attention

to Don and continued to badger the increasingly restless buffalo.

Don had been holding Buffalo Bill on a short rein, but now he released six feet of chain as he moved backward from the animal's head until he stood behind the buffalo's shoulders. "Get back, everybody," Don warned.

Still snorting and shadow-boxing, the youth circled the buffalo, stopping in front of the animal's massive head. With a roar the buffalo lunged head down at the annoying pest, and stopped, stiff-legged, his horns not an inch from the boy's chest.

Howling as if mortally wounded, the hippie leaped for the protection of the crowd, cursing Don for having such a vicious animal out where it could hurt people.

Don silenced the youth easily. "Boy, you get out of here, or I'm going to get my sheep shears and give your hair a little trimmin'."

The boy left quickly. Perhaps he'd heard of the barbering episode of a few weeks before when some idle cowboys, weekending in Denver, had tired of the noisy hippies. With flashing sheep shears the cowboys hog-tied and clipped fifty hippies, relieving them of their flowing tresses.

Don shortened the chain and began quieting his disturbed buffalo. The crowd kept growing larger even though the parking lot was secluded in the center of the block with ugly building posteriors enclosing it. Waitresses and night janitors kept slipping out the rear service entrances to check on the commotion.

Four nearly-naked exotic dancers pushed forward in the crowd to get a close look at Buffalo Bill. The onlookers fell back, opening a path, and soon only the shivering dancers were looking at the buffalo. All other eyes were drawn toward the four scantily clad girls. In the chilly night air, they bounced up and down, hugging their bare shoulders and thighs to keep warm, thus treating the spectators to a free exotic dance. The buffalo made quite a hit with the girls. Twittering and squealing, they inched toward the shaggy animal. The vast areas of their naked skin were painted with graffiti and, as they advanced on the buffalo, they looked like war-painted Indians addressing their prey.

The shapeliest and comeliest of the girls asked Don, "Does he bite, or can I pet him?"

Don's ruddy face turned a deep crimson, and grinning he answered, "No, ma'am, he doesn't bite, but I wouldn't touch him."

The shivering brunette appeared crestfallen.

From my place at the edge of the crowd I saw Bill, Don, and two other buffalo breeders go into a quick whispering huddle, accented with sweeping gestures, head shaking, and guffaws, after which the spontaneous committee of four approached the girl. We wives exchanged sympathetic aren't-husbands-silly looks while keeping a close eye on the exotic dancer and our husbands, and inwardly resolving to lose ten pounds of matronly flesh.

The conference ended, and Don led the buffalo back into his trailer house and bedded him down in clean straw. At Don's request, the bewildered parking lot attendant promised to keep an eye on the buffalo. I imagine the wide-eyed attendant kept *both* eyes on that rocking trailer all night.

While we walked toward our hotel I asked Bill what was transpiring with the exotic dancer. His eyes sparkled devilishly as he explained that buffalo fur garments were to be exhibited at the press conference the next morning. The buffalo breeders believed that the fur attire should be displayed on a live model to be promoted most effectively. One item in particular—a buffalo fur bikini bathing suit—definitely required animate demonstration. When the brunette exotic dancer had

192

appeared in the parking lot in her nearly undressed state, the buffalo breeders immediately saw her qualifications as a model. She was to be the Buffalo Gal at tomorrow's fashion display.

The next morning, still on eastern daylight time, our stomachs wakened us at 5 A.M., and we sought out the coffee shop for a hearty Western breakfast.

In the lobby we met Don Hight, just returned from his morning chores of giving his buffalo breakfast. Don joined us for coffee, and we asked how Buffalo Bill was faring in his confining trailer quarters.

"He's doin' fine," Don answered. "Bill's a good traveler, but he's sure enough dirty. I'd like to take him to a gas station for a bath, but I hate pulling that trailer in city traffic."

My fearless husband, who calmly plays crinkle-fender with the worst of city drivers, offered his chauffeuring services. Don quickly accepted.

Maneuvering the truck and huge trailer out of the parking lot, Bill and Don entered the morning traffic. They pulled into the first service station they saw, where the attendant approached the truck politely.

Jerking his thumb toward the huge trailer, Bill asked if they could wash off their buffalo.

Immediately, the station attendant's smile turned to a scowl, and he snarled, "Naw, g'wan," motioning them on. Shaking his head as he turned away, he grumbled that he ought to call the cops on early morning drunks.

Bill thought this a strange reaction. He could understand the station attendant's being surprised or even disbelieving, but Bill expected him to laugh good-naturedly, slick down his tousled hair, and look about for the hidden camera.

Driving on, Bill and Don searched for a more imaginative station attendant. They were turned away from five more gas stations until, at last, on the outskirts of Denver, they found a station serviced by a shy adolesent. The poor boy appeared frightened of the two grown men, and he stammered a bewildered "okay" to their request for a hose.

Bill discovered bathing a buffalo was a bit risky. The water was cold and under high pressure, and Buffalo Bill kept kicking his huge hoofs at the annoyance.

I had remained at the hotel during the buffalo-bathing venture. Since Dorothy Sherman and I were the only wives awake and available, we were appointed to be the reception committee for the exotic dancer. We were to get her ready for the ten o'clock press conference and style show. Neither of us ever had met this type of entertainer before, and we were nervous. We informed the desk clerk that when a young lady arrived asking for the buffalo association members, we would be seated on the red velvet settee in the lobby.

Shortly, a young girl strode up to the desk. Her clothes, her long, black hair, and jaunty step were that of any pretty college coed, but when the desk clerk nodded toward Dorothy and me, we realized this was our exotic dancer. Her body cleansed of the painted graffiti, and fully clothed, her appearance was so changed we never would have recognized her.

"Why, the poor little thing looks a lot like my daughter-in-law," Dorothy whispered. Our maternal instincts went out to the girl. We blushed to think of the lewd, hardened creature we had anticipated.

Introducing ourselves to the dancer, we led her to Dorothy's hotel room, which was to serve as the dressing room. The buffalo fur jackets and coats which were to be modeled were spread out on one of the beds. After finding the small box labeled "bathing suit," I began fumbling with the wrapping cord. I lifted the scanty bikini made entirely of buffalo fur out of its box and turned around, apologetically holding up the immodest suit.

My stammered apologies stopped as I gaped at the dancer, now entirely nude. She had shed her clothes and was posing for Dorothy and me.

"Will I be all right for the job?" she asked hopefully as she did a pirouette followed by a bump and a grind.

Our maternal feelings fled. In confusion we tried to usher her into the privacy of the bathroom for her costume change, but modesty was a trait our exotic dancer had lost. Wriggling quickly into the meager fur bikini, she began posing in front of the mirror. Dorothy and I exchanged alarmed glances. The top of the bikini obviously had been designed for a model of less ample bosom than our dancing girl's.

"My, my, that will never do," I clucked.

"Why, honey, I think it's kinda cute," the girl protested. "It's a nice change from my bunny-fur G-string. Just think—real buffalo fur!"

As the dancer admired her overflowing reflection, Dorothy and I conferred.

"How did we get into this?" Dorothy asked.

"I think it has something to do with the early riser getting the worm," I whispered.

"The first time she lifts her arm, she'll be topless," Dorothy said, barely stifling a giggle.

We debated the problem. There was no way to make the girl smaller or the bikini top larger. The solution had to lie with support. We called room service for a roll of sticky tape, but hardly dared hope that would be sufficient solution.

Dorothy rummaged through her jewelry box where she found a long brass chain necklace which she donated to the cause. Looping the delicate chain around the center front of the furry top, Dorothy fastened the chain behind the dancer's neck. We sighed with relief. If the supporting chain would just hold for the next hour, the cause of decency might prevail.

195

Wrinkling her nose, the girl shrugged, making it clear that she didn't understand some women's infernal preoccupation with modesty.

Just before ten o'clock I stepped out on the mezzanine floor to peek down on the progress of the press conference preparations in the lobby below. As several photographers checked their cameras, two busboys were assembling a folding screen which was to serve as the dressing room for our exotic model.

Like two madams gussying up one of the new girls, we helped the girl into the buffalo fur jacket which was to be modeled first. Buttoning the jacket carefully, we reminded her not to show her bikini undergarment until the end of the fashion show, as this was to be the ultimate *pièce de résistance*. The girl nodded, yawning. It *was* a bit ridiculous—two matronly housewives telling a professional stripper when to strip.

A noisy commotion rose from the lobby and the three of us rushed to the ornate iron balustrade where we looked down on the lobby rotunda. Among the milling crowd at the main entrance a path suddenly opened, and, led by Don Hight, the shaggy buffalo sedately lumbered into the lobby. Ahead of them my grinning husband moved along, opening a path. The buffalo looked clean and brushed, but Bill's wool slacks were covered with water stains. His jubilant smile, however, told me it was all worth the cleaning bill.

Don led his buffalo to the center of the lobby where the big beast uttered a tired snort and lay down on the Oriental rug. Hotel patrons hurrying by did a Hollywood-style double-take as they glimpsed the reclining buffalo. Waitresses and maids flocked to the lobby, staring and squealing, "What is it?"

The poor hotel manager paced the fringes of his lobby, wringing his hands. It was definitely the worst day of his life. He would have liked to approach Don and his one-ton pet and ask for their departure; yet

196

Don, a typical sturdy cattleman, clearly looks like the kind of man who is used to giving orders, not receiving them. Perhaps the buffalo's monstrous appearance kept the management at bay.

Patrons rushed for their own cameras as the press flashed pictures of the buffalo association members encircling their mascot.

The furriers exhibiting their buffalo fur garments huddled behind the folding screen, preparing our model. A large nine-by-twelve foot buffalo robe was spread out on the Oriental carpeting, and the style show began.

First our exotic dancer modeled a full-length buffalo coat. Clipped short, the fur closely resembled beaver with its lovely rich brown color. The long coat was followed by a succession of shorter jackets, vests, ski parkas and hoods. On the shorter coats, the buffalo fur had been cut into horizontal pelts which were joined with leather welting. Some of the sporty ski jackets and vests had the flowing hairs of the long buffalo mane incorporated into the shoulder yokes, and this hairy fringe made these fur garments unique.

Exhibiting the furs, the model twirled expertly but with more movement and undulation than a professional model. The all-male group of photographers and reporters showed their approval of this unrestrained modeling technique by a constant barrage of popping flashbulbs.

When she came out from behind the screen wearing the last fur jacket, the dancer faced the photographers with a teasing smile. Slowly and provocatively, she let the coat slide back off her shoulders to display the buffalo bikini bathing suit. As she first knelt, then reclined on the buffalo rug, the photographers cheered and whistled while clicking their cameras. No professional mannequin would have thought of such unrestrained demonstration.

The commotion aroused the buffalo bull from his drowsy snooze. Leaving his background position, he rose and approached the recumbent model. She became aware of his presence when his long, raspy tongue gave her a lingering lick up the middle of her back. As if a large spring had been released within her body, the model uncoiled to a standing position, shrieking wildly. With primitive gyrations, she wriggled farther from the buffalo, yet she was showman enough to stay within camera range. The barbaric movements blended well with her primitive furry attire, and the photographers with movie cameras grinned ecstatically as their cameras whirled footage.

In spite of the laughter and shouting, the buffalo bull remained undisturbed and lay down to finish his nap. Fortunately, he had felt only a passing interest in the young model, and this he had satisfied with one sweeping lick of his tongue. As the dancer calmed and resumed glamorous bathing-suit poses, I gave silent thanks that the chain necklace had withstood the violent antics.

That afternoon when the group met to discuss buffalo, Bill and I were introduced to whole new facets of the buffalo business. The big ranchers were intensely interested in buffalo because of the animal's great hardiness and sense of self-preservation. A severe blizzard had hit the West the previous winter, and we learned of one rancher in Montana who lost twenty thousand head of prized Aberdeen-Angus stock. We couldn't resist mentally tallying up that loss. Using a conservative price of two hundred dollars a head, the rancher lost four million dollars worth of cattle.

Roy Houck, a prominent Dakota rancher, was elected first president of our National Buffalo Association. Tall and lean, with the typical deep-lined face of one who spends his days in the sun and wind, Roy was not only a successful rancher, but a former lieutenant-governor and state senator of South Dakota. Relating how the blizzard had affected him, Roy said he had lost one hundred head of Hereford cattle at the storm's onset when freezing rain coated them with ice. Because their heavy fur shed the rain, his large buffalo herd wasn't bothered. When the blizzard subsided and he was able to get feed to both his Herefords and his buffalo, he lost another hundred head of Herefords. After their extended period of starvation the cattle over-ate and became bloated. Not a single buffalo was lost. Showing strong natural instinct, the buffalo ate sparingly for the first two days following starvation and gradually increased their intake. Since two hundred dead Herefords meant a loss of forty thousand dollars, we could understand Roy's intense interest in a self-reliant range animal.

An Oregon rancher brought out the fact that even though buffalo are nearly twice the size of domestic cows, they can live on one-third less grazing land because they will eat grass and shrubs which domestic cattle won't touch. In a bad year when the range gets short, buffalo have been known to eat cactus. On the wilder western ranges where bear and mountain lions still poach cattle, the buffalo seldom is a victim because of his protective herd instincts.

Bill and I furiously scribbled notes like eager college students at a lecture. The many new aspects and potentials of buffalo were fascinating. We learned that geneticists at Cornell, the University of Wisconsin, and in San Francisco were studying buffalo chromosomes under electron miscroscopes. The pure, unvarying configuration of the buffalo chromosomal pattern was of scientific interest. Several members reported that allergy to buffalo was unheard of, and that allergy specialists in Chicago and San Francisco were prescribing buffalo meat for patients found to be allergic to domestic beef. We were surprised to hear of the many prominent athletes whose meat diet was strictly buffalo meat because of ill effects from domestic beef.

In the discussion it was brought out that all buffalo have only one blood type, whereas domestic beef have over fifty different blood types. Apparently because of this fact, the possibility of transfusing buffalo blood into humans was being investigated. Some researchers hoped it would become possible to use buffalo blood in a single large transfusion such as is required following severe blood loss from accidents or as needed in heart surgery and organ transplants.

As a doctor, Bill was intrigued to learn that there had never been recorded a case of cancer in buffalo. Buffalo have an astoundingly high level of gamma globulin in their blood. There seemed to be many fertile fields open for medical investigation.

I leaned over to whisper to Bill, "Wouldn't it be something if buffalo became the source for developing a serum against cancer?"

Nodding thoughtfully, Bill answered, "There seem to be many interesting possibilities."

The discussion turned from the scientific to talk of the great struggle for control of the buffalo supply which had occurred the year before. Since the entire buffalo population of the United States numbers only about ten thousand animals, and since importing from the Canadian population of live animals is prohibited, it is conceivable that one man might control the buffalo supply by getting a corner on the market. With a limited supply of buffalo and increased demand for live animals and buffalo meat products, the man who controlled the supply could set his own price. A mountain state rancher who had collected the largest private buffalo herd in this country was nearing a position of control when a millionaire industrialist decided to get into the buffalo market. The industrialist tried to approach the rancher, but the rancher refused any discussion. Next, the millionaire hired cowboys to go to the ranch as advance agents, but they were driven off with shots from high-powered rifles. The rancher was extremely suspicious of any strangers since buffalo rustlers had been making inroads into his herd. Since some of the stolen buffalo had turned up in a southern state, the FBI was working on the rustling problem.

Surreptitiously, the industrialist resorted to flying three men to the ranch by plane. The invaders set up camp behind a high ridge, and with high-powered telescopes trained on the corrals and packing house, they spied on the rancher's operations. For five days they observed the handling of the buffalo, made a head count, and recorded the number of buffalo sent into the slaughterhouse. After a helicopter picked them up, they reported there were approximately four thousand buffalo rather than two thousand as had been suspected.

With this new intelligence information, the industrialist entered into concerted competition with the rancher. Every time buffalo were put up for sale, whether a single animal or a herd of fifty, cowhands representing these two moguls were flown to the site, and one or the other of them acquired the shaggy beasts.

When the buffalo-breeders first began telling about this power struggle, I thought it ridiculous. Imagine fighting and spying over a batch of buffalo! But as the tale developed, I began to reconsider. These men of great wealth seemed to smell a potential in raising buffalo. Surely they weren't going through all these manipulations without the expectation of great profit. Perhaps my husband's buffalo-breeding hobby wasn't as zany as I'd thought. I promised myself I would be less critical and more cooperative in helping with the hard labor involved in keeping our shaggy beasts.

Before our first buffalo convention ended, I made

another important resolution. A social blunder which I committed at the final evening banquet called forth this pledge.

The moment I entered the dining room that evening I knew my mink stole was a terrible *faux pas.* I should have known a buffalo breeder's wife would never advertise for the mink breeders. All the other wives were wearing buffalo fur jackets, which I admired, not only for their beauty, but also for their versatility. A mink stole can be worn only on certain dressy occasions, and never at Stanwood. Yet buffalo fur jackets, so lovely with cocktail dresses, were equally charming with country attire.

My eyes narrowed as I mentally took a census of our herd. Which was to be the sacrificial buffalo lamb to give up its furry robe to drape my shoulders? Bringing me with him to this convention was going to cost Bill more than my plane fare and meals. For the very best quality buffalo fur coat, the furriers recommended using a two-year-old heifer. To be swathed in buffalo was my desire. Immediately, I began plotting the project of Buffalo Fur Coat for Pinkie. This journey to Denver definitely would cost Bill more than he'd reckoned.

Sticks
and
Stones and
Buried Bones

13 Upon our return from Denver, it was time to disinter the buried bones of our departed buffalo, Sitting Bull. I feared a graverobber might trespass and take the bones, and though my buffalo fur coat project necessarily meant a prolonged wait, my heart was set on having a real buffalo skull immediately.

We collected a shovel and burlap bag and headed to our grisly chore. The ants and worms had done their work well. Only a sandy skeleton remained. We took home a burlap sack filled with bones. I placed the sack in a little storage shed in our backyard, high on top of a stack of snow tires, figuring in a few days I'd scrub the bones in the creek and lay them out to bleach in the sun.

Two days later, while doing the dishes, I glanced out my kitchen window and was horrified at what I saw. Sheba, our crosseyed Weimaraner, was proudly carrying the buffalo skull across the yard, heading toward her favorite bone-burying hill. I scrambled after Sheba with a banshee yell and murder in my eyes. She and I wrestled a bit, but I finally retrieved the skull, which was missing one horn-cap. I approached the storage shed anxiously, wondering what mischief Sheba had wrought upon that sack of bones. When I saw the nearly-empty sack I was heartbroken. Sheba had been a very busy dog.

Talk about looking for a needle in a haystack! Our five-acre pine-forested grounds with its many hills and gullies made looking for the bones seem a life-long hunt for buried treasure. Orders were issued to the children and their playmates that if they saw Sheba or Cleo chewing on anything—anything at all—they were to notify us immediately.

Over the next weeks we spied on our dogs mercilessly, allowing them no privacy. One by one, the bones were retrieved as the dogs dug up their buried delicacies. As each bone was recovered, we laid it out in the proper skeletal position in a mock-up, the way aeronautic officials lay out the pieces of a crashed airplane. Finally, all we needed was one missing shoulder blade. Two months later Sheba remembered where she had tucked it away. The dogs became rather neurotic from having all their bones taken away, but we had at last reassembled Sitting Bull.

Mating season appeared to be starting, and once again, up went the signs, "Kahtanka's Honeymoon, Keep Out!"

Kahtanka's disposition never did get as bad this autumn as it had the year before. Perhaps the added year had given him more finesse. But more likely, his being the only bull gave him a sense of security that mellowed his disposition. Now he didn't have to strut and growl to prove his virility to his harem. He was their only choice, and they jolly well better like it.

Kahtanka still had his extra-cranky days, though, and Bill had his second close call on one of those black days. One evening Bill didn't get away from the office until after dark to feed the buffalo. As he was spreading feed he heard that awesome rumbling growl and realized that Kahtanka had sneaked up on him. Bill scrambled frantically to the top of the nearby fourteen-foot stack of hay bales. In the darkness Kahtanka stood watching and grumbling. Finally, it began to rain, and poor Bill was cornered miserably. When at last Kahtanka tired of his threatening game and wandered off, Bill warily edged to the far side of the haystack and jumped down. But his left foot landed on a rock, and in jumping from that height, he turned his ankle painfully, tearing some ligaments. Only by crawling on his hands and knees through the wet swamp was he able to struggle to the road where his car was parked.

It was ten o'clock before I saw his headlights coming down our driveway, and I began warming up his supper. I was horrified when I saw his foot. Twice normal size, his leg was a livid purple from his toes to his knee. Slowly it healed, but at Christmas-time there was still some puffiness and a faint violet hue to remind him of the penalty for rousing Kahtanka's ire.

Since he no longer had a challenging bull to fight, Kahtanka's irascible disposition vented itself upon inanimate objects. Over-taken by an apparent urge for violence, Kahtanka would attack a fallen tree limb or an inoffensive hillock, rutting away all growth with his powerful horns. Often we saw him tossing a heavy log in the air with a casual lift of his mighty neck muscles. The log sometimes fell directly on his head, but he gave it no notice. Bill suspected this was practice for hurling a man into the air, impaling him upon the upward-curved horns as the man fell downward. This suspicion gave added material to Bill's nightmares.

Thinking that perhaps Kahtanka needed an outlet for his aggressive feelings, we decided to fashion him a toy. We fastened two old car tires together with stout wire, tucking the ends inside the tire casing so he couldn't hurt himself on the wire. We rolled his heavy new toy inside the pasture.

Kahtanka attacked the new device with vigor, heaving the toy high in the air and chasing it as it rolled. Finally, the double-tire toy landed on one horn, a perfect ringer, and dangled there crazily. Kahtanka stood motionless for a moment, considering. Instead of heaving the offending crown away, he began to prance and swagger around the pasture, showing off his new accessory. He looked more like a strutting matador than a bull.

Though Kahtanka was the most irascible animal in our herd, the other buffalo sometimes became upset and grouchy over special pet peeves. One of their fierce hatreds was dogs.

When we were building Superfence before we got the buffalo, we always took our dogs with us to the ranch, letting them run off their winter blubber and restless energy. After the herd arrived, that was changed. The first time the buffalo saw our dogs, they charged up to the fence, glaring and grunting at our fat, lazy mutts. The dogs got the idea right away. Tucking her tail between her legs, Cleo cowered against my ankles. The buffalo glowered and swung their horns threateningly until we shut the dogs in our car. When safely inside the car, the dogs stopped quivering. They suspected they weren't wanted, and didn't care to argue seniority with such big, strange animals.

After that, we warned people to leave dogs in their cars, but occasionally one slipped by us. One Sunday afternoon we arrived at the buffalo pasture just as a family with several children and a dog were trooping up the path, having already visited the buffalo.

Bill spoke to them, telling them that they should get the dog in the car, that buffalo hate dogs.

"Oh, no," the wife protested. "They just loved our dog. That big bull ran up to the fence and pawed the ground, he was so excited to see our Brutus. He wanted to play with Brutus so badly he even dug his horns into the ground and hopped around."

We just groaned.

Perhaps the buffalo's hatred of dogs is instinctive. On

206

the plains, wolves followed the herds, attacking the old or weak stragglers, and occasionally were able to get a newborn calf. The bulls had to be on constant guard against these predators, and maybe the dog's ancient kinship with the wolf rouses instinctive memories in Kahtanka.

Another sure sign that the herd is uneasy and ready for trouble is when they raise their tails. Then we know they're agitated, and we take pains to see that nothing provokes them further. The expression, "They high-tailed it out of there," comes from the mustangs' habit of raising their tails before galloping away from danger. When our buffalo raise their tails, they aren't the ones who retreat.

Late in August we noticed with great dismay that the grass in the buffalo pasture was getting scant. Our thirteen animals had cropped it short. Soon we'd have to begin feeding them if something wasn't done. We had counted on their grazing for themselves until December, and extra months of buying feed would ruin our budget.

Forty acres of grassland adjoined our buffalo pasture. This meadow had lain unused for years and was cover-ed with knee-high lush grasses, but, unfortunately, there was no fence around it. There was but one thing to do, though we shuddered even to think of it. The toil of building Superfence was yet too fresh in our memo-ries. But distasteful though it was, this pastureland must be fenced.

This time it should be easier, though, for we decided not to build a Superfence, but an Ordinary Fence. An ordinary, five-strand barbed wire fence might be suf-ficient if we used that pasture only in the quiet winter months. We figured we could move the buffalo into the confines of Superfence before calving season began, thus avoiding their most agitated periods. The pro-posed new pasture would be the winter pasture, and the

Superfence enclosure would be the summer pasture, used from March through October. Rotating the pastures in this way would be beneficial to the grasses, giving them a chance to recover from the heavy trampling and feeding of the hump-backed browsers.

Back to fence-building our family went. We were all two years older now, and considerably wiser in the ways of fence-building. One big disadvantage was that we were no longer naive. We knew what lay ahead of us, and knowing this didn't make us wide-eyed and eager—just grim and resigned. I reminded myself of my resolve to be more industrious in ranch work, but as with New Year's resolutions, my determination was fading.

The hot, dry weather of late summer had made the ground rock-hard, stubbornly resistant to our post-hole diggers. The mosquitos had a grand time, and with all the bottles of insect repellent we used, the chemical and pharmaceutical industries must have declared an extra dividend. Barbed wire is miserable stuff to work with; without warning, it cuts and scratches. During the entire fence-building project we looked like victims of a den of lions. We never became irritated to the point of quitting, though, for just across the hayfield we could see our thirteen shaggy buffalo moving about their closely-nibbled pasture in search of tender green sprouts. This reminded us that we must keep working—in fact, hurry!

There was a bright side. Since we were digging ordinary-sized holes for ordinary-sized posts, it seemed child's play compared to the rigors of building Superfence. Actually, I shouldn't say "child's play," but "child's work," since our children did a large share of the labor. We found they were quite capable of digging post-holes in the sandy spots, and they seemed to withstand the heat better than we old folks did. Occasional bribery with cold soda pop kept them digging expertly.

While toiling on Ordinary Fence I discovered that an eleven-year-old boy is stronger than his mother. I learned that a nine-year-old daughter *thinks* she's stronger than her mother, and after two hours' work under a broiling sun, she is right.

As the eldest, and because he was serious and dependable, Bruce was given the responsibility of driving the buffalo car to deliver barbed wire and fence posts where needed. Beth, our extroverted and effervescent redhead, always proud of her physical strength, proved to be the best post-hole digger. Though perspiration was streaming down her face, she would finish one hole and move on to the next spot for digging. My shoulder muscles ached just from watching her determined industriousness. Bill and I suspected that Beth was not only the youngest post-hole digger in Mecosta County, but probably the most diligent.

Since Brenda was only four years old and lacked the strength needed for farm labor, she was our errand girl and messenger. Her job entailed fetching water for us parched workers, delivering hammer and fence staples where needed, and carrying messages of progress from one work detail to another. Brenda felt demeaned by this childish job, and, as her short little legs carried her off through the tall grass on an errand, she muttered her dissatisfaction. Her desire for responsibility had grandiose goals. Feeling mature enough to drive the buffalo car, Brenda brushed off her midget size, ignoring the fact that she had to stand up on the car seat in order to see where the car was going. Brakes and clutches were beyond the worry of a four-year-old.

One torrid day we were working in a swampy area where the mosquitos buzzed around us like swarming bees. It was a steamy, insect-infested jungle. All we lacked were pith helmets and beating tom-toms. Working conditions were utterly miserable, and the air became dense with self-pity.

209

I kept hoping some sympathetic soul driving past would at least stop momentarily and say, "What's a nice girl like you doing in a place like this?" But I suppose the smeared mud and mosquito dope obscured the fact that I was a girl, to say nothing about being a *nice* girl.

As Beth and I were tamping muck around a cedar post, trying to firm it, Beth suddenly stopped in disgust. With the positiveness of a nine-year-old, she said, "Well, I can tell you I'll never marry a farmer!"

"Oh?" I grunted. "How come?"

"I hate building fences!"

"I know," I sighed, "so do I. But I didn't marry a farmer, and look at me."

Beth looked at me sympathetically. "You just never know, do you?"

Another one of those spontaneous lessons in life. I hope it hasn't damaged her psyche. What if she becomes a spinster-career girl, all because she fears a husband might make her build fences?

With all those mosquitos hovering about in the swampy areas, it was hard to converse. If you opened your mouth, a mosquito was apt to go exploring within. One afternoon, while straw-bossing the stretching of a strand of barbed wire, I frequently had to shout orders to my work crew. While issuing three consecutive orders, I inhaled and swallowed three mosquitos. I can't describe what fresh mosquito tastes like—they went down whole. I tell you it was a traumatic experience for one who won't eat even an oyster or a sardine.

When school began following Labor Day, our work schedule had to be revised, and fence-building was done after school hours.

Each day I collected the children's work clothes and drove to the school where I picked up Bruce and Beth, thus avoiding their long bus ride home.

After a few days of school followed by fence-building, the children began to grumble about slave labor, threat-

210

ening to invoke the child labor laws against us. Even though I always parked in a prominent spot in the school bus loading zone, Bruce and Beth never seemed to see my car. They developed a blind, deaf jog toward their school bus, and my honking and waving attracted no attention. Along with every other Stanwood citizen, the bus driver knew we were expanding our buffalo pasture, and daily, he turned them away from the school bus toward me, the mother taskmaster. They rewarded him with disgruntled frowns.

While driving the short distance home after two hours of fence-building labor, the children collapsed in the back seat, appearing near complete exhaustion. Once home, their recovery was miraculous. Without fail, while I was preparing our evening meal, I could glance out the window and see them playing a rough game of football with the neighborhood children. Not a sign of fatigue lingered.

What a happy moment it was when we drove the last staple into the final fence post, thus adding forty acres of lush hay and grasses to our pasturage! Though near dusk, we wanted to turn our hungry animals into the verdant, untouched meadow, releasing the buffalo from their Superfenced pasture for the first time. While the two older children climbed nearby trees to watch in safety, Bill opened the gate into the new pasture, then scrambled up into the tree branches. Taking Brenda with me, I chose the security of our car parked on the macadam road, just outside the new fence.

When they found the opening in Superfence, the animals seemed dazed and confused, and they wandered through the gate unsurely. Moving slowly, they grabbed huge mouthfuls of alfalfa as they walked. After crossing nearly half the new pasture in hesitant dignity, two of the heifers kicked up their hoofs in glee over the new freedom and abundant food supply. That started the entire herd off on a thundering inspection tour.

211

Galloping fast, they headed straight toward the new fence. I held my breath. Our buffalo were used to the huge posts and woven wire of Superfence. Would they even see the thin strands of barbed wire which were supposed to set their boundaries? As usual, Kahtanka and Old Cow were leading. Ten feet short of the fence Kahtanka skidded to a halt, turning the herd toward the south, where they ran the length of the new pasture. What a relief! The buffalo had recognized our Ordinary Fence as a fence and had respected it.

After thirty minutes of jumping and cavorting, performing a buffalo dance, the herd settled down to gorging themselves on the long grasses.

We watched the contented animals for a while, feeling great contentment of our own—the satisfaction of another hard job completed. Now I anticipated a period of leisure.

"I think I'll spend the next week in the hammock," I sighed as we were driving home.

Bill cleared his throat. "No hammocks yet, I'm afraid." He threw me an uneasy look. "Before the ground freezes we have trout ponds to dig."

Horrified, I stared at my husband, while unrolling in my mind was the image of me swinging a pick and shovel.

"No," I answered firmly. I was still shaking my head in the negative when I stalked into the house. None of my sins had been so dastardly as to condemn me to a prison chain gang detail.

Though my jaw was set in firm rebellion, Bill persuaded me to look at the material he spread out on the kitchen table. There were topographical and aerial maps of the ranch, surveys, elevation reports, water and fish studies, trout stream regulations, and blueprints. Bill had been very busy learning about and planning trout ponds.

His plan called for three ponds to be dug in a series,

each one a different shape. The ponds would be located in a low, marshy area where clear creek water would be partially diverted to fill them and provide the constantly changing cold water necessary for brook trout to survive. The ugly, mosquito-infested swamp would be eliminated, giving way to clean, deep ponds, both beautiful and productive.

Bill's scheme made sense, but I scented another one of those back-breaking Big Projects in the wind.

What a relief it was when a monstrous dragline and bulldozer arrived at the ranch and began scooping up huge bites of earth! I'd have no more nightmares about digging ponds with a shovel. As these pieces of heavy equipment dug the fourteen-foot deep excavations, I fully appreciated our machine age. In two weeks' time, the big machines finished the ponds and the final task of smoothing the excavated earth into the landscape. The roar of diesel engines ceased, and the trilling calls of flocking birds could be heard once again.

It had all been too easy. Surely, I thought, there must be something left undone. My suspicions were correct. Bill explained that we must build a twenty-foot-wide dam to divert some of the creek into each of the three ponds. Constructed entirely of rocks, the dams would be handmade by us.

Thousands of years ago, when the Ice Age glaciers began their melting retreat from Michigan, they left behind countless grapefruit-size stones. These smoothly scoured rocks littered the landscape. Since they were harmless to the tall pine forests which eventually sprang up, these stones were ignored until the twentieth century farmer decided to till the soil. Before plowing and cultivating, the farmer's family had to gather all these glacial remnants.

Scattered about our buffalo pasture were several cairns where these ancient, round rocks had been heaped. Every plowing and every heavy rainstorm

213

brought to the surface a new crop of these pesky stones, which then had to be picked up and added to the existing rock piles.

Bill explained that our dam-building procedure would mean filling the trunk and back seat of our buffalo car with rocks, then driving to the dam site, where we would throw the rocks into the creek. Suffering broken fingernails and bruised fingers, the children and I labored at this task. It was tedious work, but I was grateful for the presence of the rock piles. At least we didn't have to explore the buffalo pastures, gathering stones. While tossing the cobblestones into the trunk, I often thought of the poorhouse inmates whose back-breaking labor had collected the stones into cairns years ago. Whenever tides of self-pity threatened, I thought of those pitiful stone-gatherers, and tossed rocks with more energy.

Even though Beth's right arm was then immobilized in an unwieldy plaster cast, she was not released from her obligation to serve on the rock pile. Breaking an arm by falling off a horse was not considered sufficient excuse for exemption from duty.

While throwing rocks, Bill and I discovered a new method for meting out punishment. The slightest misbehavior from one of the children brought on an additional allotment of rocks for that child. "That's ten rocks!" was the penalty for spilling milk at the dinner table, and forgetting to put the cap back on the toothpaste tube added twenty-five rocks to the transgressor's quota. Each child scrupulously remembered not only how many rocks he owed, but how many each sibling had accumulated. Though it worked much like a demerit system, our discipline-by-rocks was faintly reminiscent of the old-fashioned farm punishments of chopping kindling or having to fill the woodbox.

In a short while the children became adjusted to this new punishment system, and their behavior improved so drastically that Bill and I had to add newer rules of deportment. We decreed that Bill was to be addressed as "sir," and I, as "ma'am." Forgetting to so address us brought a penalty of ten rocks.

Even with the added impetus of this penalty system, the dam construction progressed slowly, and the chilling air warned that autumn was nearing an end. I despaired that we would ever finish. After bruising my thumb between two rocks one afternoon, I announced my retirement. "Bill," I said, in disgust, "erosion will turn these rocks to pebbles before we get that dam finished."

"Don't be a quitter now," Bill urged. "I'm working on an idea that may speed things up a lot."

The next Saturday Bill returned home from the hospital early, excitement glittering in his eyes. "Boy," he addressed Bruce, "do you remember when you were little, how much you wanted a dump truck for your sandpile, but we couldn't afford one?"

With an indifferent shrug, Bruce nodded.

"Well," Bill continued, "I've always felt guilty about that, and now that I can afford it, I've bought you one."

Bruce's mouth pursed indignantly. "Oh, come on, Dad, cut it out. I'm too old for that sort of toy."

Bill insisted we all must see Bruce's new toy. Sullenly, Bruce slouched in the back seat of the car, silently condemning the misdirected devotion of fathers.

Bruce was totally unprepared for the specter parked at the back door of Bill's office—a sixteen-ton, rusty, red dump truck, complete with double rear wheels, hydraulic dump box, and numerous gears.

Racing to the rusty monster, Bruce climbed into the cab where he began studying the levers, gauges, and gears. The new toy was a hit.

We named the twelve-year-old truck, "Rockmobile," and immediately put it to work on the rock pile Picking up and throwing rocks into the steel dump box was still a slow, manual job. It took the five of us nearly an hour to fill it with two tons of rocks. When full, it was time to drive Rockmobile to the dam site and disgorge its load.

After carefully studying the operating mechanism of the truck, Bill and Bruce felt ready to attempt the maiden voyage. I took Brenda's hand and began walking to the creek, warning them not to dump the load until Brenda and I got there to watch.

Beth begged that she be allowed to ride atop the load in the dump box and was granted permission.

Brenda and I had walked some distance when I heard the rumble of the truck's engine starting. Glancing backward, I shielded my eyes from the sun, and what I saw forced a shrill scream from my throat.

Gradually, as in slow motion, the dump box was tilting upward. I could see Beth clinging to the rising forward end of the dump box. I knew she would be howling with terror, but the noisy engine would blot out her screams. Waving frantically, I prayed that Bill would realize the dump box was ascending and get it stopped before Beth was dumped along with two tons of crushing rocks.

While I stared in helpless horror, the dump box finally stopped lifting. Bill jumped out of the cab and rescued his terrified daughter.

Later, Bill told me that the moment the truck started he realized the dumping mechanism lever had somehow become engaged. In his rear-view mirror he saw the box began to rise. He kept yelling, "Hang on, Beth," while frantically searching for the proper lever to disengage the hydraulic system. We were all thoroughly frightened by the scare and acknowledged that our new entry into mechanization was going to require practice and caution. Rule Number One governing Rockmobile was agreed upon unanimously: No one was ever to ride in the dump box again.

As soon as Bill and Bruce became efficient and safe

dump-truck drivers, our dam-building project progressed swiftly. When Rockmobile dumped its dusty avalanche of rocks with one earth-shaking roar, the height of the dam was increased more than from one week's tiresome hauling with the buffalo car. After only one week of Rockmobile's services, the first big dam and spillway was completed. We demonstrated our engineering skills by driving the sixteen-ton dump truck over our cobblestone dam.

I shouldn't give the impression that when we worked with our children it was steady toil. The concentration span and patience of children is limited, and our work details were liberally sprinkled with diversions. Instead of coffee breaks, we scheduled horseback-riding breaks, kite-flying sessions, buffalo watching, and excursions into nature lore. By teaching the children how to recognize and collect elderberries, huckleberries, wild strawberries, and mushrooms, Bill demonstrated how he and his family survived back on the reservation during the great Depression. He taught them how to catch fish and frogs from the creek.

"Nearly everything in nature can be used if you're smart enough to find it or catch it," he preached.

During one of these work breaks Beth learned an unplanned lesson on the negative side of nature. Bill was giving Rockmobile a transfusion of motor oil as I lay on my back studying a wispy jet trail.

Suddenly a distant, shrill howl came from upstream where Beth had gone to catch frogs. Many kinds of screams and yells come from children at play, but a mother usually can tell which sounds can be ignored and which are serious. Before Beth's scream tailed off into silence, I was on my feet, running. Never before had I been able to jump over our six-foot-wide meandering creek, but without breaking stride I leaped across without muddying a foot. As I ran, I was calling, "Beth, where are you?" Finally another wail directed me

217

into a dense elder thicket, where I found her kneeling, white-faced and terrified.

"A snake! A snake!" She shrieked.

"Where?" I asked, looking all around.

"I don't know. It's gone, but it bit me!" She thrust out her sturdy brown hand, and there were two faint scratches below the base of her thumb.

Bill came running up. Intuitively, he grasped the situation and immediately began sucking on the tiny wound. Bruce and I paced alongside the creek, looking for the attacker, which we had to assume might be a rattlesnake.

Poor Beth was convinced she was going to die. She hadn't gotten a good enough look at the snake to describe it for identification, except that it was only about eighteen inches long. As Beth had been about to pounce on a frog she'd been patiently hunting, the snake writhed in and grabbed the frog. Indignantly, Beth had struck the snake to make it release her quarry, and the snake whirled at her. Beth's reaction time had been almost as quick as the snake's, however, for there were no fang punctures. The fangs had only grazed the skin as she retracted her hand, and very little venom could have been released. While searching for the culprit, Bill concentrated on calming Beth, as fright is a big danger to snakebite victims. When she finally became convinced she would not die, Beth vented her wrath on that nasty snake who had stolen her frog.

Two days later Bill killed a timber rattlesnake near the creek. He showed the children its identifying marks, and how the retractable fangs released their venom. We would never know whether this snake had been Beth's assailant, but a good lesson in caution had been dramatically demonstrated. No one would argue possession with a snake again.

Once our cobblestone dams were completed, we

found yet another use for our rusty, red dump truck. It made a passable buffalo-herding vehicle. By lining both outer edges of the dump box with bales of hay, comfortable, though scratchy seats were formed. Visiting city friends considered it quite an adventure to climb aboard the dump truck, seat themselves upon bales of hay, and be driven among the buffalo herd. It was sturdy, and its heavy double tires defied getting stuck. Still, when riding in the dump box enthroned upon a hay bale, I felt insecure. What if a passenger in the cab accidentally touched the dump lever? Being dumped in the midst of a buffalo herd is the stuff nightmares are made of! Surely there was a better buffalo-herding vehicle somewhere—a perfect Buffalo Buggy.

One day I finally saw it! I was parked outside a bank when this perfect buffalo-handling vehicle double-parked right beside me. In financial circles it's known as an armored car, but to an old buffalo hand it looked like a perfect roundup wagon. With its slit-narrow windshield and steel-armored sides, it'd be like a steel cocoon midst a mass of charging horns. Certainly we should have one of those.

At my first opportunity I approached a banker. "Where do old armored cars go to die?" I asked waggishly.

He didn't understand. Bankers aren't waggish.

"Where can I buy an old, second-hand armored car?" I repeated slowly.

The puzzled but friendly smile vanished immediately. His ledger-book mind had taken the logical thought process:

1) Bankers use armored cars.
2) Bank robbers would like to use armored cars.
3) This woman is not a banker.
4) Therefore: she must be planning a robbery.

He cleared his throat. "Armored cars are not made available to private citizens."

219

I let it drop there. The banker would never believe me if I tried to tell him what I really wanted it for.

Perhaps someday when I feel brave enough I'll run a sedate advertisement in the classified section: "WANTED: Used armored car, reasonable. References and fingerprints furnished."

Surely somewhere there's a used-car dealer who's stuck with a "white elephant" armored car. Someday he'll find us, or we'll find him, and we'll have our Brink's Buffalo Buggy.

Unless, of course, the war surplus stores have a fire sale on Sherman tanks. Now a tank might be just the thing . . . .

It
All Started
With
Buffalo

14 In their new winter pasture, the buffalo could be seen easily from nearby Highway 131, a busy north-south highway. It was amusing to watch the speeding cars suddenly slow to a crawl, necks popping out of car windows. Often they'd turn around at the first convenient spot and drive back to check their eyesight.

"I thought those were buffalo!" they'd gasp.

One man said he was sleeping in the back seat and happened to open his eyes. His first thought when he saw the buffalo herd was that he was having a Western nightmare.

Many tourists didn't have cameras with them, and they were disappointed not to get pictures to prove they had visited a buffalo herd. This prompted us to have some picture postcards made up from a color photo of Kahtanka. The children thought this an excellent idea. They offered to sell the postcards, expecting to make themselves a fortune. More profitable than a childish lemonade stand, they were sure.

The postcards finally arrived from the printers in two huge cartons. On the picture side, Kahtanka glared darkly at us with Old Cow and their reddish calf in the background. On the message side of the postcard was our poem:

> Me Kahtanka, mighty leader,
>
> Feeder, breeder, and stampeder.
>
> Have no wish to be among
>
> White man with his fork-ed tongue.

The children eagerly began hawking their postcards on weekends when the most tourists were viewing the herd. They learned many things about the ways of the business world. Some days their successes astonished them, when some big-time spenders bought three cards at once. Then there were days when nickels came slowly. The slow days started them thinking about branching out.

If people bought pictures of buffalo, they reasoned, why wouldn't they buy a chunk of buffalo fur, or buffalo leather?

The children collected pieces of buffalo wool and wrapped it in plastic wrap, carefully labeling the package in their grammar-school printing, "Genuine buffalo fur, ten cents." They conceived a deluxe package which contained a ball of buffalo fur and a small buffalo shape cut from buffalo leather, hopefully marked "twenty-five cents." They entered the marketing world with these new products and had some success.

One other buffalo by-product kept drawing our attention. That was buffalo chips, and we had plenty of those. The settlers of the treeless plains, always short of firewood, had really appreciated the burning qualities of buffalo chips (dried manure). The prairie farmers had a saying that they "let the buffalo chop their wood."

Oldtimers say food cooked over buffalo chips resembled the flavor of meat cooked over hickory. Every

222

self-respecting backyard barbecue chef sprinkles damp-ened hickory chips over his charcoal. What could be more nostalgic than steak broiled over buffalo chips? With a little promotion here was a huge market just awaiting our product. We could package it in plastic bags, and . . . then the whole project fell through. We couldn't get any volunteers to gather the buffalo chips. A fortune would continue to slip through our fingers!

Too young to sell buffalo by-products or help with the feeding of the herd, Brenda passed the winter prepar-ing herself for her enrollment in kindergarten the next fall. While learning her ABC's from children's alphabet books, her round face scowled. She was willing to accept "K is for kangaroo" and "M is for monkey," but the "B is for baboon" vexed her.

"B is for buffalo," she protested.

There was nothing to do but prepare a buffalo alphabet for her. It went like this:

THE BUFFALO ALPHABET
by
The Rx Ranch Buffalo Herd

A IS FOR ALFALFA,
The hay that we eat.
In the long winter months
It really tastes neat.

B IS FOR BISON,
A word you might know.
But mostly we're called
By the name buffalo.

C IS FOR OUR CALVES,
In late spring they are born.
They have reddish hair
And not one single horn.

D IS FOR DOGS,
We chase them away.
They remind us of wolves
From a long-ago day.

E IS FOR EXTINCT
Which we almost became.
Our herds were destroyed,
'Twas a terrible shame.

F IS FOR THE FENCE
That keeps us confined.
It protects you from us,
And us, from mankind.

G IS FOR GRUNT,
The noise that we make.
We sound like a pig
With a bad stomachache.

H IS FOR HUMP,
There's one on our back.
It's big and it's curved
Like a farmer's haystack.

I IS FOR INDIANS,
We were their beef.
When the white man destroyed us
They called him a thief.

J IS FOR JUMBO,
Which means very large.
We're big standing still, but
Oh, boy, when we charge!

K IS FOR KAHTANKA,
Our chief, strong and brave.
Who tangles with him
Has a mighty close shave.

L IS FOR LEGEND
Of the days long ago,
When the luckiest people
Saw the white buffalo.

M IS FOR MUD,
Which we wallow in.
It keeps the mosquitos
Away from our skin.

N IS FOR NICKEL,
The buffalo kind.
But just like with us,
They're so hard to find!

O IS FOR OLD COW,
She leads us around.
A better cow leader
Could never be found.

P IS FOR PALEFACE,
They killed off our herds.
What we think of them—
They're strictly for birds!

Q IS FOR QUICK,
By speed we are ruled.
We look slow and clumsy
But don't you be fooled!

R IS FOR THE RANCH,
Which we call our home.
It is the place where
We buffalo roam.

S IS FOR STANWOOD,
Our home in the East.
It is a nice haven
For both man and beast.

T IS FOR TAIL,
It's really quite short.
When angry, we raise it
And give a loud snort.

U IS FOR UNRULY,
Which means we are wild.
To civilized ways
We are unreconciled.

V IS FOR VAGABOND,
We wandered the West.
With freedom and space
We doubly were blessed.

W IS FOR WOOLLY,
Our thick, dark-brown hair.
No cold can phase us,
Even deep arctic air.

X IS FOR RX,
"Rx Ranch," the whole name.
We buffalo are
Its big claim to fame.

Y IS FOR YAK,
A black, shaggy beast.
Since they're distant kin,
We can bear them, at least.

Z IS FOR ZOO,
You can see bison there.
But we love open spaces
And fresh, country air.

The children were receiving a very buffalo-centered education, and it sometimes had disadvantages for them. Once at Sunday school Beth was greatly embarrassed by her farming knowledge.

The Sunday school class was discussing The Lord's

Prayer, and the teacher asked what was meant by "Forgive us our trespasses."

Beth's hand shot up quickly.

"It means asking God to forgive us for the times when we walked on somebody else's land," she said.

The whole class laughed uproariously, and Beth sank back in her chair, blushing and bewildered. She certainly couldn't see what was so funny. She'd nailed up enough "No Trespassing" signs to know what they meant.

Like something weird out of science fiction, the buffalo were gaining control over us steadily. They devoured our leisure time, our thoughts, our conversations, both with friends and with strangers.

When spring arrived we resumed buffalo watching in earnest, counting the number of pregnant animals. One of our buffalo cows was obviously not with calf.

One of the main things we'd learned thus far about buffalo was that they are always inconsistent. Only in their inconsistency are they consistent. For instance, buffalo cows are supposed to wean their offspring when the calves are four or five months old. Old Cow weaned Wanji Sidga right according to the book's timetable. But Good Cow, soft-hearted, tender soul that she is, just couldn't bear to wean Nopa Sidga. On her first birthday the four-hundred-pound, gangling Nopa was still a suckling calf. Her horns tended to get in the way, and she practically had to get down on her knees to get at her dinner, making a ridiculous sight.

While buffalo calves are nursing, they periodically bunt their mothers to make the mother let the milk down. It is instinctive and by the time they are a day old, the calves are very adept at it. It always made me wince to watch those little calves give their mothers' tender undersides such a hefty whack.

Still nursing, the big yearling, Nopa, could give her mother such a bunt it would raise Good Cow's hindquarters off the ground. After one of these tortuous thumps, Good Cow always walked away from her daughter, grunting disgustedly. Because she was still mothering her overgrown calf, Good Cow was not pregnant this spring. She was skipping a whole year of calf-bearing. We hoped Good Cow didn't entertain any grandiose notions of making Nopa her only child. That we couldn't have. To earn her keep, we expected each cow to present us with a calf every year.

The first calf of the season arrived June 11. For the next eight weeks, calves dropped at two-week intervals, with one being stillborn. Of course, during this period we weren't just sitting around, counting our multiplying herd. The sun was shining, so once again our family project was making hay.

By the end of July we had put up nearly two thousand bales of hay. When the last bale was neatly stacked, the word "hay" was designated a naughty word, never to be used within our hearing. None of us wanted to see, touch, or smell hay for a long time.

The last calf of the season was born to Old Cow, making a summer's total of six living calves. The first and last born were little heifers, and the middle four, little bull calves. What a mischievous, cavorting group they made! Chasing each other, they scooted beneath the legs of the cows, bunting with their nubbins of horns.

The herd calmed and gentled during this period, the mothers indulgently watching their children romp. Even the imperious, cranky Kahtanka was gentle and fatherly toward his six new offspring. He'd give them a gentle lick with his rough, purple tongue in acknowledgment of his paternity. The calves had no fear of their monstrous black father. Often one or two calves dozed near his side. Kahtanka didn't seem the benevolent, fatherly type to me, but it shows how wrong one can be judging by appearances.

228

ne warm, sunny afternoon Kahtanka heroically demonstrated his fatherly instincts. Old Cow and Pocahontas, her four-day-old calf, walked past Kahtanka, headed in the opposite direction. A young calf is quick to follow anything, and Pocahontas followed Kahtanka while Old Cow wandered several yards away, grazing. The hungry and curious Pocahontas began to nuzzle her mighty father. Beginning at his tremendous head, her investigating quickly took her to Kahtanka's underbelly in search of warm milk. As soon as Kahtanka sniffed her, he stood perfectly still to avoid injuring the fragile bundle of fur. When Pocahontas found the spot where mother's milk is produced, she became impatiently hungry and gave her father a vigorous bunt. Kahtanka let out a deep groan and sank several inches in pain, but he didn't move a hoof. Unaware of her agony-rendering indelicacy, the little calf was about to give Kahtanka another whack when he was saved by Old Cow, whose grunting calls attracted Pocahontas away from her father.

Old Cow was the only mother having her second calf. All the others were first-time mothers. Old Cow and her first-born, Wanji Sidga, now a gangling yearling, had months ago parted company. Wanji had been on her own for some time. When Old Cow retired to the outskirts of the herd to have her second calf, it surprised us that it was Wanji who accompanied her mother to serve as midwife. Another cow always seems to accompany the mother-to-be to her nesting spot and remains with her for the first few days after birth. However, long after the birth, Wanji stayed near Old Cow and her new little sister, Pocahontas, serving as baby-sitter while Old Cow attended to her herd-leading duties. Wanji seemed to feel no jealousy, just a fond sense of duty.

Since the first-born calf was two months older than the last-born, we had before us a real panorama of the maturing schedule of buffalo calves. With each new arrival we marveled how small it seemed, and how much growing a buffalo calf does in just two weeks.

By mid-August when the last calf was born, the two June calves were losing their auburn coats and were almost a solid dark brown like their mothers. The two July calves were mottled with dark brown splotches, and a dark brown streak covered their backbones from neck to tail. The two recently-born calves still gleamed soft and red in bright contrast to the others.

The fifth calf of the summer, a little bull born to Bleeding Horn, attracted our interest immediately. He was tiny, seemed to have no neck at all, but he had the energy and spunk of three ordinary calves. He was certainly something to watch—a promising calf, perhaps even a future helper to Kahtanka. Since we were trying to maintain the proportion of one bull for every ten cows, in just a few years we would need two bulls to keep all our cows bearing calves yearly. We named this cocky, bouncing little calf Little Big Horn, and are hopefully watching his development. If he matures into a beautiful, first-rate bull, we can always drop the "Little," and he can bear the more pretentious name, Big Horn. If he doesn't live up to his calfhood promise, Little Big Horn will be sacrificed to one of Stanwood's buffalo barbecue celebrations. It's a case of shape up!—or be served with parsley.

Roly-poly Angie didn't shape up in the proper manner. Rotund with blubber, she was the fattest black Angus heifer we'd ever seen, yet Angie remained barren, producing no Angelos for us.

Twice during the preceding year we had pronounced a death sentence on the unproductive Angie, but each time she conjured up a false pregnancy and received a stay of execution. On those occasions her udder swelled to milch cow dimensions, and motherhood seemed

230

imminent. Though I'd heard of false pregnancies in women, I had no idea a cow's psyche was so strong.

While the last brilliant leaves were dropping from the maple and birch trees, her final false pregnancy began to recede.

"That does it!" Bill passed sentence. "Angie goes into our freezer."

Sentimentality and squeamishness had to be overcome. With our limited supply of grass and hay, unproductive animals had to be sacrificed for those who earned their keep by reproducing and multiplying their numbers.

For some time we had discussed eating Angie. Now she began to look quite delicious. Upon looking at her square figure, I could almost taste a bacon-wrapped filet, crumpy on the outside and juicy pink within.

Yet when the slaughterhouse truck arrived to take Angie to her doom, I turned my head guiltily. It was even worse than taking an old faithful dog to the veterinarian for disposal. We weren't disposing of Angie—we were going to eat her, and, even worse savagery, I intended to make a rug out of her hide.

In home-decorating magazines I'd seen black and white cowhide rugs made from spotted Holstein cows and thought them attractive. Suspecting that Angie's ebony coat would make a stunning rug for our den, I began investigating how one turns a cowhide into a rug.

The process sounded deceptively simple at first, involving only cleaning the hide and tanning it. I collected a half dozen tanning recipes, all meant for small animals. Apparently, no one does-it-yourself anymore when it comes to cowhide tanning. I selected the simplest sounding recipe for a raccoon skin and multiplied by ten the required ingredients. This arithmetic indicated I needed a fifty-gallon brewing kettle. I was stumped momentarily until Bill suggested a fifty-gallon oil drum. Ten pounds of alum and twenty-five pounds of salt completed my ingredient collection.

I gathered an assortment of tools. A fleshing knife was the proper tool for cleaning a hide, but I discovered I wasn't strong enough to wield it more than a few minutes at a time. I had to resort to other tools, butcher knives and putty knives. Bill donated some old dull scalpels, which turned out to be the best tools, but I had to work very slowly to keep from cutting the hide.

Spread out on the garage floor, hair down, Angie's hide was ten feet wide and twelve feet long. The slaughterhouse skinners had left her tail on the hide, and I decided to leave it that way. A rug with a tail would add that certain personal touch.

Fleshing a hide is miserable, back-breaking work. One must crouch over the hide in uncomfortable positions, and the work requires both strength and delicacy. I had worked several hours at the gruesome task when the children arrived home from school. Immediately, I drafted them as assistants. With much groaning and declarations of queasy stomachs, they worked alongside me. When I reminded them that Indian squaws had once done this all the time, they retorted that the squaws should have joined a union and gone on strike.

Speed was important. I had to hurry before the hide turned bad. Angie's hide was so large I worked far into the evening and all the next day before finishing. Even putting the hide in the tanning solution was difficult, for it weighed seventy-five pounds. It was quite a struggle for me to move it around and get it in the oil drum, but determination seems to make the weak strong. For ten days the hide had to soak, with frequent stirring. Every few hours I hurried to the garage where, like a witch stirring her cauldron, I poked around in the tanning solution with a broomstick.

Following the tanning period I stretched the hide out

in the yard to dry. Men who had tried tanning deer hides with the hair on warned me that there would be bald spots where the hair slipped off. "Only the tanning factories can do it right to keep the hair from slipping," they said.

How happy I was to discover not a hair had been lost! I had performed a perfect tanning job. As I proudly showed my results to Bill, I bragged, "I bet the squaws back on the reservation can't do any better."

Bill patted my shoulder. "Pinkie, nowadays, back on the reservation even the squaws don t know how. You've out-squawed them."

No better praise could come from Bill.

All that remained to be done with Angie was softening the hide. To do this, I arranged sawhorses in the basement. Over these I would pull the hide back and forth, breaking down the fibers over the blunt edges.

His dark eyes glittering rougishly, Bill reminded me that Indian and Eskimo women softened hides by chewing them. I withered him with a sharp look and a warning that I'd sic my dentist on him.

As I knelt, pulling the stiff hide back and forth over the sawhorses, I realized that this tiring stage would take many moons. Upon each trip to my basement laundry room I put in five minutes at the sawhorses. In this sporadic manner the softening work progressed. Then disaster struck.

One awful morning our furnace fuel oil tank ruptured, spewing a hundred and twenty-five gallons of dark, smelly fuel oil into our basement. Rushing down the basement stairs, I gasped when I saw laundry baskets and lifejackets floating in fuel oil. Then I saw my prize, Angie's hide, soaking up oil like a lantern wick. I slid across the slippery floor to the cowhide rug and heaved it on top of the pool table. It was too late. Sections of my beautiful black rug were thoroughly soaked with the reeking fuel oil. There were many other losses of more valuable possessions, but it was Angie's ruined hide which made me cry.

As we began the tremendous cleanup job and took inventory of the destruction, I discovered another irreplaceable loss—the buffalo hide which we'd had tanned professionally after Sitting Bull died.

The insurance adjustor was a nice young man, and I didn't mean to give him a hard time. Yet as we discussed buffalo skins and cowhide rugs, I could see the young man wished he'd been assigned to a million-dollar fire loss instead of to buffalo people. Angie, especially, gave him difficulty in arriving at a settlement.

He shook his head sadly. "How am I going to face the home office with this?" he moaned. "It'll be hard enough to explain how I arrived at a dollar value on a buffalo hide, but how the dickens do I describe a rug with a tail on it which is called "Angie" by the owners?"

Though I have no shining black rug in my den, slaving over Angie has been good experience. Tanning her hide had not only strengthened my biceps and my character, but given me new respect for the toiling squaws of long ago.

It's peculiar how one hobby or interest often opens the gates to another related interest. I never dreamed our buffalo-breeding venture would lead us down so many strange avenues.

For three summers we had been woolgathering—gathering buffalo wool, of course. Every year when the animals shed, we'd gathered all the buffalo fleece we could find, carefully stowing it away; for what reason, we really didn't know. No piece was small enough to be ignored. Sometimes, dangling from a fence wire or nestled in the grass, we found huge patches bigger than a breadbox. Since Worms and Good Cow loved being scratched, we cheerfully obliged, peeling off matted chunks of their winter coats. Four huge shopping bags of buffalo wool were stashed away in our basement.

We're chronic savers. We preserve everything from bent nails to broken Tinker Toys. Yet sometimes I did wonder why we were collecting buffalo fur. On house-cleaning day I felt we had enough buffalo items. Bill had his extensive collection of buffalo figurines which were efficient dust collectors, and I had my accumulation of buffalo books.

When we first started researching buffalo lore, I discovered that our local community and college librar-ies couldn t supply such esoteric information. They had to cater to the informational needs of the masses, and the masses just weren't stampeding the library to find out how Pothole Pete skinned a buffalo back in '76.

The poor librarian got so she could hardly stifle a groan when she saw me coming. She runs a tight ship of a library and is proud that it satisfies the needs of the community—except for me. She was chagrined that her library had so little buffalo information. It was worse when I arrived looking for buffalo fur facts. Helpfully, she tried inter-library loan and mailed off my want-list to the state library. Even the state library had to admit defeat.

This convinced me that I would have to collect my own library of buffalo books. From bibliographies, I compiled a long list of books we should have. Nearly all of them were out of print. I started by frequenting rummage sales and auctions. For many of the rarest books, I turned to professional book-searchers, who had some success finding the old books for me, and we assembled a quite respectable library of books on buffalo.

Upon consulting my buffalo library concerning uses for buffalo fur, I could find only one short reference to the use of buffalo wool in the past. Nearly one hundred years ago there was a cloth factory in Winnipeg, Canada, which specialized in manufacturing buffalo wool. Each buffalo yields from ten to twelve pounds of wool yearly. According to this reference, the buffalo cloth factory was successful until it had to stop operations because of the near-extermination of the buffalo.

One day we received a letter which made us thankful we were collectors and savers. An elderly Swedish lady, Martina Lindahl, of Hartland, Michigan, wrote us asking if we had any buffalo wool. Explaining that she'd read of our .buffalo project in a magazine, she wanted to try spinning some buffalo wool into yarn. Mrs. Lindahl had spent her lifetime doing spinning and weaving work, and she was curious about the kind of yarn buffalo wool would make.

We immediately shipped off to Mrs. Lindahl a shopping bag filled with buffalo fur.

A week later she returned a package containing various samples of buffalo yarn. Mrs. Lindahl had labeled each step in the transformation of the wool into yarn. First, there was a sample of the dirty, matted wool as it came directly from our animals. Next was a cobweb-like piece of wool that had been cleaned of seeds, washed, and carded on thin, wire teeth (wool cards). The exhibit showing the third stage was a frothy tube called a "rolag," which is the carded wool rolled into a gossamer tube. The rolag is fed into the spinning wheel and twisted into strong yarn. There was a skein of one-ply yarn and another of two-ply buffalo yarn. The color was a rich gray-brown, the texture unbelievably soft, and the fibers strong.

Mrs. Lindahl and I began a pleasant correspondence discussing yarns, and I began a search for a workable spinning wheel. Since I was ten years old I had enjoyed knitting; now I felt inspired to learn how to spin. Mrs. Lindahl promised to help me learn this dying art.

236

With a purpose now in woolgathering, we searched the pasture for every scrap of fur. I hoped to collect enough wool to make Bill a buffalo wool sweater.

My search for a spinning wheel proved difficult. When I occasionally spotted one in an antique shop, it always had missing parts. I wasn't interested in a wheel as an antique or a conversation piece. I wanted a sturdy, workable spinning wheel.

My search through antique shops and catalogs rewarded me with some additions to my buffalo library, and these additions gave further mention of uses of buffalo wool.

The early Jesuit explorers had recorded that the Indians wove buffalo wool, making fabrics and ornaments from it. The Illinois Indians were cited for being able to spin buffalo wool that would equal that of English sheep. One explorer even claimed that buffalo wool surpasses the wool of merino sheep, making gloves nearly equal to silk. This rave notice sounded suspiciously like making a silk purse out of a sow's ear.

I also learned that following the destruction of the great buffalo herds, when the bone-pickers were gathering bones, they gathered the long, coarse hair from the buffalo bull's head. This hair is never shed, and on some of the older animals, reaches a length of twenty inches. The bone-pickers received seventy-five cents a pound for the hair, and it was used for stuffing cushions and mattresses. If we were to peek inside the upholstery of some of those sedate Victorian sofas, we might find they weren't stuffed with horsehair after all, but with the long chin whiskers of a granddaddy buffalo.

My search for a spinning wheel began to get expensive. Though I couldn't seem to find a suitable spinning wheel, I never came home empty-handed from a day's antique-hunting. I accumulated an Indian peace pipe, a pair of snowshoes, and a stovepipe beaver hat—little

237

necessities I couldn't resist. Bill began to get nervous every time I mentioned I was going someplace to look for a spinning wheel.

One day I came home with a seventy-year-old buffalo robe. Bill just shook his head and mumbled something about taking coals to Newcastle. Using a can of flea powder (just in case), I cleaned up the robe and laid it in front of the television set as an "occasional rug." But it isn't used occasionally; it's used often. Dogs and children are drawn to its curly softness like cats to catnip. The first child done with his homework dashes for the buffalo rug. It's considered the choice seat in the house for televison-watching.

As it turned out, I never did find a spinning wheel. Bill found it. I think he was getting desperate to stop my antique-hunting excursions before our home looked like a museum. He bought the wheel from a couple who graciously agreed to teach me to spin on it. It's a lovely, century-old Swedish wheel and very workable.

I'd like to report that I am now a good spinner. I'd like to report it, but I can't. Spinning is another one of those things that looks easier than it is. It takes a tremendous amount of practice to get smooth, even yarn. The lumps and bulges in yarn are called "character, and my yarn is full of character. It varies from very thin to knotty to nubby. Everything has to go evenly to get even yarn. The foot treadle must be pumped with uniform speed. The finger tension placed on the rolag must be unvaried. Even irregular breathing is bad, and a sneeze spells complete chaos.

I intend to become a good spinner, but I fear I've undertaken another long-term, Big Project. I suspect I'll need trifocals and a cane by the time my yarn loses its character.

Bill did the next bit of collecting. I still think he did it to get even with me. He was most uncomplimentary about some of the antiques I brought home during my spinning wheel hunt. He insisted on referring to them as "junk." Can you imagine—that rare, unpainted, wooden bowling pin? Someday I'll surely find a use for it.

Sheba, our Weimaraner, had tangled with a raccoon and lost, and our household dog population declined to two—which was still one too many as far as I was concerned. I was thoroughly relishing the diminished dog census when Bill made an announcement one evening.

"Tomorrow I'm bringing home a new pet for the children."

I said, "No," but this accomplished as much as saying "no" to a charging buffalo.

Bill made us guess what kind of pet we were getting.

"Dog" was one of the very first guesses.

"You're half right," Bill said. "It's half dog."

This caused a moment of silent thought.

"*Half* dog?" Oh, come on, now!

"His father is a malamute, an Eskimo husky." Bill's smile was very smug.

"And his mother?" my voice quavered.

"A full-blooded wolf."

More silent thought. "No," I said again. "Absolutely no."

The wolf moved in the next day. The wolf was at our door, and also on my davenport, in my kitchen, and under my feet. Though only eight weeks old, he'd already mastered a blood-chilling howl. Bill proceeded to train him to howl when anyone said, "General George Armstrong Custer!"

We named him "Shung"—what else, but the Sioux word for "wolf."

Shung immediately adopted the buffalo robe. He slept on it, licked it, nuzzled it, and had accidents on it. All the time he kept growing larger and larger. His fangs grew longer and sharper, his eyes more slanted

239

and wolfish. Sometimes when he looked at me I felt just like Little Red Riding Hood.

My spinning wheel is set up right next to the buffalo rug. I sit and spin, and Shung lies there on the shaggy, brown relic, studying me with what I hope is adoration. Sometimes I suspect the look is downright hunger. Then I get prickles on the back of my neck.

"Oh, well, he's *half* dog," I reassure myself, trying to read the thoughts in his pale eyes. His wagging tail is a hopeful sign, but when he opens his mouth I want to say, "But Granny, what large teeth you have!"

One day a man came to the door to collect payment for some fence posts he'd delivered at the ranch. The children led him into the room where I was spinning.

"I'm here for my money," he announced.

I found my checkbook and began to write out a check.

Making polite conversation, the man said, "Those buffalo of yours are really something, ma'am. They . . ." He stopped short and stared. His eyes darted from the buffalo skull on the coffee table to the peace pipe over the doorway, then to me, sitting at the spinning wheel, and to the wolf reclining on the buffalo robe.

The man leaned forward, craning his neck to get a better look at Shung. Cocking his head, Shung returned the stare. Just then, his nose tickled by a wisp of buffalo fur, Shung sneezed, exhibiting all of his long teeth.

The man left quickly, saying I should just mail him the check.

Bawdyhouse
Banquet

15 When we received notice of another National Buffalo Association meeting forthcoming in Denver, we decided to make a family vacation of it by driving and taking the children with us.

In preparation Bill began squaring away his practice by postponing all but emergency surgery. After arranging for a buffalo-sitter, Bill persuaded his office nurse to be our dog-sitter. While I had the car tuned up for the trip, the children and I packed suitcases, keeping our fingers crossed that no gallbladders or appendices would flare up and prevent our departure. I never actually count on going anywhere until we're at least one hundred miles from home. At that distance I assume we're out of telephone range and have eluded any pursuing patients or the state police. Because of the state police radio-communication system, there had been times in the past when we were stopped by a trooper and sent homeward to care for a newly risen emergency.

When we finally crossed the state line into Indiana, I cheered. We had escaped and were on a vacation. However, "vacation" may be the wrong word, as it developed into more of a buffalo study-tour.

By afternoon as we were crossing the parturient cornfields of Illinois, we saw the first signboard saying,

"Live buffalo ahead." Even east of the Mississippi River we couldn't seem to escape buffalo.

Bill slowed the car, his eyes searching ahead for more signs. Like the old buffalo hunters he was scanning the prairie for buffalo signs—though the printed kind.

The buffalo signs became more frequent until the last one said, "Live buffalo, one-quarter mile." By that time we were moving at wagon train speed. Obviously, Bill intended to stop and see live buffalo.

And that's just what we saw. One live buffalo. We paid fifty cents each to see it. Tourists and their money are soon parted.

At suppertime we crossed the mighty Mississippi, Father of Waters. The children and I were famished, but every time we hinted at our hunger, Bill answered, "Westward, Ho! We can't stop, we've got to keep heading west!" It appeared Bill might keep heading west indefinitely.

We were saved by another sign. It read, "LeClaire, Iowa. Visit Buffalo Bill's boyhood home."

To me, it seemed slightly illogical that we stop and pay our respects to Buffalo Bill Cody. We were going to a great deal of trouble to undo his lifetime work of destroying buffalo herds. But I said nothing. My hunger kept my tongue silent. Anything to stop and eat.

That's the way our whole trip went. I think we visited every buffalo between Stanwood, Michigan, and Denver, Colorado. All along the way we visited the buffalo association members we'd met at that first meeting in Denver.

As we sped across Iowa, we said a quick hello to my family and to the Sherman's buffalo farm, the birthplace of our animals. The Shermans would also be attending the Denver meeting, and we agreed to meet there in a few days.

Veering north, we turned into South Dakota, where our first destination was a visit to the Triple U Ranch, the vast family enterprise of Roy Houck, our buffalo association president. Roy, his charming wife, Nellie, and their two sons, Jerry and Tom, run this fifty-thousand-acre spread, which is home to thousands of registered Hereford cattle, quarter horses, and fifteen hundred buffalo.

The Houcks' ranch is thirty-five miles from town, and on that rolling, grass-mantled prairie there wasn't a house to be seen all those miles. The only signs of human life were two rural mailboxes perched alongside the dusty road, hinting of a remote homestead out of sight from the road.

The third mailbox stood sentinel at the entrance gate to the Triple U Ranch. Driving through the arched gateway, we assumed we had arrived at the Houcks. The driveway dipped into a draw, climbed up a divide, and curved onward over the rolling plains. We drove for five miles before rounding a gentle slope where we saw the settlement of barns, sheds, and ranch houses which was home to the Houcks and their hired hands. The very length of their driveway gave an indication of the size of this family empire.

The Houcks greeted us with warm Western hospitality. Though I'd met Nellie Houck only briefly the year before, her friendly, gracious ways made us friends immediately.

Still awed by the remoteness of their ranch, I said, "You're really way off by yourselves here."

Roy nodded, smiling. "Our neighbors are so far away we have to have our own tomcat."

When the Houcks drove us on a tour of their buffalo pastures, we were amazed at the size of their operation. Enclosed in buffalo fence like our Superfence was thirty thousand acres, and this was divided into nineteen separate pastures. Comprehending that fencing task was like trying to understand the immensity of the universe—beyond my mental capacities.

Even though buffalo were a common sight to us, it was thrilling to see such an enormous herd in one place. Some ambled about, grazing; others lay ruminating and dozing. The herds of long ago must have looked like this when they were spread out over the treeless plains.

Not far from the buffalo herd we discovered a prairie dog town. The fat, curious little animals stood up on their hind legs and stared at us.

"Aren't they cute?" I purred.

"You wouldn't think they were cute if your horse stepped in one of their holes and broke his leg, and maybe your neck, too," Roy retorted. "We'll have to get out here tomorrow and poison the whole village."

Nellie explained to me that any burrowing animal was anathema on a ranch because of the danger to horses. Prairie dogs and badgers could not be tolerated.

While preparing lunch, Nellie and I got acquainted. The Triple U was presently without a cook, and Nellie explained this was a frequent condition. The cooks who were hired assumed their duties with good intentions, but a few weeks of remote isolation soon drove them back to neon lights.

Lunch proved to be a hearty meal. The hard-working ranchers needed much more nourishment than the soup and sandwich of the sedentary businessman. From the mealtime conversation I quickly gathered Nellie was a most versatile woman, equally at home in the governor's mansion and state political activities, or on the back of a cutting horse. One of the hired hands proudly boasted that Nellie was the most skillful hand on the ranch when it came to working and cutting cattle. A slight, white-haired, attractive woman, only her wind-tanned skin hinted that she was a rancher's wife.

Roy obviously adored and respected his wife, and thoroughly enjoyed telling tales on her. His blue eyes twinkling with amused affection, he told of the time

244

Nellie was helping round up some wandering buffalo. Spotting a bunch across a flood-swollen draw, she tried to urge her quarter horse to wade across. The horse balked, refusing to move into the water until Nellie became thoroughly incensed at the horse's disobedience to her command. Finally, the horse obeyed, stepping into the water, which to Nellie's surprise, but not the horse's, was over six feet deep. As her horse plunged through the icy water, struggling to regain a foothold, the heaving lunges threw Nellie onto the saddle horn which snagged fast her borrowed oversized blue jeans. When the horse and Nellie reached the other side, separately, Nellie was without pants, her jeans hanging jauntily from the saddle horn.

Joining with the others, Nellie laughed heartily, recalling her predicament. "There I was," she chuckled, "standing there in soggy long Johns."

The conversation moved to the methods of checking on their cattle. Though cattlemen still do a lot of horseback riding, mechanization has become a time-saving way of keeping track of livestock. When you consider that the Triple U cattle and buffalo can wander over a range of one hundred and eighty square miles, it would take a lot of jeep driving or time in the saddle to cover this territory. The Houcks maintain two airplanes with which in a few hours they can check their entire holdings by air.

"How about an aerial view of the ranch?" the Houcks' son-in-law, Jim, asked Bill and me. Bill accepted immediately, but I began mumbling excuses about helping with the dishes, and finally, I had to admit my cowardice over being more than three feet from the ground.

To Westerners, cowardice is nearly as bad as wanton immorality. I had lost face and shown I was of weak moral fiber. As Bill and Jim rose to leave, Houck's granddaughter, Mary, spoke up. "Well, then, if you're not going for a plane ride, you can go horseback riding with me."

Bill turned in the doorway, grinning at my predicament. He knew I hadn't ridden a horse in twenty years, and was frightened at the thought of climbing aboard any four-legged beast. I gulped, torn between two terrifying alternatives. I dared not decline both.

Mary settled my dilemma by grabbing my clammy hand and tugging me toward the back door. "Come on, you can ride Dan. He's real gentle. My three-year-old cousin rides him all the time."

With trembling knees, I heaved myself into the saddle of the big horse. Looking at the hard, baked ground far below I shivered at the altitude. Just as I was wishing I'd chosen the plane ride, where at least I'd have a seat belt, I heard the roar of the Super Cub making its take-off run down the grass runway. It disappeared in a valley, then rose above a slope, its nose tipped heavenward in a steep climb. I clutched the saddle horn and decided the horse wasn't so tall after all.

Bill's airborne tour proved exciting. First climbing to seven thousand feet, Jim pointed out Standing Butte and other ranch landmarks, then put the plane into a steep dive. Bill is not a brave flier, and before the Super Cub leveled out at fifteen feet above the buffalo grass, his pulse and blood pressure had risen to amazing heights. Jim pointed toward a herd of antelope racing through a coulee, and they chased them across the rolling prairie. After upsetting several small bands of antelope and checking on the cattle and buffalo herds, Jim turned the plane back toward the ranch house.

At such low altitude, Bill spotted a badger just leaving a water hole. He nudged his pilot and pointed down toward the animal. Instantly, Jim banked, his practiced eye calculating wind speed and direction from the waving grass, and settled the plane down on a gentle slope near the badger. Even before the prop had stopped whirling, Jim had removed his seat belt, opened the door, and began removing the two control sticks.

"Choose your weapon," Jim said, thrusting the two sticks toward Bill. The twelve-inch metal pipes were the only weapons available aboard the plane. Jim and Bill dashed after the badger, each racing on one side of the waddling animal. Cut off from his den and enraged, the badger began to attack his tormentors. Cornered, he fought savagely. When he ran at Bill, Jim would throw his control stick at the badger, and when the animal turned on him, Bill struck. After two sharp head blows from the continuing double flank attack, the badger staggered. Jim quickly leaped to the stunned animal and swung a crushing blow to the animal's skull. Another hole-digging animal had been eliminated.

The two hunters wanted to take their prize back with them to show to all of us their resourcefulness in the wilds. Not daring to put the odorous, bleeding badger inside the plane, Jim's eyes narrowed as he pondered how to manage.

Suddenly, he knelt. "Our shoelaces, Doc—they'll do it fine," he said. The two men removed their shoelaces and tied the badger's four legs to the wing struts.

Bill nervously wondered how the one-sided weight of the badger would affect flying, but after a quick test of the wind, Jim took off smoothly, and they were airborne.

My horseback tour had just ended, and I was wondering if I would ever sit again, when the plane circled low over the ranch houses.

One of the ranch hands pointed, "Look, they have something tied to the wing."

"It looks like an animal," Nellie said.

Expectantly, we all watched the small plane land, practically in the front yard, and taxi up to the front door. Wondering what the afternoon hunt had yielded, we ran up to the plane. As soon as the engine stopped, strange, guttural, rasping sounds could be heard coming from the trussed animal.

The windy ride on the wing had resuscitated the badger, and as he struggled against his shoestring bindings, he growled savagely. One of the ranch hands brought a pistol, and the hardy animal was destroyed.

Bill counts the spontaneous badger chase as one of his fondest hunting episodes.

After leaving the Houcks and their Triple U ranch, we stopped to see Don and Adeline Hight and their trained Buffalo Bill. Though our car radio had just announced the temperature was one hundred and one degrees, we found them putting up hay. Just as in Michigan, during Dakota hay-making time the thermometer always seems to climb to record temperatures. Don insisted upon quitting, which left his teen-age son and nephew with the hot, dusty work. Bruce was sent in as a substitute for Don, and the three young boys took off on the tractors and hay-loaders to do men's work.

Though we had seen many thousand acres of Hight's land, I hadn't yet seen a buffalo, but when we drove up to their house I saw the first buffalo signs. Buffalo skulls decorated nearly every stave of the picket fence. On Hight's back porch was a most unusual hatrack: a huge, mounted buffalo head with two cowboy hats and a horse halter hanging rakishly from the curving horns.

As we entered the kitchen I discovered we had interrupted Adeline in the final stages of filling rows of glass jars with clear, crimson-colored jelly. Appropriately, it was buffalo-berry jelly. I had heard of Indian squaws gathering buffalo berries long ago, but never dreamed it was still done. The jelly's bright color was beautiful, and Adeline spread some on a slice of homemade bread for me to sample. Deliciously tart, it reminded me of currant jelly, and I resolved to investigate whether buffalo berry bushes could be grown in Michigan. Buffalo berries might do for buffalo hump steak what cranberries have done for turkey.

Late in the afternoon we prepared to leave for the Black Hills where we had reservations for the night. We invited the Hights to join us on our leisurely, roundabout journey to Denver, but their son was scheduled to compete in a rodeo that evening. Participating in rodeos is to ranchers' sons what Little League baseball is to suburban boys.

Though the Black Hills, the legendary Paha Sapa of the Indians, is one of the most spectacularly beautiful places on earth, our reason for going there was to visit Custer State Park, where one of our friends, Wes Broer, was a ranger. Bill wanted to study their corral and cutting chute arrangement as a model for our future needs.

At Custer, Wes, who was also secretary of our buffalo association, drove us around the seventy-four thousand acre park in his bright red forest ranger car. Only a ride on a speeding fire engine would have excited the children more. Even though the park has one of the largest herds of bison in the world, finding buffalo to see wasn't easy in that large an area. Through reports of other rangers over the car s two-way radio, we did locate two different herds, each consisting of several hundred fine buffalo.

As we drove about the park on our buffalo-hunt, Wes pointed out the old decaying movie location sites of "How the West Was Won," and the "The Last Hunt." We listened, fascinated, to his tales of how the buffalo stampede and shooting scenes were managed. There is no more beautiful scenery in the world than the rolling, pine-swathed Black Hills, with the green valleys, red rocks, and brilliantly blue sky. No wonder so many Western movies are filmed there.

As we walked about surveying the huge corrals and

squeeze chutes used in separating and vaccinating the buffalo, we had to be cautious of rattlesnakes, throwing rocks ahead of us as we walked. Wes told us that the previous summer no visitors had been hurt by the free-roaming buffalo, but sixteen people were bitten by rattlesnakes.

Custer is a state-owned park, and it shares its long, southern boundary with a national park, Wind Cave National Park. Both parks have large herds of wild animals, especially buffalo, and there appears to be some good-natured rivalry about the quality of their respective buffalo herds. The gate joining the two parks is open so tourists may have access to both parks. However, to keep the state-owned and federally-owned animals from integrating, a cattle guard is fixed within the gate. This is a metal grating set into the roadbed, consisting of parallel metal bars, close enough together so an automobile can drive over, but far enough apart so an animal cannot, or will not, attempt to walk over it. A latticework grating in a sidewalk presents the same barrier to women wearing high-heeled shoes.

As we drove near the boundary between the two parks, we noticed a solitary, huge buffalo bull at the southern end of Custer State Park. He appeared to be heading purposefully toward the entrance to Wind Cave Park.

Wes laughed. "I want to see this," he said. "That old bull is one of Wind Cave's bulls. I suspect he goes back and forth freely between our two parks. I've been wondering how he does it."

We sat still in the parked car, watching.

The monstrous, shaggy bull finally reached the dirt road, where he ambled ponderously toward the gate with its restricting cattle guard. He never hesitated or even slowed down. When he reached the parallel metal grating with its deep holes between, he plodded on, placing his huge hoofs on the slippery metal bars. Once a hoof slipped on the slick metal, yet he didn't fall. Three more steps and he was back in his federal park. The crafty rascal had probably increased the buffalo population in both state and national herds, unwittingly messing up their genetic records.

After our meandering course to take in all the important sights of the buffalo world, at last we arrived in Denver. Many of the buffalo association members already were there. We met the Shermans, Hights, and Houcks in the hotel lobby where they were planning the evening activities. Roy Houck knew of a nearby dining spot he was sure we'd all enjoy.

While reservations were being made, I quickly settled the children in our hotel room. With a hamburger and milkshake supper in front of the television set, they considered themselves living in high style. Bill and I left to join our buffalo-breeding friends.

Our dinner club was directly across the street from the hotel, and as we descended the five steps into the vestibule of the French restaurant, we praised Roy for his choice of such a convenient place. Roy's sly grin said that its accessibility was a minor asset.

Inside, our chatter hushed when we confronted a life-sized oil painting of a bare, well-fleshed blonde in a reclining posture. Following the maître d', we passed through the main dining room decorated in ornate, authentic Victorian fashion. Beyond a magnificent hand-painted, hand-carved bar, a small jazz combo entertained.

We were led upstairs into one of the many small, private dining rooms, and as we seated ourselves at the long, linen-covered table, I stared in awe at the huge mosaic fireplace in the center of the room. Directly over the table hung a delicate crystal chandelier. While looking upward, I saw we were surrounded by gilded framed oil paintings similar to the one which had greeted us downstairs. Nude women encircled us, smil-

251

ing down from the walls, their full, almost portly figures showing the tastes of the past. The art objects, the furnishings, even the building itself, were authentically nineteenth century.

"What's the history of this place, Roy?" I asked.

His pale eyes twinkling mischievously, Roy tipped his chair back on its hind legs. "This place is a Denver landmark, nearly one hundred years old; a very popular spot in its heyday."

He paused, grinning pointedly at each of us four women seated around the table. "Until the turn of the century, this place was an elite, high-class brothel."

We four wives gasped collectively.

Roy threw back his head and roared over our confusion.

The men in the group suddenly took on new life, sitting up straight and looking about with new interest. Until now, they had been secretly wondering why a rugged cattleman like Roy would bring them to a French restaurant.

Unconsciously, I looked upward at the voluptuous, unclothed women portrayed in the paintings.

Roy saw my glance. "Yes, you're guessing correctly, Pinkie," he chuckled. "Those girls are all former occupants of the place. But don't stick up your nose at them. Many did very well for themselves. With true Western democratic spirit, a Colorado governor married one of them, and she became a society leader."

Ghosts of the past seemed to float about the room, and exotic history exuded from the *fleur de lis* flocked wallpaper. How strange it seemed!

Assuming a haughty look, I said, "Well, at least *I* can say *I've* never been in a place like this before."

From across the table, Francis Sherman laughed. "Well, just wait until I tell your father I saw you at a disorderly house in Denver."

Maddeningly, I blushed at his teasing.

Deciding that the men were having too good a time making the ladies squirm, Nellie giggled, "Roy, you seem to feel quite at home here."

The repartee continued as Roy described the underground rail line which still existed under the building. By way of a tunnel, the tracks ran under the street and terminated in the basement of our hotel just across the street. This little nicety had made it possible for prominent men to visit their "lady" friends surreptitiously.

"Scoundrels!" we wives exclaimed. Imagine those proper Victorian gentlemen settling their wives and children in a hotel suite, then slipping through the tunnel to say "howdy" to the painted women!

The steward arrived with huge menus printed entirely in French. In true cowboy fashion, the men, many of whom had studied French in college, suddenly feigned total ignorance. With exaggerated country bumpkin manner, they besieged the confused Creole steward with requests for translations, and threw him into suffering agony by asking why there weren't any beans or hog jowls on the menu.

The steward's clipped mustache quivered against his reddening skin. When he returned, carrying the tray laden with salad bowls, his hands were trembling noticeably, and Francis Sherman added the last straw to the waiter's nervousness.

Softly tapping the Creole's arm, Francis smiled sweetly and said, "This is sure a nice place. It's really swell of you to let us bring our own women."

The salad bowl in the steward's hand spun across the room, spewing lettuce against the mahogany wainscoting. With something close to a sob, the poor man fled.

When the steward returned, he was reinforced by the company of the maître d' who helped clean up the carpeting and stayed for some time to lend moral support to the disarranged waiter. The dignity and unflustered manner of the maître d' showed his years of practice in handling unruly cattlemen.

What with the excellent cuisine and the titillating, licentious atmosphere, camaraderie and good conversation flourished. Inevitably, talk turned to buffalo and finally to the ruggedness and superiority of the beast which was our common bond.

Wes Broer, the park ranger, told about one of his duties which was shooting buffalo. Annually, the Custer State Park herd was thinned through sale and slaughter to keep the herd population within the feeding capability of the range. For years, Wes had been shooting buffalo, and he knew exactly where to hit them.

Don Hight told of the time he shot a bull and ran up to the fallen animal to slit its throat for bleeding it. As he began to cut the supposedly dead animal's throat, the bull jumped up, and Don had to leap away. With only its windpipe severed, the buffalo galloped off, clouds of frosty breath forming in front of his slashed throat. Without stopping, the bull ran for eight miles and disappeared into the badlands. After this traumatic experience, the buffalo was so wary and cunning, a hunting party had to track him down like a wild animal.

When buffalo-breeders really want to boast about the toughness of buffalo, one of their favorite stories concerns James "Scotty" Phillip, a well-known cattleman around the turn of the century. Mr. Phillip was married to an Oglala woman who persuaded him to raise some buffalo to save the species from extinction. After building a fine herd of bison, Mr. Phillip made the statement that one of his buffalo could easily defeat a Spanish fighting bull. This boast was challenged, and ultimately, Mr. Phillip took a buffalo bull to Mexico to make good his brag.

At the Mexican bullring, the buffalo bull was turned into the arena first. The shaggy brown beast ambled

254

into the ring, glanced sullenly about, and lay down on the dusty ground. The Mexican crowd roared, howling whatever is the Spanish for "boo!", convinced the American buffalo was a quivering coward. Next, the black fighting bull, the toro bravo, was released. Snorting and glaring fiercely, he came trotting into the ring. When the bull saw the reclining buffalo, he galloped straight at him, but stopped thirty feet short, glaring and pawing the ground.

The buffalo heaved himself up, lowered his head, and charged the Spanish fighting bull, killing him instantly. With a satisfied grunt, the buffalo calmly walked away from the dead foe and lay down again.

We buffalo owners get a gleeful and savage pleasure from that tale. Perhaps it's a childish trait, going back to those "I bet my dog can lick your dog" times. Whatever the psychological hang-up may be, we seem to relish having the fiercest pets of all.

On our return journey from the buffalo-breeders' convention we didn't meander all over the prairies as we did on the outgoing leg of our trip. We had seen all the buffalo herds and were anxious to get home to our own herd. We allowed ourselves two side trips, both of which were to see "cattalo." Though crossing cattle and buffalo and achieving a new superior hybrid strain was one of our fondest projects, we had never seen a live cattalo. Thus far, Angie and Mable had failed us, not having produced an offspring by Kahtanka.

First, we visited Pete and Ethel Rosander at Belle Fourche, just north of the Black Hills. Pete had been crossing cattle and buffalo for twenty-five years, achieving hybrids with varying proportions of buffalo blood. Pete knew the exact ancestry of every animal. "That one's one thirty-second buffalo, and that light one is one-eighth," he explained, pointing out the different cattalo. Strangely, two of the dark brown hybrids, which looked very similar to full-blooded buffalo, contained a smaller percentage of buffalo ancestry than some of the lighter-colored animals.

Heading eastward, we sought out two cattalo kept in a feed lot in eastern South Dakota. Don Hight had told us about these two animals of his which he had produced after a great deal of trouble. Don had put twenty shorthorn cows in a pasture with a buffalo bull. Seven of these cows did not become pregnant. Eleven died during their pregnancy. Two successful cows each produced a bull calf, both of which proved to be sterile. These two sterile bulls were now four years old, and Don's description of their size had made us anxious to see them.

The sight of these two magnificent specimens was most impressive. Each weighed thirty-four hundred pounds, larger than their buffalo father or their short-horn mother. In the feed lot these animals were putting on eight pounds of good meat every day, a fantastic weight gain, almost unbelievable to beef producers. The protein diets fed to animals in a feed lot were utilized more efficiently by the cattalo than by domestic beef, which customarily gain two and one-half pounds of body weight daily in the feed lot.

Creamy white in color, Don's two hybrids were freckled all over with auburn spots. Their humps were not as pronounced as those of full-blooded buffalo, but their hindquarters were heavier and their tails longer and bushier.

Seeing these animals spurred us homeward to continue our crossbreeding investigations. We were anxious to learn why domestic cows had problems with their pregnancies, developing too much water around the unborn calf. Apparently, the mother's system treated the half-buffalo calf as a foreign body, attempting to reject the invader. The problem seemed similar to that encountered in humans receiving transplanted organs,

256

where the recipient's immunity system tries to reject the transplanted organ.

Perhaps the most extensive project ever undertaken in crossing buffalo and cattle was done in Saskatchewan in the Wainwright experiments. Subsidized by the Canadian government and lasting over a period of fifty years, this project should have been successful since a large herd and extensive facilities were available for the experiment. However, upon reading the reports of this project, we found many flaws in their genetic records. They had not used practical selection in choosing bulls to improve their herd. Instead of using selective breeding, the Canadians apparently established this as a nature study to see how well these animals would cross and produce beef animals when left to their own resources.

By selective breeding, we hoped to save the good qualities of domestic beef—the large hindquarters which produce good steaks—and add the large front quarters and hump roasts of the buffalo strain. In addition to improving the meat carcass, we hoped to instill in the hybrid animal the endurance and rugged individualism of the buffalo.

Upon our return to Stanwood we were greeted by a conflicting hospital situation. The enactment of Medicare had changed the picture for Mecosta Memorial. Patients who before had been unable to pay for their hospital care, thus being treated on a charity basis, now were covered by Medicare, and the hospital received payment for their care. Though there was now more revenue for the hospital, there was another side to the coin. With Medicare came added regulations, making necessary many expensive changes if the hospital were to continue to be approved for treating Medicare patients.

To meet these new regulations, architects had evaluated the hospital building and determined that the necessary changes would cost $300,000. Raising that sum of money seemed nearly impossible. Even with volunteer help available locally for some of the construction work, electricians, plumbers, and other skilled help would have to be paid.

Though worried over the longevity of Mecosta Memorial's existence, the doctors, nurses, and hospital personnel went about their work, now busier than ever. Anticipating the arrival of Medicare, many elderly poor people had been postponing medical treatment for over a year, awaiting the time when they would be covered by the new plan. Once their coverage was in effect, they sought their long-needed care, and empty hospital beds filled.

More than ever, Mecosta Memorial was needed; yet its chances for surviving seemed dim indeed.

The
Will to Die

16 Indian summer is the nicest time of year for buffalo-watching. After the first killing frost the insects disappear, allowing the buffalo to graze contentedly. The scarlet maples and yellow birch form a brilliant background for the darkening animals. This is the time of year to sit on the hillside, chew a stem of grass, and gaze on the tranquil, browsing animals. Our oldest calves were already dark, and the auburn coats of the two youngest were well mottled with dark brown. Very appropriately, the Sioux called September "the moon of the black calf."

The buffalo often take a siesta in the early afternoon, snoozing in the weak autumn sunlight. Without the aggravating flies, they lie still for nearly an hour, the only movement being the fluttering buffalo-birds.

Buffalo-birds are the constant companions of our buffalo, hopping among the huge hoofs and perching on the woolly backs. The buffalo appear entirely indifferent to them, but we suspect the buffalo-bird serves to keep insects off the buffalo's hump and back, an area he can't reach with his short tail. Buffalo-birds better be good for something. They are known as the laziest birds in the world. They don't even make nests for themselves. Instead, the female sneakily lays her egg in another bird's nest, and always in a nest of a bird smaller than she.

To the poor bird whose nest is selected, it's like discovering a foundling on your doorstep, only we humans are smart enough to know the foundling isn't our baby. When the unsophisticated bird discovers the huge egg in her nest, however, she thinks it's hers, and dutifully sets on it along with her own smaller eggs. The big trouble comes when the egg hatches and the baby buffalo-bird, twice the size of his foster brothers and sisters, demands twice the amount of food. The foster mother and father sometimes actually kill themselves trying to fill the huge mouth of their adopted baby. Their own nestlings are short-changed, and sometimes not one of them survives except the baby buffalo-bird.

No one loves a buffalo-bird, except a buffalo with a pesky fly on his hump.

One afternoon as the buffalo were taking their usual siesta, Bill decided to let the animals move into the alfalfa field for a few days of richer pasture. Opening the gate, he called the animals and retreated to the safety of the truck. The buffalo stretched to shake off sleep and happily entered the lush hayfield. For quite a while Bill watched them eat. Then he noticed a dark lump back in the pasture where they'd been sleeping. Right away he feared he had a sick or dead animal lying there.

He drove the truck back into the pasture, and as he got closer, sure enough, there was one of the calves lying very still on its side. Jumping from the truck, Bill walked up to the quiet little thing. He held his hand up to the small muzzle to feel for breath. The little nose began to twitch and sniff. After a half-minute of sniffing, the calf began to blink and squint. His glazed eyes rolled around, then suddenly focused on Bill. The eyes bulged in horror and with a shrill bleat, the calf jumped up and tore off, bawling for his mother. That little calf had been sleeping so soundly the whole herd had moved off, and he hadn't wakened. We laughed at the

260

poor calf's predicament, yet we were surprised that his mother went off and left him. Usually, mother buffalo are, by human standards, over-protective. Her casualness was amazing.

As we watched the animals, we grew more and more worried about Ringo. She appeared listless and thin. Finally, there was no doubt; she was definitely ill. Unable to eat, she lost weight quickly and seemed to have one hoof in the grave.

A friend who has a large farm ten miles east of ours had shown a keen interest in our buffalo. When he heard we had a sick buffalo, he immediately volunteered to take her to his place and admit her to one of his sick pens. There she could be examined and treated in confinement.

One chilly October afternoon he arrived in his pickup truck, which had been well reinforced with stout boards. A canvas was stretched over the top, a precaution which darkens the interior and calms an animal during shipment. Bill called the herd into another pasture, but closed the gate before the trailing Ringo could join them. We now had her alone, confined in a fifty-acre pasture. A makeshift corral of snow fence was set up, and, if we could entice her into the wide end of the corral, we could slowly move the snow fence inward, forcing her to enter the truck.

It sounded simple, but when Ringo realized she was completely cut off from the protection of the herd, and that human beings were trying to push her around, she made a quick recovery from her drooping, sluggish ways. She tore around the pasture, galloping, charging, wheeling, and glaring. Forming a huge human circle around her, we slowly forced her toward the side of the pasture where the truck was waiting. People driving by stopped to see what the commotion was about, and several of them joined us in our big roundup circle.

The volunteers grinned, and I could imagine them

261

thinking, "My wife will never believe me when I tell her what I did after work today."

Thirty to forty feet separated each of us in the circle, and every few minutes Ringo tried to dash through one of these open spaces. The grass was knee-high and thick. Running through it was like a horrible nightmare where you're trying to run through water, except that even in my worst nightmares I've never had a buffalo charging me at the same time. Whenever Ringo made a charge toward an open slot near me, it took all my courage to dash toward her, waving my arms and yelling. Though hornless and sick, she loomed mighty large as she bore down. When she'd finally whirl off and charge toward another opening, I'd just stand there with my knees shaking. It takes real fortitude to buffalo a buffalo.

At last we got her confined within our flimsy corral, facing the truck. The final problem involved getting her to step up the ramp into the truck. No amount of pushing or goading from behind worked, so Bill decided to try honey instead of vinegar. Well, not really honey: it was ground feed covered with thick molasses. Bill climbed into the truck and started calling softly to Ringo, holding out a juicy fistful of sweets.

For ten minutes Ringo stood her ground, snorting and shaking her head. I held my assigned section of snow fence and worried about what would happen when she entered the truck. Would she crush Bill against the side, stomp on him, kick him? At that moment I wished Bill had taken up some nice, safe hobby like racing in the Indianapolis Five Hundred.

When she finally walked up the ramp, it was an anticlimax. She calmly licked the food from Bill's hand and stood there patiently as if to say, "Well, all right . . . if you really want me to go."

Now that Ringo was being given attention all seemed

262

right with the world. The days grew shorter and the nights nippier as the season of Halloween approached. The children were especially excited this year, as they had been invited to a real old-fashioned, bob-for-apples Halloween party. We'd spent days preparing spooky costumes, and all was excitement as the big day arrived.

Early that morning the farmer who was nursing Ringo called with bad news. Ringo had just passed on to the happy hunting ground. I wasn't surprised, for her medical reports had been getting progressively worse. After she was placed in a barn, her condition went downhill fast. The confinement seemed to break her spirit and will to live.

Puzzled about what sort of arrangements must be made, I asked him to notify Bill. Buffalo disposal wasn't my line. Vaguely I recalled something about a rendering works which took dead animals and turned them into glue. At least, my second-grade teacher always said, "Now, children, don't eat glue. It's made from dead horses."

I felt a tinge of sadness for poor dead Ringo. She'd always been such a pathetic outcast. But I didn't let it ruin my day, not until Bill called later in the morning.

"We're going to have an autopsy performed on Ringo. I want to know what her trouble was," he said.

"Good idea," I said, giving my approval.

"Well. . . ," Bill hesitated, "I'm going to be tied up at the hospital all day, so you'll have to deliver her for the autopsy."

"Me?" I screamed. Take a buffalo to an autopsy? I sputtered and tried to laugh, but I knew he wasn't kidding. Finally, I gasped, "Take her where?"

"To Lansing, of course," Bill tried to sound matter-of-fact. "That's where the diagnostic center is."

"Forget it," I said. "Me, drive a truck a hundred and thirty miles to Lansing? You know better than that."

Bill patiently explained that I wouldn't have to drive a truck. "I've emptied the trunk of my car and I'm sure we can cram Ringo in there. She's real thin."

This was going too far. Even I have to draw the line somewhere. Bill had it all planned out, and I had to think fast.

"Bill, this is Halloween," I protested. "The kids are invited to a party this evening, and I have to drive them there and pick them up." The party was ten miles away. He couldn't say, "Let them walk."

Instead, he said, "Drive fast, honey! If you scoot right along, you can be back in time for the party."

I tried to argue, but he went right on. "I'm in a hurry now. I'll go pick up Ringo and get her in the trunk. You meet me at the hospital in half an hour and trade cars with me. Now don't waste time thinking of excuses. Just hurry!"

I was left sputtering into a dead telephone. He'd hung up.

I muttered grimly as I changed to suitable traveling clothes, checked my purse for money and gasoline credit cards, and studied a map. I've run some crazy errands, but delivering a dead buffalo to the state capital was something else.

As I concentrated on the best and quickest route to Lansing, my mind began to wander, Walter Mitty style. I pictured myself speeding along the expressway at seventy miles an hour, racing time. My imagination conjured up blood—slowly drip, drip, dripping from the trunk. Soon a state policeman picked up my bloody trail, and a siren screamed me off the road.

In my vision, a grim uniform approached, but instead of a perfunctory, "May I see your driver's license, lady?" I was greeted with a drawn pistol.

"Okay, sister, out of the car!" he barked. "Put up your hands."

He motioned me away from the car; then he reached

inside and snatched my car keys. "Now let's have a look inside that trunk." He glared at me with repugnance.

"But it's only a dead buffalo, officer," I blubbered.

"Yeah, sure," he snarled, "and I'm Crazy Horse and this gun is a peace pipe."

The ringing telephone brought me out of my daymare. It was Bill.

"Glad I caught you before you left. You don't have to go to Lansing after all," he announced apologetically. "The local veterinarian can do the autopsy here."

A big sigh of relief was the only thanks I could muster. But another person should be even more grateful for the trip's cancellation. Somewhere between Stanwood and Lansing an unsuspecting state trooper had just been spared a most traumatic confrontation.

Ringo probably would have died anyway, but Bill was convinced that confining her in a barn precipitated her death.

"Being cooped up killed her off," Bill mourned.

"You mean Ringo lost her will to live?" I asked.

"It's not that passive a thing," Bill explained. "She didn't lose her will to live. She exerted her will to die." Bill continued, describing that, not just in buffalo, but also in humans, there is a determination to live which makes some people survive what are usually fatal illnesses or injuries.

"These people struggle to survive because they want to live," Bill said. "Other people, just as determinedly, want to die. It's more than losing their zest to live; they actively will themselves to die."

"Oh, Bill," I protested, "surely no one can just decide he wants to die, and then die."

"Yes, they can, and I've seen it happen," Bill insisted. "Don't you remember my telling you about the first case of this will-to-die I ran into? It was back during my residency."

As a young surgical resident, Bill had been upset and

puzzled by this first inexplicable case. An attractive young mother of five children had been admitted to the surgical floor for a simple pelvic procedure. The night before her surgery, Bill was taking her history and writing up a pre-surgical evaluation of this pretty, thirty-two-year-old woman.

When he asked the usual questions of whether she'd had mumps or scarlet fever, she said, "It doesn't make any difference what you find out about my past illnesses, because I'm going to die, anyway."

Before undergoing an operation, many patients express a fear of dying, but it bothered Bill the way this patient said, "I'm going to die." Though her voice was dull and flat, there was a tone of strong determination in her statement. Bill tried to draw her out, wondering why this woman with five dependent children would wish not to live. She was reticent, and Bill managed to get only the impression that there was an insoluble problem in her life.

Trying to cheer her by commenting on her attractiveness, Bill also reminded her that all problems eventually recede and fade away; that she had a great deal to live for. She remained unresponsive.

Following her surgery the next morning, the young woman appeared to be in good condition, physically. All signs were normal, but her appearance was lacking in spirit. Lethargically, she answered the questioning of her doctors, but, as if in a severe depression, she showed utterly no concern for pain, suffering, or her health.

On the second day following surgery she was causing great concern among the doctors. Although all laboratory tests were normal, her condition was deteriorating. A psychiatrist was called in on the case. He spent a great deal of time working with her for two days, and finally decided it was necessary to give her shock treatments. Even following these, the young mother remained unresponsive, continuing her same lack of concern for her own life. Hour after hour she lay unmoving, her eyes half open, not even interested in sleeping. Seven days after her operation she fulfilled her prediction by dying. An autopsy revealed a moderate amount of pelvic inflammation, yet her white blood count had never risen markedly. White blood cells combat infection and increase in number tremendously whenever an infection is present. In seeking death, this young woman seemed to have inhibited the production of white blood cells, thus suppressing her body's defenses for fighting disease.

This power of the mind over the body made a deep impression upon Bill. That a young woman who seemingly had much for which to live, could will herself to die, taught him the importance of each patient's mental attitude.

During his second year of practice in Stanwood, he acquired forty-two-year-old Vivian for a patient. Her flat monotone, accented only occasionally by a whine or whimper, touched off a warning buzzer in his diagnostic thoughts. He had heard that same dull drone from the young mother who willed herself to die.

Vivian had many chronic complaints and desperately wanted to be operated upon. For some time Bill refused to do the surgery, but when she lost fifty pounds in a sixty-day period, he had no choice but to tackle her gallbladder-duct pathology.

Before surgery, she became even more depressed, and her blood pressure dropped alarmingly. Vivian did very poorly during the surgery, remaining in shock continuously, unless supportive medications were given. These medications were extremely toxic, and she developed severe side effects following surgery.

In a semi-coma, Vivian lay sluggishly in her intensive care bed, with continuous fluids and medications dripping into her veins to keep her out of shock. For five days Bill remained with her constantly, even sleeping at

267

the hospital. With so many intravenous fluids going, the veins in both arms and ankles became ruined, and on the fifth day, Bill prepared to dissect out a thigh vein to use. Vivian's kidneys were functioning well, and her blood level was being maintained, but she would not hold up a blood pressure without drugs. Tests showed a low white blood count, which reminded Bill that the body's defense mechanism was not fighting.

As Bill bent over Vivian, dissecting out the thigh vein, the ankle vein presently receiving the fluids broke down, and medication could no longer enter. Immediately, her blood pressure fell to nothing. Bill felt a weak heartbeat and very slow respiration. Comatose, and in obvious shock, her skin became clammy. Bill shouted her name twice, but her eyelids never fluttered. Hurrying on with the vein cut-down, Bill feared Vivian would die before he was able to get the fluids started in the newly-prepared vein.

Tense and perspiring, Bill glanced at his patient's face to see if he were hurting her. Amazingly, one wide-open eye was staring at him with a clear, lucid look. The minute Bill looked up, the eye snapped shut.

Bill was enraged. Vivian was frighteningly near death, yet she was aware of what was happening. Bill realized she was enjoying his intense attention and anguished concern over her suffering. Saying nothing, he quickly finished the cut-down and got the blood pressure sustaining fluids dripping once again.

Immediately, Vivian's blood pressure rose, and she became responsive. After asking the nurses to leave the room, Bill leaned over his patient and said, "Vivian, what's your minister's name? It's time to call him and your family, so you can make peace with everyone before you die."

Bill was attempting a tremendous gamble. Vivian was flirting with death—in fact, actively seducing death—but Bill guessed that she really didn't mean it. She wanted to cause concern and appear to be dying, but Bill suspected she really wanted to live.

When Bill spoke of death being imminent, Vivian's mouth flew open. "Oh, Doctor, I feel much better. I really think I'm going to be better now."

Bill shook his head soberly. In his most somber voice, he intoned, "This often happens just before the end. I must get the minister and your family now."

Vivian's round eyes were snapping angrily when Bill walked out of her hospital room.

The minister and family assembled, but within two hours after Bill's desperate gamble, Vivian's blood pressure rose to normal limits, and the flow of medications could be decreased drastically.

By early the next morning she was maintaining a good blood pressure with no intravenous fluids needed, a truly astounding recovery. Vivian had trifled with death flirtatiously, not realizing that wooing death is usually fatal. She had willed her body to die, but fortunately her spirit still wished to live.

When Bill finally came home after those five days of continuous tension and lack of sleep, he yawned, gave me a drowsy kiss, and sighed, "I think she'll make it now. She wants to live."

When I saw the tight, white look around his eyes and the new wrinkles in his forehead, I speedily ushered him off to bed. It looked as if the years he'd added to Vivian's life span had been taken from his own allotted time. Every time he waged a long battle to keep a patient alive, Bill injected some of his own vital forces into the patient.

Giving part of himself to each patient is one of the sacrifices a country doctor makes, because he becomes so involved with each patient. The demands of country practice are wearing, but the rewards are also great. I have never yet met a pompous country doctor, perhaps because they are ruled by the idea of being servants to

269

mankind, rather than striving to gain admittance to the most exclusive yacht club.

City doctors usually aren't close enough to their patients to know all that goes on behind the scenes. In a small town there are very few secrets. Even your doctor knows whether you are following his orders. If city doctors knew some of the things their patients did, they might reevaluate some of their medical ideas.

Faith-healing is a much more common practice than most city doctors suspect. The very thought of faith-healing makes most doctors gnash their teeth and roar, so naturally their patients don't tell them when they participate in anything medically unapproved.

Bill knew of one instance of faith-healing at Stanwood which would have made a city specialist tear his hair, had he ever learned of it. A local woman had been involved in a terrible auto accident in which she suffered severe lacerations, internal injuries, and many fractured bones. For three months she was hospitalized at a large medical center, after which she was sent home, still wearing a long cast on her right leg and a cast on her left arm. When she returned for her six-month check-up to the nationally-known orthopedic surgeon who was caring for her, he could not encourage her about her future. From the results of his examination of her injuries and from the X-ray findings, he concluded that it was unlikely she would ever walk again, and so informed her. The thirty-year-old woman took the dismal news stoically because, to her, the opinion of a famous orthopedic surgeon meant little compared to her faith in the power of prayer.

The following Sunday evening her wheelchair was pushed to her regular place for the weekly prayer meeting in the church. The gathering had heard of the unhappy medical prognosis, and this evening they united their prayers, appealing for heavenly intervention for the woman. The prayers for intercession continued for some time until one of the congregation received the message that their sister was healed, and that the cast should be removed.

Taking off the heavy plaster casts might have been quite an obstacle, except that one of the prayer-meeting participants was Jake, the janitor at the hospital. Quickly he went to the hospital emergency room, where he found the cast cutters.

Since he worked at the hospital, Jake was in the position of being the most medically-oriented person present, and he wielded the cast cutters, removing both the arm and leg casts.

"Thou art healed," intoned the preacher. "Rise, sister, and stand before your Lord."

Tremulously, the young woman leaned forward in her wheelchair, slowly letting her weight settle on her legs. With an angelic, radiant smile, she stood upright, straight and tall. After taking three hesitant, faltering steps toward the altar, the woman bowed her head in thankful prayer, tears streaming down her cheeks.

The congregation cried, "Hallelujah! It's a miracle!", and joined her in prayer.

Even before arriving at the hospital the next morning, Bill heard about the faith-healing meeting. The head nurse called to report that the cast cutters had been used during the night.

Once at the hospital, Jake, the janitor, met Bill at the rear entrance to report the medical miracle.

"I seen it with my own eyes, Doc!" he exclaimed. "I cut off the casts myself. I was going to be a doctor once. Guess I'd a been a pretty good one."

As a doctor, Bill was not involved with the case at all; he could stand back and watch with uninvolved interest. Besides adding a small prayer for her full recovery, Bill also believed there might be some scientific sense to her premature escape from the casts. Because the leg fracture had been healing so slowly, he believed that a little

271

stress at the fracture site might stimulate healing, where prolonged immobilization in the cast had not done so.

The woman's doctor would have been infuriated at this breach of his medical directions, but he was spared any knowledge of the sudden cure. The young woman never returned to him. Gradually, over the next few weeks, she increased exercise and weight-bearing on the leg fracture. After two months, she was walking normally and had good function of her arm. What had promised to become a medical failure and personal tragedy for the woman became, instead, a triumph of faith and belief. Some call it faith, some call it God, and others call in "mind over matter," but Bill had seen enough of it that he never scoffed over the power of the human will.

There had been several times when his own patients had ignored the currently acceptable medical regimen Bill had placed them upon, yet had recuperated even better than would be expected. Because of these instances, Bill accepted the fallibility of current medicine. There are still many unknowns in medical practice, and he was willing to keep an open mind.

Bill's grapevine informed him of the times his patients went to the old Indian herb doctor, or to a faith-healer, but instead of becoming livid with rage, as many doctors do, he accepted these illegitimate consultations as a part of the patient's search for health and vigor. Too many doctors alienate their patients by ridiculing their extra-medical searches. By accepting the fact that many of his patients were also seeking unapproved consultations with the herb doctor and faith-healer, Bill kept them under his watchful medical surveillance, not turning them over entirely to unscientific personnel.

A patient's desire to get well was many times more important than all the medications and surgical intervention a doctor could provide. Bill looked forward to the day when more was understood about how to infuse in a patient the will to recover and to live.

Constantly hanging over our heads was the specter of the three hundred thousand dollars needed by the hospital if it were to remain open. Each time a new crisis arose, Bill and I suffered pangs of insecurity. If the hospital were to close, our life at Stanwood would have to end. A surgeon without a hospital could not be a surgeon.

Feeling as if we were living temporarily, I postponed buying new bedspreads and kitchen curtains. So many times we had suffered through these threats to the survival of the hospital! Now I understood how wives of factory workers must feel when their husbands' industries are threatened with a shut-down or strike. We all yearn for security and permanence, conditions so elusive in Stanwood.

Early in December the first blizzard whistled in from the west. The ground was completely covered with snow, and huge drifts formed on the lee of fences. Winter closed in upon us, but with a good supply of hay, we felt prepared, and anticipated an uneventful winter. There was one experience, however, we had yet to endure.

People often asked, "What do you do if your buffalo get out?"

After an involuntary shudder, we had always been able to reply that our buffalo never bothered the fence—that they'd never gotten out.

But then at suppertime one very cold evening the telephone rang. It was Bill's office nurse, Wilma, panting and gasping for breath.

"One of the buffalo got out!" she cried. "It wants back in the pasture, and I can't get the gate open! Can you come and help me open the gate?"

Another crisis! The children and I hastily donned our jackets and boots and sped to the ranch.

Dusk was deepening to darkness as we pulled into the office parking lot, just in time to see the dim hump-backed shape of one buffalo heading eastward, outside the fence. In the knee-deep snow, Bill was stumbling along behind the shape, calling and pleading softly for its return to the fold.

Inside the office I found Wilma, shivering and stamping. She breathlessly reconstructed the escape.

It seems Bill had opened the pasture gate just wide enough to admit the truck with its load of hay. As he maneuvered the truck through the narrow opening, Worms had spotted the haystack outside the fence and quickly slipped out. Swiftly, Bill shut the gate to prevent any more escapes. Then he drove the hay-laden truck to the far end of the pasture, to entice the remaining animals away from the gate.

While he was Pied-Pipering the herd away, Worms suddenly discovered what she had done. She stopped nibbling on the haystack and stared bug-eyed at the pasture. The herd and her only child were out of sight. Starting for the gate, she found it shut (though a white-uniformed woman was frantically trying to force it open). With this provocation, Worms staged a one-animal buffalo dance. Her legs stiffened and her tail shot up in the air. The white-uniformed figure abandoned her post at the gate and shinnied up the tractor, to stand shivering on the slippery metal seat.

Worms jumped and snorted, pogo-sticking about the yard and parking lot. It was a dramatic tantrum. Since she couldn't speak, it was her way of saying, "Let me in! Let me in!"

Tiring from her buffalo dance tantrum, Worms decided to seek another way back into the pasture. She started plodding along the fence line, looking for another opening in the fence. Bill returned just as she was heading eastward. He followed, calling softly and offering handfuls of grain.

This was the situation when I arrived. I kept peering into the darkness, trying to see distant shapes, but Worms and Bill were far away. I kept brushing aside nightmarish thoughts of Bill lying out there, trampled and gored.

Meanwhile, back at the east end of the ranch, Bill was having his own thoughts of a violent end. He followed along behind Worms for several hundred yards, until she left the fence line and entered a grove of four-foot high Christmas trees. Then Bill lost sight of her. He waded ahead slowly and warily, for there were no trees big enough to climb, and the fence was far away. The fence wasn't much protection anyway, for now there were buffalo on both sides of it.

At each step he listened, but could hear nothing. Suddenly he got that neck-prickling feeling that somebody or something was watching him. Just as he started to turn, from behind him came a warning snort, that awesome sound which usually precedes a lunging charge. Worms was glaring at him from behind a small pine tree. He had passed her in the darkness, and now she was stalking him, like a tiger.

After half an hour of this who-is-stalking-whom game (during which Bill aged ten years) Worms headed for the hospital. Evening visiting hours were in full swing just then. You can imagine how some visitor would feel if he stepped from his car and confronted a grunting buffalo. Fortunately, the lights of civilization didn't appeal to Worms. She turned away again, heading back toward the office and the gate.

As her shape materialized out of the darkness, I ran to the gate. In my excitement and fright I opened it one-handed, though under normal circumstances I can't open it at all without help. Worms calmly walked through the gate to rejoin her child and friends. Our two-hour ordeal was over. With great relief we collapsed in the snow, patting each other on the back, gasping congratulations, and expecting hero's praise.

Now we have an answer to that question, "What do you do if your buffalo get out?"

We reply, "We get them back in."

Everything
From B to Y

17 A diverse and varied collection of humans live in Mecosta County. There are the natives, who live there because it is the homeland; they can't imagine wanting to live elsewhere. Then there are the immigrants, people like us, who are enticed to the country by the piquant fragrance of pine, and the clean, sparkling waters that freckle the land.

To the natives we are "new people," and new people we will remain for at least twenty years. We are considered one rung above the many summer people who arrive from the south on Memorial Day, but close their lakeside cottages on Labor Day. In late fall, the deer-hunting crowd descends upon our woodland. We must then keep our children and dogs indoors while the high-powered rifles carelessly boom at anything moving in the forests.

Several unusual and interesting people had migrated to Mecosta County, making it their permanent home. There was a young, retired, big-league baseball player who became a lake-project developer. Among our friends, we counted other professional people, college professors, and management consultants, all of whom had chosen rural living for various reasons.

Through our buffalo herd, we met many fascinating people. Eager' to see these strange American beasts they'd viewed in Western movies, visitors from foreign countries sought out our buffalo. A Swedish sculptor came to sketch our animals, as he was interested in the anatomical differences between American bison and their European cousin, the wisent. Before he returned to Sweden, we had formed the Swedish-American Bison Society. We entertained a South American ambassador, who fortunately had brought along his own interpreter. Our halting high-school Spanish proved insufficient when discussing animal husbandry. There were visitors from Alaska and from Hong Kong. Like a vortex, the buffalo drew interested and interesting people to Stanwood.

We became good friends with a couple living in the small village of Mecosta, fifteen miles east of Stanwood. There, Russell and Annette Kirk chose to live in Russell's ancestral home, built nearly a century ago by his great-grandfather. After accumulating degrees from several universities, including his doctorate from St. Andrews University in Scotland, Russell settled in Mecosta, where twenty years of further study established him as one of the chief social thinkers in America. A man of letters, philosopher, political historian, and lecturer, Russell pursued his scholarly studies and writing amid the rural quietness. He purchased an abandoned factory and converted it to a charming and impressive study and library to house his vast collection of books and journals.

Bill and I first became acquainted with Russell through his nationally-syndicated column, *To The Point.* A strong believer in individual effort and enterprise, Russell became interested in the cause to our unsubsidized country hospital, and his chairmanship helped make a fund drive successful.

About the time we acquired our buffalo herd, Russell won the hand of the beautiful Annette Yvonne Cecile Courtemanche, a raven-haired young teacher from

278

ong Island. Taking his bride away from flamboyant suitors and sophisticated society, Russell brought Annette to his ancestral village.

I was fearfully skeptical that anyone reared near a large city could acclimate herself to such a sudden change, but Annette soon became an important part of her village. Her interest in young people and education led her to become deeply involved in the education of Catholic youngsters; she strove to instill in them the thought that there is more to life than marrying at sixteen. She took part in establishing a community library in Mecosta, making available to the villagers the world of books. All this she accomplished between her travels to Spain, Africa, and Britain, as she accompanied Russell on his lecture tours and adventures.

As Annette and I became better acquainted, we sometimes discussed the far-off world of New York City, Lincoln Center, the art galleries, and museums. Once I told her of the morning spent at Central Park Zoo, and Bill's and my infatuation with the pair of yaks housed there.

Annette's always-animated face lit up immediately. She, too, had been fascinated by that same pair of yaks and had taken Russell to see them, where they had watched the long-haired animals exchange nuzzling endearments.

"You really ought to have a pair of yaks, Pinkie!" she exclaimed.

It wasn't a completely new idea. For several years, Bill had been interested in yaks and had developed a theory that yaks, buffalo, and musk oxen all might have descended from an ancient wild ancestor. The fossil remains of *Bison antiquus* and *Bison athabascae* showed the path the species had made coming from Asia, across the ancient Arctic land bridge, to this continent. These were ancient predecessors of the buffalo, and perhaps

279

the musk ox was a cadet of this same line, having adapted to the local Arctic environment, never spreading farther south.

In studying musk oxen, Bill had learned of a Kellogg Foundation project in Alaska, in which an attempt was made to establish a means of livelihood for Alaskan natives. Musk oxen were crossed with domestic beef, producing an animal which produced annually eleven pounds of very fine wool and provided milk for the Indians. This wool graded superior to even the finest cashmere goat wool, and greatly exceeded the four-pound annual yield of goats. This project intrigued Bill and whetted his appetite for such a project on our Rx Ranch. Bill knew that musk oxen would not breed in warmer than Arctic climates, so he could not consider them. But, Bill had learned, yaks would thrive in our climate, and for some time he had wished he could locate a pair of yaks. He was eager to try crossing them with buffalo and domestic beef.

"Bill would love to have yaks," I told Annette, "but he's never heard of any yak breeding ranches outside of Tibet, behind the Bamboo Curtain."

Annette hummed thoughtfully. "I have a great idea!" she said. "First I'll talk to Russell about it; then I'll let you know what it is."

Bubbling with excitement, Annette telephoned me a few days later. The great idea involved the method of payment of an obstetrical fee. The Kirks were expecting the arrival of their first child in a few months, and Bill was going to deliver the baby. Since he emphatically refused to charge our friends an obstetrical fee, the Kirks had been puzzling over the choice of a gift to take the place of a fee. Through her Eastern contacts, Annette actually had located a game farm having baby yaks for sale.

"We'll give the good doctor a yak for his delivery fee," Annette laughed.

I remembered that during the depression of the 1930's, cash-short farmers occasionally had paid my lawyer-father's legal fees with livestock. Once it was a hog; another time, a vicious goose was delivered to our back door; but nothing ever so strange as a yak.

"Paying for our baby with a yak!" Annette giggled. "I must remember to write that in the baby book!"

In earnest, Bill and I began to bone up on yaks. We kept remembering the congeniality of the two yaks we'd seen at the zoo, and this convinced us that we should get a matched set, a male and a female. We entered into partnership with the Kirks, whereby we each purchased one yak.

Annette placed the order, and the Catskill Game Farm promised that the yaks would be shipped in the early autumn, as soon as they were weaned from their mothers.

The baby yaks we were getting were of the ancient, wild, gray-muzzled strain, quite rare now, with just twelve thousand left in the world. Only fifty years ago the first pair of wild yaks was brought to the United States, where they thrived and multiplied in the New York Zoological Park. They and their descendants produced twenty-four calves in the following two decades.

Wild yaks are black, with a touch of gray about the muzzle. The outstanding characteristics of a wild yak are its long black hair that hangs nearly to the ground, and its pronounced shoulder-hump. Their horns can measure up to thirty-eight inches. Reaching a height of six feet at the shoulder, bulls may weigh up to twelve hundred pounds. Domestic yaks, a cross between wild yak and Mongolian cattle, are smaller, more docile, and come in a wide variety of colors.

Yaks originally wandered in enormous herds all the way from Kashmir to China, but now there are just a few wild herds left in the inaccessible regions of the

Tibetan mountains. For centuries, the domesticated yak has been used in Tibet as a beast of burden. It is also ridden, milked regularly, and slaughtered for its fine meat and furry hide. The mountain people of Asia have made the same intensive use of the yak as the plains Indian made of the buffalo. Perhaps because the Tibetan people had been around the yak for a much longer period of time than the plains Indians' span of only a few decades with the buffalo, the Asians made even more extensive use of their native animal. By crossbreeding it with their cattle, they developed the domestic yak, which could be used more intensively than a wild animal. The Indian, of course, never domesticated the buffalo.

In our reading, we learned there were many similarities between yaks and buffalo. Like buffalo, the yak makes grunting noises; it is sometimes called "the grunting ox." The bulls of both species are very protective and will form a circle around a calf, protecting it from danger. When we read that yaks eat lichens, moss, and yak grass, we groaned. Our pastures contained no yak grass. We had the feeling that we had passed this way before, when we had read that buffalo eat buffalo grass. We mused that we'd never heard of horses eating horse grass, cattle eating cattle grass, or sheep munching sheep grass.

The long fur of the yak covered its entire body down to its ankles, in contrast to the cape the buffalo have only over their front quarters. The yak has a prominent hump, something like that of Brahma cattle, but it is not so large as a buffalo's hump. The yak's horns sweep outward, being longer than buffalo horns. Agile and sure-footed as a mountain goat, yaks love to climb rocks and hills.

We couldn't determine what we would get from crossing yak and buffalo. There seemed to be no pictures or records of such a hybrid, yet zoological

282

journals asserted the two species crossed readily. We didn't know what the crossbreed would look like, but we did know it would be called a yakalo.

As for crossing yaks and domestic cattle, again we couldn't find any articles about such a hybrid, but we coined a name for them. We would call the crosses "cattlyaks." Assuming these animals would produce a superior grade of meat, we look into the future to the menus of the better restaurants, which might read, "Our meat is choice cattlyak—The Cattlyak of beef." Cattlyak would be to the meat industry what the Cadillac is in the automobile field.

Seven calves were born to our buffalo herd in June and July. Three were little heifers and four were bull calves.

Old Cow had the best record. Of the three calves she had presented us in three years, all were heifers. Though she was cantankerous and temperamental, she was the largest and best-looking cow in the herd. Her three daughters promised to be large, statuesque females. They could hardly be otherwise, with Old Cow for their mother and the mighty Kahtanka, their father. We still waited eagerly for Old Cow to have a bull calf, as he would make an excellent herd-bull partner with Kahtanka.

Kahtanka grew slowly taller and heavier in the shoulders and hump. His massive head, so black it appeared almost bluish in sunlight, was twice as large as that of the cows, and his heavy beard reached toward the ground. Already Kahtanka weighed a ton, and he would continue growing for another three years. Prancing and adolescent strutting were things of the past. He no longer needed to make a big fuss to prove he was the monarch. Kahtanka knew he was the chief, and he knew everyone else acknowledged his reign. He became a brooding, stern dictator. At five years of age, he was reaching his prime, though it would be many years before anyone dared say he was past his prime.

283

One sweltering summer day the Rx Ranch inflicted another wound upon Bill; this time the culprit was not a buffalo, but a small piece of steel. While Bill was tightening a sagging fence, a steel fragment flew into his eye, cutting the cornea and lodging there.

At the hospital he found Dave, his physician companion, who removed the tiny bit of steel and put soothing ointment in Bill's reddened eye. Dave suggested that Bill wear dark glasses for a few days to shield the injured, light-sensitive eye.

The morning after Bill suffered his eye injury, a pale pink was beginning to streak the eastern sky when our bedside telephone rang at four o'clock. It was Annette Kirk, reporting that she was in early labor. Since her half-hour drive to the hospital was over bumpy, pot-holed gravel roads, Bill insisted she leave for the hospital as soon as possible.

As so often happens when expectant mothers arrive at the hospital, Annette's contractions ceased. She was dismayed, but Bill assured her this was very ordinary, perhaps because once in the hospital atmosphere, the mother relaxes, thinking "Well, I made it here!" and this allows all her muscles to relax, postponing active labor.

"Once you get to the hospital you have to keep active," Bill advised. "That gets things going again. For a starter, let's go see the buffalo."

Annette, Russell, and Bill climbed into the car and headed for the drive-in gate to the pasture. Instead of parking on the road to watch the herd, Bill opened the gate and drove into the pasture. Morning mist was rising off the dewy meadow grass. Shaking off sleep, the buffalo tossed their damp manes and stretched.

Long plowed furrows, spaced six feet apart for Christmas tree plantings, ran east and west across the pasture. When inside the buffalo pasture, we tried to do most of our driving in an east-west direction, since driving across the furrows made a very bumpy ride.

Bill purposely turned the car south, driving the wrong way over the furrows. This gave his passengers a jolting toss at each knobby ridge.

Annette groaned and laughed simultaneously. "Now I understand why you wanted us to see the buffalo. This must be your prenatal treatment for reluctant babies. Did you learn this trick back on the reservation?"

Bill answered with a droll smile. The dark glasses protecting his injured eye also hid a puckish gleam.

Driving directly into the center of the browsing buffalo herd, Bill turned off the ignition. Kahtanka and Old Cow ambled up to check out the visitors. Old Cow began rubbing her neck on the grill, stretching out over the hood of the car. Suspecting that Old Cow had discovered an excellent rubbing post, Kahtanka joined her in scratching his heavy shoulders across the hood. The whole vehicle swayed, rocked, and rolled.

Turning pale, Annette squealed, "That's enough. We've seen the buffalo now. Let's leave."

"Sshh," Bill cautioned her, "you don't want to make noise when they're this close. They'll smash the car."

Squirming, but not daring to make a sound, Annette stared in alarm as Kahtanka leaned far over the hood and glared through the windshield at the three occupants. His huge nostrils pressed against the thin glass, forming circles of steam on the windshield.

"Sshh," Bill repeated.

After some time, Kahtanka and Old Cow meandered away, having soothed their itchy spots.

Annette expelled a long breath. In a tight voice, she whispered, "It's time to go to the hospital—right away!"

One look at her pinched face caused Bill to agree with her suggestion. The buffalo herd had spread out all around the car, and Bill had to maneuver and cramp his wheels to avoid the roadblocks of shaggy, unmoving animals. On the way out of the pasture, he avoided crossing the bumpy furrows, not being anxious for the Kirks' baby to be born in a buffalo patch.

"This was all part of your plot, wasn't it?" Annette scolded good-naturedly. "Frightening me to death to hurry up the baby!"

"Oh, it's just an old Indian custom," Bill grinned. "Haven't you heard how the Indian braves used to help their squaws have their babies quickly? When a squaw first went into labor, they tied her to a tree. Then the husband would mount his pony and gallop straight toward the helpless woman, veering sideways only at the last moment. Pure fright brought on the papoose."

"And I thought being eyeball-to-eyeball with Kahtanka was bad!" Annette laughed. "Now drive faster, please."

Just a few hours after little Monica Rachel Kirk was born, I hurried to the hospital to visit Annette and offer my congratulations. I found her bubbling with excitement, and I fondly recalled the marvelous feeling of well-being which follows giving birth to a much-wanted baby. Annette was ecstatic over her perfectly-formed, dark-haired daughter.

"And I had her by natural childbirth, Pinkie, just as I'd hoped!" she exclaimed. "Your dear husband insists the natural childbirth was due to his Indian treatment—can you imagine?"

I laughed with her. FAll through her pregnancy, Annette had faithfully practiced the prescribed exercises and breathing practices in preparation for natural childbirth. Now Bill was trying to usurp the credit, claiming that the menacing buffalo were instrumental in allowing natural childbirth.

The ebullient Annette described the thrill of seeing her own baby born. "Oh, Pinkie, she was so red! Then they told me she was a little girl and just fine, and I heard her begin to cry—the most beautiful sound I'd ever heard!"

Suddenly throwing back her head, she began to laugh and laugh. "After they put the baby in the bassinet, I looked up at your husband, and he was still wearing his sunglasses!" she giggled. "He had the proper full regalia—green scrub suit, hat, and surgical mask, but those crazy big sunglasses!" Annette burst into laughter again.

Monica Rachel's arrival on earth was by no means ordinary. A child whose obstetrical fee is paid for with a live baby yak must certainly be marked for a prodigious life.

In a few days the Kirks took their tiny daughter home from the hospital. Though it would be a while yet, the Kirks and we anxiously awaited word from the game farm that our baby yaks were ready to be weaned and shipped to Michigan.

Late one autumn evening the phone rang. It was the operator of Stanwood's only tavern.

"Mrs. Cummings," he said, "there's a trucker here who says he has a couple yaks for you."

"Thanks, we'll be right down," I answered.

We drove up in front of the tavern, and there was the stock truck, its bed loaded with huge crates. We peered into the boxes, but most of them appeared empty. Still munching his hamburger, the trucker came out and explained that our yaks were his last delivery. He had left camels in Cleveland, llamas in Milwaukee, and now yaks for us.

At the ranch, we opened the gate to the new yak pasture. After the truck was backed into the opening, the trucker and Bill began juggling crates around on the truck bed to get at the yaks. In the darkness it was very hard to see, but I could hear their hammers pounding on the crate. After a loud rip of splitting wood, two dark forms moved toward the end of the truck, jumped off, and disappeared into the blackness of the pasture.

Bill trustingly signed a receipt for two (2) yaks, but I wondered. Did we, or didn't we have yaks in the yak pen?

After the truck left, we moved our car so the headlights would shine toward the pasture. Then we saw them—two yard-high ebony animals, huddled together, sides touching, staring at our blinding headlight beams. They must be yaks, I conceded. They didn't look like anything else I could put a name to.

We walked into the pasture, hoping to approach them, but they moved warily away, walking side by side. Their bushy tails nearly swept the ground, so very different from the short tuft that is a buffalo's tail. No wonder they were hard to see at night. They were entirely black, except for their silvery-gray muzzles. We'd chosen ancient wild yak instead of domestic yak because, like the buffalo, the wild yak had approached extinction. Also, we wanted the original genes for our crossing experiments.

Weary of trying to see something black in the darkness, we decided to return in the morning for easier viewing.

The next morning we were surprised that we could find not one sign of a yak in the small enclosure. It was surprise at first, then real concern. The woods were full of bow-and-arrow hunters stalking deer. If our yaks had wandered into the countryside, what would a hunter think if he came upon one? With their long, black hair and bushy tail, they didn't look like deer. An eager hunter might persuade himself that he had in his sights a black bear with horns. Hunters aren't really to be trusted. Every year many of them manage to shoot their hunting companions, in spite of the fact that a man in a red coat only dimly resembles a brown buck with antlers.

We looked around uncertainly. How does one go about reporting two missing yaks? Surely the sheriff and the conservation officer had better things to do than go on a yak hunt. We couldn't wait for the lost-and-found column. By the time the afternoon papers were out, a yak's head might be decorating somebody's trophy room. We could just see the great white hunter standing proudly beside his trophy saying, "Yes, this beast is a strange mutation I stalked down in the north woods of Michigan."

Off in the next pasture, we noticed the buffalo herd moving out of a valley to the hillside. Automatically, Bill began counting the distant dark shapes. As he finished counting, he yelled a relieved "Whoopee!" The missing yaks were found.

The yaks had joined the buffalo. Somehow in the night they had found a gap in the barbed wire fence and crawled through to join the herd. Perhaps they hoped the dark shapes were their parents, or maybe, being herd animals themselves, they just preferred the company of many other animals. We thought of our donkey who preferred being with the buffalo. In spite of their grunting, menacing ways, our buffalo seemed awfully popular in the animal world.

We found a sheltered spot just outside Superfence and sat down to observe how the social adjustment of the yaks was progessing. The buffalo didn't seem exactly hostile to the newcomers. They tolerated them, even letting them move about with the herd. But when food entered the picture, everything changed. As Bill began to feed the animals, the buffalo charged at the yaks, snorting and swinging their horns, chasing them away from the food. The two little yak calves stood aside with Mabel, waiting for the buffalo to get their fill. As the herd finally moved off to doze and ruminate in the sun, the yaks and Mabel slipped in, seeking the leftovers. We threw in' some more food, and the American and Oriental bovines dined together.

The two yaks were inseparable. We never saw them more than a foot apart, and usually they moved about with their sides touching, like Siamese twins. They were so nearly identical that it took close study to tell the male, Panchen, from the female, Dalai. Though Panchen eventually would be larger, his only present difference was a broadness between the eyes and between the horns. Undoubtedly his head would be much heavier and larger than the female's, just as a buffalo bull's head is nearly twice as large as a buffalo cow's. The concealing shaggy hair of the yaks prevented the more usual method of differentiating the sexes. The society that promotes the clothing of "naked" animals needn't bother with yaks: they are covered very modestly. When winter blasted in, the children discovered a new way to tell the male from the female. "The one with icicles on his tummy must be Panchen," they said seriously, with no intention of being sly or ribald.

We'd planned to keep the yaks separate from the buffalo, at least until breeding age. Since they were so young, it was our intention to work with them and tame them. Several times we tried to entice them into their own yak pasture, but they would have none of it. The lithe creatures were like goats in that they could creep through small gaps in the fence. Always, they returned to their adored buffalo herd.

Such determination finally defeated us. "Why fight it?" we shrugged. If you're going to deal with strange animals, you've got to expect strange behavior. As our menagerie expanded, we were getting wiser.

Although the young yaks were docile and affectionate with each other, we discovered they were even more short-tempered than buffalo. They had a tendency to

290

attack quickly, with no warning. If irritated in the slightest way, they jumped at us, hooking their horns menacingly. At least the buffalo had always signaled their annoyance first, by showing the whites of their eyes and raising their tails.

"Feisty little critters, aren't they?" Bill laughed as he jumped back from a swift lunge of the little yak bull.

I nodded, uneasily wondering if we would laugh at their irascible dispositions once they were full-grown.

Bill had discovered a new type of food for the animals. It wasn't intended to take the place of hay or grain, but was a treat food, to be used for enticing the animals near the fence so we or our visitors could see them. Before, when grain was used to coax the animals close, it had been necessary for Bill to climb inside the fence and spread out many piles of grain. This was dangerous for Bill when the buffalo came thundering up before enough mounds of grain were poured out.

One day, when driving past a bakery advertising day-old bread, it occurred to Bill that buffalo should enjoy bread. Inside the bakery, he discovered not only day-old bread for the thrifty, but week-old bread for true misers. Bill figured week-old bread would be fine for animal consumption. For two dollars, the baker happily filled the trunk of Bill's car with scores of torn packages of buns, rolls, and bread.

The buffalo, yaks, and Mabel all loved old bread. Slice by slice, we tossed it out into the pasture, without the danger of entering inside the fence. Also we could feed them by hand through the fence. It took a bit of nerve to keep a steady hand as hot buffalo breath approached the hamburger bun on your flattened palm. Only Bill fed the mighty Kahtanka this way. The children and I were afraid of Kahtanka, and we knew Kahtanka smelled our fear.

The yaks loved the old bread, and we wanted to keep them tame by hand-feeding. However, the buffalo

291

chased them away, not letting the yaks get close to us at bread-feeding time.

Because yaks have an acute sense of hearing, Bill was able to remedy this situation. The buffalo had learned that after we closed the trunk of our car, there would be no more bread forthcoming, and they soon wandered away to graze. When the buffalo were some distance away, the yaks often sauntered nearer to us.

Quietly, Bill called to the nearby yaks, "Phsst! Phsst!" and held out another piece of bread, stealthily, so the buffalo couldn't see it. The inquisitive yaks came up to Bill and received their nutritious reward. Before long, this developed into a conditioned response, so that Bill's quiet "Phsst!" brought the yaks every time.

There were many rock piles remaining in the pastures, even after their extensive use in our dam-building project. Joyfully the yaks discovered them. Like goats, they clamored over the big piles of rocks, playing king-of-the-mountain with each other.

When the first biting winds of winter arrived, the yaks cavorted playfully, reveling in the frigid temperatures as the buffalo do. Since they were only a generation removed from their ancestral home in the freezing altitudes of the Himalayas, their bodies were meant to withstand cold. Their cold-weather friskiness sometimes led them to mischief.

One bitterly cold day, when Bill was out of town attending a medical seminar, I received a telephone call from the proprietress of Stanwood's general store.

"One of your animals is out, Pinkie," she said. "A lady just came in here and said when she drove past your ranch, an animal was out in the middle of the road."

I groaned, "Oh, no!"

"From her description, I don't think it's a buffalo," she added hopefully. "She says it was a black, funny-looking thing."

"Thanks for letting me know, Helen," I sighed. It

must be a yak, I figured unhappily, though I reminded myself I should be grateful it wasn't Kahtanka.

The children were home from school, and I instructed them to dress warmly for a yak roundup. As I began to pull on layers of heavy clothing, I had a sly thought.

I should call Annette, and say, "Annette, *your* yak is out of the fence." But little five-month-old Monica couldn't be expected to perform as a yak-herder yet, and I had three children capable of helping me.

As we drove down the black-top road bordering the west boundary of the ranch, the children and I saw the dark shape of Panchen loping up and down the fence line, vainly looking for reentry into his pasture I was sorry the escapee was the bull, since he was even more testy than Dalai, the heifer.

The children and I tried to form an Indian-type surround, encircling the peppery animal. Though he was only a six-month-old calf, his horns loomed long and sharp when he charged, and none of us had the nerve to hold our ground against his lunges.

When the little Panchen tired of attacking us, he turned upon the fence. Plunging angrily at this wire barricade to his pasture, he threw his hefty shoulders at the fence. Again and again, he heaved his weight against the creaking wire, forcing it to sag inwardly a few inches. The fencing wire was stapled on the inside of the fence posts, giving the fence strength to withstand impact from animals within the pasture. Bearing up under the lunges of an angry yak was not usually required from the outside surface of a fence. This was Ordinary Fence, not Superfence. The children had pounded the staples into the posts, and I prayed their staples would hold. At last, the little bull gave up on battering the fence, and turned again on us.

We wanted to herd him down the fence line to a gate we could open for him. We were making very slow progress until Beth remembered Bill's food-call of "Phsst." With this enticing sound, she coaxed him up to the closed gate. Now the obstacle was the buffalo herd, milling uneasily around the gate. If we opened the gate to let Panchen in, the buffalo might get out.

I checked my station wagon, and luckily, found a few dried-out, dusty bread slices there. Hugging these to my jacket, I trotted up the fence line a distance, then called the buffalo, waving a bread crust enticingly. The buffalo took the bait. With relief, I saw the whole herd moving toward me.

The moment the tail-end buffalo was ten yards removed from the gate, Bruce untwisted the wire fasteners and threw open the gate. The impudent yak stared at the opening, unmoving. Bruce remembered the code word, "Phsst!"; and responding to this, Panchen jumped through into the pasture. Bruce quickly swung shut the gate.

Another time a few months later, Panchen, now heavier and longer of horn, again found his way through the fence. Again, Bill was out of town. I accused him of harboring some strange extra-sensory premonition of trouble and leaving town to avoid it. I threatened offering Flaming Filet of Yak, Peking Style, for next Sunday's menu.

This second yak escape occurred during school hours, so it was Wilma, Bill's master-of-all-trades office nurse, who joined me in braving the thrusting yak horns. As nurse to The Buffalo Doctor, Wilma collected many scrapes and scratches from duties not mentioned in her *Medical Assistant's Standard Office Procedure* manual.

Caring for our growing number of animals took more and more time. To Bill, I grumbled, "I hope you don't intend to collect the whole animal alphabet from A to Z."

"Of course not," Bill retorted. But with an impish grin, he added, "But we have a good beginning on everything from B to Y."

■
The
Spirit
Returns

18 Under the tepid April sunshine, Bill prolonged his daily visits to his herd. He reclined on the spring-dampened ground, one arm holding his head up; Bill's spirit seemed to gain nourishment whenever he watched the peaceful, grazing animals. The solitude and quiet were relaxing, but it was more than that: almost a communion of his soul with the spirit of the buffalo herd. He always returned from the buffalo pastures looking as if he had absorbed strength and gained endurance.

There was trouble to endure. The remaining two family doctors, who had been practicing in nearby villages, were moving away. One was leaving to specialize, and the other was going to the city to practice. Where there once had been nine doctors, now there were but four. These four were all specialists: surgeon, anesthetist, internist, and radiologist, an excellent nucleus for a medical group, but only a nucleus. These four could not maintain for long the heavy practices necessary to keep the hospital full of patients.

The three hundred thousand dollars needed for hospital remodeling to meet the newest regulations was a steady worry to everyone. For months, George, the radiologist, had been contacting sources in financial circles. Finally, he had obtained a fair commitment from the money people that a loan for this large sum could be given Mecosta Memorial; yet to lend this sum, the lenders wanted assurance that this country hospital was a stable operation. To insure stability for the hospital, more doctors were needed in the area.

For years we had been trying to entice doctors to our area. With the uncertainty of the hospital's survival, how could we ever get doctors to join us now? They would surely have to be dedicated physicians to be interested in our struggling cause.

Still, all was not gloom. Spring's arrival brought positive signs that a calf was going to be born to Mabel, our sexy red cow. Jubilant that Mabel had seduced Kahtanka, the only possible father, Bill envisioned the resulting calf as the beginning of his dream of developing a new breed of livestock to improve northern beef herds.

Soon Mable's waistline began enlarging—too rapidly. Bill recognized the symptoms of polyhydramnios, which meant that Mabel was becoming engorged with too much fluid. Slowed down by her unwieldy shape, Mabel began to stay on the periphery of the buffalo herd, making it easier for Bill to supervise her pre-natal condition. When her ankles began to swell, indicating early congestive heart failure, Bill grew terribly concerned.

Daily he encircled her round body with a rope, recording careful measurements of her girth. The first entry on Mabel's obstetrical chart read, "Girth: nine feet, two inches." At first the excessive fluids increased her waistline half an inch a day, but by the end of that week, Mabel was ballooning one and a half inches daily.

When her udder became swollen with milk, signaling impending delivery, Bill was ecstatic.

Cliff, the neighboring farmer to the north, had been watching Mabel's touchy condition. Sympathetically he offered the use of his barn for her imminent confinement, and Mabel was made comfortable in a roomy, straw-carpeted box-stall.

Two veterinarians checked the bloated patient and predicted calving within a day or two. After only two days in the barn, Mabel was retaining fluids, and her ankles puffed up alarmingly. Remembering Ringo's quick deterioration once put in a barn without sunlight and fresh air, Bill decided to return Mabel to the pasture. Once she was out-of-doors, her ankle swelling receded slightly, but Mabel's waistline now measured eleven feet.

Bill probingly searched for a sign of a fetal heartbeat. Bumping the unborn calf is supposed to elicit a quick return kick from the calf; but because of the many gallons of water encasing Mabel's calf, no signs could be felt. Impatient with suspense, Bill thought of his stethoscope.

Daily he listened to different areas of Mabel's monstrous tummy, but was rewarded only with gurgling, digestive sounds. It was during one of Bill's intent searches for the fetal heartbeat that the awful thing happened.

With the stethoscope's ear pieces in his ears, shutting out all outside sound, Bill was not aware of the approach of the buffalo herd. Suddenly he was rammed from the rear. Head first, he slammed into Mabel's flank, and then crumpled to the ground, dazed.

Though only half-conscious, Bill instinctively rolled under the fence to escape the yet unknown danger. Lying on the outside of the fence, his brain began to clear, and his eyes regained their focus. Bill looked up through the barbed wire into the red, hate-filled eyes of Kahtanka. Snorting his wrath, Kahtanka roared and pawed the ground. Bill lay very still, making no sound. Taking account of his injuries, Bill could feel no pain, but there was an aggravating numbness and tingling in his right arm, as though the arm had gone to sleep.

The whole herd approached the fence near where Bill lay. They sniffed around, with little interest, then hopped off into a gay, springtime buffalo-dance. Unable to resist joining in, Kahtanka pounded off, to jump and cavort through the fields.

Once the buffalo were a safe distance away, Bill started to move. Only a light movement of his head brought excruciating pain which radiated out into his tingling right arm. Struggling to his feet, Bill gingerly picked his way through the brush to his car.

Except for his dirty clothes, there were no marks of violence upon him when he walked into the hospital emergency room, but the pain evident in his strained face brought immediate attention. X-rays showed a broken bone in his neck. An extension neck-brace was applied to exert traction on the neck. This relieved some of the pain, but not the persistent numbness and cramping of his right arm. Besides suffering physical pain, Bill sagged in spirit. He was terrified that his surgical career might be over.

Following his injury, every morning Bill attempted to get out of bed and make it to the breakfast table. After only a few minutes of upright posture, his pain became so great he became nauseated, and it would be necessary for me to help him back to bed. With the rigid brace holding his neck in an uncomfortable chin-upward position, Bill's nights were filled with restless moaning and struggling. After many sleepless nights of helpless listening, I began camping on the davenport. It was torture to see him suffer, and there seemed to be nothing I could do to help. From the outset, with typical physician's logic, he assumed the worst and would not eliminate the possibility of permanent paralysis until there should be some positive sign the injury was of lesser degree. I felt sure he would recover, and told him so.

298

With a despondent sigh, he asked, "When did you become a neurologist?"

I remembered a nurse telling me once, "There's only one thing worse than a sick man, and that's a sick doctor!"

Bill received daily telephone reports on Mabel from Cliff, who was taking care of the animals. Mabel's condition had been rapidly deteriorating. Bill prescribed some dehydrating water pills to rid her of the excessive fluids, but Cliff reported she was too sick to eat.

Bill felt sure Mabel was dying, and he instructed Cliff to take her to the slaughterhouse. To save the calf, Bill gave detailed instructions on performing an immediate Caesarean section to remove the calf as soon as Mabel was killed. He told how to clear the breathing passages and give artificial respiration by tugging on the forelegs of the calf.

Cliff tried to dissuade Bill from the slaughter, suggesting that we wait until Mabel died, and then take the calf. Bill feared that the calf's condition might decline along with Mabel's deterioration, and both calf and cow might be lost. Once Mabel died, the calf would have to come within minutes, and there was no one able to carry out a constant, twenty-four hour vigil, watching for Mabel's probable death.

From the slaughterhouse, Cliff telephoned, his voice despondent. "We have the calf—a little bull—but he's too premature; he'll never make it."

Forty-five minutes later Cliff called back. The calf had just died.

The disappointment pushed Bill farther into the deep pit of pain and hopelessness. Still, he insisted upon seeing the little calf. Moving painfully, he struggled to the car and slowly eased himself into the back seat.

Though perhaps seventy-five days premature, the

little bull already showed the superior markings of the rugged animal we had hoped to breed. The rounded head was small, like a buffalo calf's head, necessary for range animals because they must be delivered unassisted. Its short neck, deep chest, and short legs were the characteristics of a good beef-producer. Because of its prematurity, the calf had tufts of hair only on the top of its head and on the tip of its tail. The yet hairless body was a light tan color.

Bill turned away from the pitiful little body, his shoulders drooping despondently. He murmured, "How sad to think what might have been."

Gradually Bill was able to stay out of bed for longer periods. If he didn't overdo himself, or ride in a car very long, he managed to keep somewhat free of pain. Still, the nagging numbness and muscle-cramping in his arm remained.

By mid-summer he was once again able to perform surgery, removing his neck-brace in the operating room, but he was not yet able to take on prolonged, difficult cases. These he referred to other surgeons.

The exodus of the two busy general practitioners threw a heavy work load on the remaining doctors. Though the four survivors were specialists, each one carried on an extensive general practice in addition to his specialty. Taking care of the added numbers was a real burden to both the doctors and the patients, who often suffered long, futile hours in the crowded waiting rooms. Many of the patients drifted away. Some returned to their old habits of doctoring themselves with patent medicines; others slipped off to the willow grove to patronize the old herb-doctor. At the hospital, empty beds became common, and the prognosis for the hospital seemed bleak.

Always having been athletic and muscular, Bill was dismayed over the extreme loss of muscle tone he had suffered since his neck injury. More devastating, though, than the weight and strength loss, was the depletion of his spirit. As I watched his listless motions of living, I sometimes hardly recognized my husband. Before, the most ebullient of men, Bill now seemed only an apparition.

Besides losing his spirit, Bill had lost his companionship with Kahtanka. From the moment of the ramming attack, the big buffalo bull had taken a different attitude toward Bill. No longer would Kahtanka take bread from Bill's hand. Whenever Bill approached the fence, Kahtanka began snorting and pawing the earth. If Bill walked along the fence, Kahtanka would stalk him, glaring and shaking his head. At last Bill realized what menacing thoughts lurked in Kahtanka's brain. Believing Bill was a competitor for the affection of his harem, Kahtanka was attempting to instigate a battle, just as he would with a rival bull.

Bill was heartbroken. He had always spoken blithely of how Kahtanka and he would grow old together over the next forty years. "With my cane, I'll hobble up to the fence," he often had chuckled, "and Kahtanka and I will grunt and complain over our stiff joints together."

Now, after only four years, the companionship was at an end. A mean bull cannot be tolerated. When aroused, bulls are too strong to restrain, and an ill-tempered buffalo bull, with his powerful shoulders and deadly horns, was sure to kill. Bill feared for the safety of Cliff and his teen-age son, who were caring for the herd during Bill's convalescence.

For this summer's annual Buffalo Barbecue, we had promised to donate two of our two-year-old buffalo bulls. Slaughter arrangements had been made for these two animals. The chairman of the meat committee was astonished when Bill called him, announcing his intention to substitute Kahtanka for the two young bulls.

"When dressed out, Kahtanka should give even more meat than the two bulls," Bill told the surprised man.

"Not Kahtanka!" the man sputtered. "Not *the* Kahtanka, surely!"

My reaction was the same. I couldn't believe Bill really meant to sacrifice his beloved Kahtanka. Though I was personally terrified of the big bull and enraged at him for nearly making me a widow, I couldn't imagine Bill without Kahtanka. The collaboration of their spirits had made them appear to be one. Though I would feel relief to be rid of the dangerous beast, I feared for Bill's spirit if he disposed of his friend.

A taxidermist in the southern part of the state heard that Kahtanka was to be shot. He telephoned us, explaining that when passing through Stanwood, he often had stopped and admired the beautiful black head of our herd bull. He was hopeful we would let him have the head to mount. When he explained that he didn't intend to sell the mounted head, but to display it in his shop for visitors to admire, we agreed. We reasoned it would give Kahtanka a semblance of immortality. For generations to come, Kahtanka's regal head would impress viewers with the magnificence of Great American Bison.

Even when they saw the slaughterhouse truck arrive at the buffalo pastures, the community could not believe Bill would shoot Kahtanka. Kahtanka was an institution, like Lassie or Man o' War.

As in a time of mourning, on the day of the shoot a few close friends gathered to be with us. Bill would not be persuaded to let anyone else shoot Kahtanka. He wanted him dropped painlessly with a single shot. This he wished to do for his friend. If the shot were muffed, Bill chose to be the culprit.

Everyone was very quiet, realizing this was the end of a very special relationship. Because Kahtanka was so antagonistic toward Bill, Cliff called the buffalo up to us, and by spreading feed and coaxing with bread slices, he managed to entice Kahtanka into the adjoining pasture.

I leaped forward to close the gate, keeping the rest of the herd from following him.

Alone under the solitary old oak tree, Kahtanka sniffed the feed, but did not eat. His animal brain strained to size up the situation. The morning sun beat down on the shaggy black head of the herd master. A true monarch, he ignored the tempting ground feed until he assured himself his herd was in no danger. Slowly he lowered his massive head toward the mound of golden grain.

Bill pulled the trigger. While the boom of the high-powered rifle was still echoing against the hills across the valley, Kahtanka's legs folded; he dropped straight down onto his belly, and then rolled onto his right side. A hind leg twitched once, and he was dead.

Bill turned away quickly, struggling back into his neck-brace. With wooden motions, he locked the rifle in the trunk of the car and walked off alone. Nervously watching his dejected figure, I saw him disappear into the dense woods. As I had feared, Bill's spirit was now entirely gone. I did not follow, knowing he needed to be alone. The soothing quiet of solitude among the leafy spires of the forest might provide solace.

Uncomfortably I kept vigil on Kahtanka while the slaughterhouse people performed their gory duties. It is distressing to see a fallen giant. Gazing downward upon the fallen Kahtanka seemed disrespectful. Erect, he had been a monarch. Sprawled in the reddening meadow grass, he was a dead animal. Why must life end with indignity?

Kahtanka was winched onto a flat-bed wagon pulled by a tractor. Making its way out of the pasture, the procession headed through Main Street toward the slaughterhouse. I remained behind, wishing to avoid the sight of this final humiliating ride, an affront to the once-proud beast.

I went to Bill's office with Wilma, and together we

Sipped coffee and tried to make light conversation. Since we both knew the severity of the affliction, disappointments, and worries borne by Bill in the past few months, we kept peering anxiously out the window, nervous over his lengthening absence.

After two hours, we could force ourselves to wait no longer. "Let's go find him," I said.

When we stepped out the back door of the office, we were greatly relieved to see Bill striding toward us through the hayfield. His step seemed almost sprightly as he approached.

Above the white plastic neck-brace tipping his chin in an upward angle, Bill's face was placid and serene—an extreme change from his haggard, lifeless expression upon entering the woods two hours before. Nature apparently had replenished his spirit.

Bill's eyes shone with excitement. "Kahtanka is back with us again!"

Bewildered by this incoherent announcement, Wilma and I stared dumbly at each other. My mind groped frantically to reject the possibility of Bill's derangement.

Perceiving our consternation, Bill laughed. "I mean Kahtanka the Second. Only a half-hour ago, Old Cow gave birth to the finest bull calf I've ever seen. We've been anticipating what a fine bull Old Cow and Kahtanka would have, but up until now their combination had produced only heifers. Wait until you see him! What a calf!"

Enthusiastically, Bill motioned us toward the car. "Come on. You've got to see him!"

Still awed by Bill's renewed good spirits, I slid behind the steering wheel. As we drove down the gravel road, I marveled at our good fortune. All the calves of the season had been born, except this one of Old Cow's. We had awaited the bull calf which would result from the joining of the blood lines of Old Cow and Kahtanka,

304

either animal a superior specimen of majesty, dominance, and appearance. We knew the son of their alliance would be the crown prince. The birth of this posthumous son less than two hours after his father's death seemed almost a miracle to me. I blinked back tears of thanksgiving.

An exceptionally large calf, baby Kahtanka II stood calmly beside his mother. As we neared him, instead of darting away, as other young calves usually do, he gazed at us watchfully.

"He's different from the other calves, isn't he?" Bill commented. "Instead of wobbling about like a newborn calf, he stands there with dignity and pride. I think I can see a look of haughty disdain in his eyes. He has his father's spirit. Kahtanka's spirit is in his son."

Kahtanka had been resurrected through the birth of Kahtanka II. Continuity was restored.

The birth of Kahtanka II reinvigorated Bill. With new effort, Bill worked to regain his former strength and vitality. Carefully regulating his life to include generous amounts of exercise and rest, Bill strove to recapture good health.

As Bill mulled over the consequences of killing Kahtanka, he realized there was a real advantage, a bright side, in not having Kahtanka around. Since there would be an interregnum of two year's time between Kahtanka's death and the accession to the herd-bull throne by Kahtanka II, our crossbreeding project could be advanced.

First, Oscar, a Hereford bull, was added to our herd. Fearing for the safety of his children, the farmer who owned Oscar disliked keeping him around his barnyard. Oscar was needed only occasionally by the farmer's dairy cows, and with relief Oscar's owner brought him to the ranch to stay.

Waving goodbye to Oscar, the farmer called, "Keep him as long as you like, Doc."

305

We acquired two more domestic cows to replace Angie and Mabel, and wished we could afford others.

Since Panchen, the yak bull, was maturing, we foresaw long strides ahead in our cherished hybrid project. With Kahtanka out of the way, Oscar and Panchen now had free access to all the buffalo cows. For the next two years, these bulls could seed our herd, fathering two annual crops of hybrid calves—cattalo, sired by Oscar, and yakalo, by Panchen. Their ascendancy will terminate when Kahtanka II becomes two years old. At this age, the young crown prince will become a mature herd-bull, tolerating no rivals. Then Oscar and Panchen will have to retreat to the shadows, hopeful that Kahtanka II will be busy enough with his buffalo harem to leave them their domestic cows and yak. Getting rid of Kahtanka might turn out to be a real catalyst for our crossbreeding plans.

Throughout the following winter, Bill slowly recuperated. By faithfully sticking to his program of exercise, Bill was rewarded by a wider range of motion in his neck and arm, and he suffered less pain. By late winter, he was free of pain much of the time. Only on days when he toiled fourteen or sixteen hours at the hospital, did the sharp jabs of pain return, warning him to slow down.

One Sunday afternoon not long ago, Bill and I lounged on the green hillside, lazily watching the lumbering shapes of our grazing animals. The stillness of the scene was broken only by the twittering calls of birds.

The yak heifer, Dalai, moved about slowly, appearing heavy with calf. As the thick fur coats dropped away in patches from the buffalo cows, their full figures promised maternity. We anticipated a fruitful season. Once our crossbreeding project was launched by the birth of several hybrid calves, it would be still only the beginning. We realized it might take the rest of our lifetime to achieve a truly new hybrid as a new breed. In order to be registered as a new species of animal, a new breed must prove itself capable of reproducing itself with uniformity. When a registered Hereford bull is crossed with a registered Hereford cow, one can predict exactly what the calf will be. It would take many generations before cattalo and yakalo were stabilized into a new animal which would breed true. Though our first crossbred calves would be only a tiny step forward, we awaited their arrival with eagerness. Undoubtedly there would be many problems and setbacks, for we had much to learn about the genetics of animal husbandry.

From our hillside perch, we watched a little fastback sportscar come down the gravel road and park near the trout ponds. Three young men climbed from the car and began waving at us. With a sigh, Bill rose and walked down the path to meet them. As Bill talked with them, he began waving his arms enthusiastically. Without a doubt he was delighted to see them.

Soon the four of them began climbing up the gently sloping path toward me. Bill's step seemed unusually springy.

Bill introduced me to his companions with his usual, "This is Pinkie—my first wife."

They were three doctors, just finishing their internships and looking for an area in which to practice.

Ken, the tallest of the three, explained, "We've been looking at various places around the state, trying to decide where we would prefer to practice." He looked around at the verdant, rolling hills and took a deep breath. "Ah, that unpolluted air!"

Turning to me, Ken asked, "Do you find this a nice place to live and raise a family?"

Before I could open my mouth, Bill answered for me. His face beaming, and in a hearty voice, Bill spoke expansively. "Your families are going to love it here. Pinkie says she wouldn't raise our children anywhere

307

else. The children have things to do out here in the open. They get a chance to learn a natural way of living before they're put into the city to learn about juvenile delinquency, teen-age pregnancy, and drugs."

"Someone said you need family doctors out here?" asked Paul, the dark-haired, studious-looking intern. "We're interested in practicing where we will be most useful—some place that needs us and wants us."

I felt sure Bill had never heard a sweeter tune. Seldom did he find someone who sang in his key. I remembered how Bill had been enticed to Stanwood by the plea, "We need you."

"Do the other doctors here really want us?" Paul asked Bill. "Would we be welcome on the staff at Mecosta Memorial?"

Would they be welcome? I thought. Is a life-line welcome to a drowning man?

As he assured the young doctors they would be most welcome, Bill's voice reverberated enthusiasm. "You're going to find practice here in the bush different from that in the city. You'll be taking care of everything from coronaries to diaper rash. You'll have to keep on your toes, but you're going to love it!"

Chewing blades of grass, the three young men sat on the meadow slope, listening to Bill describe the advantages of rural practice. Even when he began to review the near-overwhelming difficulties and stumbling-blocks imposed upon our country hospital, Bill spoke with fervor. As in the past, his eyes shone with optimism.

The bad times, the pain, the discouragement of the past year were over. Goose-bumps of happiness and relief covered my arms.

Down on the road, a pickup truck skidded to a gravel-spraying stop behind the interns' sportscar, and a wild-eyed, middle-aged man leaped out. Stumbling, he dashed toward us.

"The Buffalo Doctor! Where's The Buffalo Doctor? They said at the hospital I could find him here!"

Bill rose to meet the gasping man. "I'm The Buffalo Doctor."

"It's my little boy," the man gulped. "Hit by a car—in the emergency room now."

Bill took the frantic father's elbow. Turning quickly toward the three young doctors, Bill said, "You fellows might as well get started right now. Let's go take care of this boy. If he has a ruptured spleen, I can sure use your help!"

As he and the father raced down the path toward the truck, Bill called back over his shoulder, "Meet me in the emergency room in a couple of minutes!"

With a dusty U-turn, the truck sped toward the hospital. The three young interns rose to follow, brushing the grass from their clothes.

"Buffalo Doctor!" the blond intern exclaimed. "Is that what they call him?"

Smiling tenderly, I nodded. "Yes, that's what they call him—The Buffalo Doctor."